Between East and West

Between East and West

Sufism in the Novels of Doris Lessing

Müge Galin

State University of New York Press

Published by State University of New York Press, Albany

© 1997 State University of New York

All rights reserved

Printed in the United States of America

For information, address State University of New York Press
State University Plaza, Albany, NY 12246

Production by Dana Foote • Marketing by Fran Keneston

Front cover charcoal drawing by Müge Galin, 1997.
Back cover photograph by Heiderose Forby, 1997.

Library of Congress Cataloging-in-Publication Data

Galin, Müge.
    Between East and West : Sufism in the novels of Doris Lessing /
Müge Galin.
        p.   cm.
    Includes bibliographical references (p.   ) and index.
    ISBN 0–7914–3383–8 (hc : alk. paper). — ISBN 0–7914–3384–6 (pb :
alk. paper)
        1. Lessing, Doris May, 1919–   —Religion. 2. East and West in
literature. 3. Sufism in literature. I. Title.
PR6023.E833Z67 1997
823′.914—DC20   96–42446
                                                                                                CIP

10 9 8 7 6 5 4 3 2 1

Credits: My sincere thanks go to the following publishers for their permission to reprint extracts from longer works published by them. A. P. Watt granted permission on behalf of Idries Shah for quoted anecdotes from *The Exploits of the Incomparable Mulla Nasrudin* (New York: Dutton, 1972) and *The Subtleties of the Inimitable Mulla Nasrudin* (New York: Dutton, 1973). Doubleday, a division of Bantam Doubleday Dell Publishing Group, Inc. granted permission to quote excerpts from *The Sufis* by Idries Shah (New York: Doubleday, 1964). Part of a poem was reprinted, by permission of the Octagon Press, from *The Secret Garden* translated by Johnson Pasha (London: Octagon Press, Ltd., 1974). Penguin USA granted permission to quote an excerpt from *Tales of the Dervishes* by Idries Shah. Copyright © 1967 by Idries Shah. Used by permission of Dutton Signet, a division of Penguin Books USA Inc. (New York: Dutton, 1967). Penguin USA granted permission for excerpts from *The Way of the Sufi* by Idries Shah. Copyright © 1968 by Idries Shah. Used by permission of Dutton Signet, a division of Penguin Books USA Inc. (New York: Dutton, 1970). Redhouse Press granted permission to quote an excerpt from Yaşar Nuri Öztürk's *The Eye of the Heart*, translated by Richard Blakney (İstanbul: Redhouse, 1988). Threshold Books, RD 4 Box 600, Putney, VT 05346 granted permission to quote lines from *This Longing: Poetry, Teaching Stories and Letters of Rumi*. Trans. Coleman Barks and John Moyne (Putney: Threshold, 1988). Threshold Books, RD 4 Box 600, Putney, VT 05346 granted permission to quote excerpts from *Open Secret: Versions of Rumi*. Trans. John Moyne and Coleman Barks (Putney: Threshold, 1984).

For
Marilyn Robinson Waldman,
who thought with her heart

In Memoriam

Marilyn Robinson Waldman
April 13, 1943 – July 8, 1996

Between East and West is dedicated to my mentor, associate, and friend, Marilyn Robinson Waldman, in gratitude for her friendship, her love, and support. She taught me the history of Islam, the Sufis, and the art of comparison, suggested the title for this book, and insisted that I take equally seriously *both* sides of the equation, East *and* West.

We may read some truths and theorize about human capabilities in books but when we come across someone who embodies many of those truths, we are reminded of what a human being *can* be. Then a different kind of hope arises within us, which can have an enormous impact on us. In some convents, such a person is called *une règle vivante*, or "a living rule." I believe I am not alone when I say that Marilyn Waldman was a living rule for me. Marilyn set high standards for herself: "our reach should always exceed our grasp, else what's a heaven for?" she posed. She applied the same passion, vigor, fairness, and kindness and devoted the same quality of time, care, and attention to all that she did, from mothering, being a wife, gardening, knitting, sewing, or making friends to teaching, researching, writing, and giving public lectures. She took special trips with her husband, Loren, to England and Canada to see gardens and to get new ideas for their own garden. She took delight in knitting and sewing exquisite baby clothes and blankets, because, she said, "it's an honor to make a gift for a newborn." Learning that her first grandchild (who turned out to be a boy, Jeremy Aaron) was due in August 1996 to Amy, their only child, and her husband, David, gave her immense joy.

She went to great lengths to impress upon her students "what it means to be educated." She spent hours with students outside of class, believing she would make a difference, one student at a time. Only in the last couple years of her life did "thinking with her heart" lead Marilyn to limit her contacts, when her illness limited her ability to play the role of the giver and caretaker.

Marilyn Waldman was a product of Harvard and the University of Chicago. In her twenty-five-year career at The Ohio State University (OSU), she taught comparative religion, history of religions, the history and civilization of Islam, world history, historiography, and social science theory and methodology. She was of Eastern European Jewish descent, from Dallas, Texas, with unusually strong commitments, knowledge, and convictions regarding Islam and the Muslim peoples. She wrote *Toward a Theory of Historical Narrative* (1980) and edited *Muslims and Christians, Muslims and Jews* (1992); she coedited *The Islamic World* (1973), the periodical *Papers in Comparative Studies* (1981–96), which included *Religion in the Modern World* (1984) and *Understanding Women* (1992), among other titles that explored issues of fundamental human concern from a cross-cultural perspective. She also prepared translations and textbooks and wrote reviews in several academic fields. She presented nearly fifty scholarly papers at professional meetings and served on more than forty committees at The Ohio State University. As Director of the Center (later Division) of Comparative Studies in the Humanities (1980–91), she was instrumental in the design, establishment, and implementation of the Religious Studies Program. In recognition of her distinguished, sustained, and balanced achievements throughout her career in the areas of teaching, research, and service, she received the College of Humanities Exemplary Faculty Award in 1996. If one were to focus Dr. Waldman's scholarship on one point, one would have to say she was fascinated by the "interrelatedness" of all things.

Dr. Waldman's sense of obligation to carry knowledge into the wider world led her to cultivate a "second career" as a public speaker on issues of broad general concern. She gave more than five hundred public presentations which earned her the 1992 Richard Bjornson Distinguished Service Award from The Ohio Humanities Council. She covered topics such as "Islam in International Affairs," "Women Leaders: Why Are There More Outside the U.S.?", and "Behind and Beyond the Gulf War." As she said in her acceptance speech, she believed "in disseminating the public significance of academic scholarship as widely as possible." Her public scholarship, she said, improved her academic scholarship, "not just the other way around." She insisted on searching and teaching what it means to be human, doing away with the mainstream approach to the study of history, and fighting stereotypes that sneak upon us in all shapes and sizes, in all fields of study. A quote from Spinoza, pinned to the bulletin board outside her office, sums up Marilyn Waldman's commitments: "I have made a ceaseless effort not to ridicule, not to bewail, nor to scorn human actions, but to understand them."

Recognized internationally for her scholarship in comparative religion, Dr. Waldman received numerous awards and honors, including a Woodrow Wilson fellowship and special recognition for public work from the Islamic Foundation of Central Ohio. Although ailing with cancer since 1991, she remained active in her field(s) and continued to make significant contributions. A recent grant she received was from the Office of Research at OSU for the interdisciplinary research seminar that she organized, entitled "Comparing Comparisons." As always, she was interested in comparative thought and in *how* the process of making comparisons varies across disciplines. She combined her comparative skills and her knowledge of, and experience in, the field of Islam to write her book *Inviting Prophets and Entertaining Comparisons* which was still in progress when she died on July 8, 1996. Although this book was "finished" at various points in time, Dr. Waldman continued to revise, reorient, and rewrite it, the more she read and lectured on the subject. She applied the same thorough fairness to concepts and theories as she did to people whose paths crossed hers. While writing about the differential impact of Muslim images of Muhammad on other religious communities, for example, she commented in a letter to me: "It's hard to take other people's wonderfully detailed work and make it serve your own quirky purposes—very complicated, especially since I feel I have to pluralize everything to avoid reductionism." Her purpose was to close the gap between special and general knowledge of Islam and "to help the study of 'religion' find its place in human studies as a whole." She believed, as she wrote in the preface to her book, that "the commitment to cross-cultural interpretation is a moral act, a practical necessity, and an intellectual challenge; the circumstances of our time make it possible for us to address all three, and unwise to neglect any of them."

Among the things Marilyn and I shared was our love for the legendary figure Mulla Nasrudin and the Sufi poet Mawlânâ Jalâluddîn Rûmî, whose tales and poems we frequently exchanged with each other. I am sure Marilyn would be pleased to be remembered by the jokes she liked to tell. In her Inaugural Address at The Ohio State University on March 2, 1988 titled "The Meandering Mainstream: Reimagining World History" she introduced the following story, thus: "I feel some urgency about the need to reimagine world history. For me, it's not just a question of *whether* we survive, but *how* we survive, and what human possibilities we open up for ourselves in the process. That sense of urgency, like many things, is best captured for me by a story about my favorite folk-hero Mulla Nasrudin."

> Nasrudin sometimes took people for trips in his boat. One day a fussy pedagogue hired him to ferry him across a very wide water. As soon as they were afloat the scholar asked whether it was going to be rough.
> "Don't ask me nothin' about it," said Nasrudin.
> "Have you never studied grammar?"
> "No," said the Mulla.
> "In that case, half your life has been wasted."

The Mulla said nothing.
Soon a terrible storm blew up. The Mulla's crazy cockleshell
was filling with water.
He leaned towards his companion.
"Have you ever learned to swim?"
"No," said the pedant.
"In that case, schoolmaster, ALL your life is lost, for we are
sinking. (Shah, *Exploits* 18)

Marilyn would also be pleased to be remembered along
Rûmî's lines in the *Divan-e Shams-e Tabrîzî* (trans. Nicholson).
Let me allow her to introduce it, as she did in "The Meander-
ing Mainstream":

I see the academy as locked in an unresolved, in fact not yet fully
engaged conflict between two positions I like to pose as competing
alliterations: the pursuit of the perspectiveless perspective and
the pursuit of plural perspectives. The attempt to go beyond perspective to an absolute truth is hardly new. Even though the children of the Enlightenment see themselves as finally capable of
transcending the parochialism and localism of religious worldviews, the attempt to transcend time-bound and space-bound perspective has often been the product of religious faith itself, especially of mystical insight, which often viewed the transcending of
perspective as the attainment of an altered state of consciousness.
Listen to the verses of the Persian poet Rûmî, to whose music the
Mawlawî dervishes still turn, more than 700 years later:

What is to be done, O Moslems? I do not recognize myself.
I am neither Christian, nor Jew, nor Gabr [Zoroastrian], nor
     Muslim.
I am not of the East, nor of the West, nor of the land, nor of
     the sea;
I am not of Nature's mint, nor of the circling heavens,
I am not of the earth, nor of water, nor of air, nor of fire;
I am not of the empyrean, nor of the dust, nor of existence,
     nor of entity.

IN MEMORIAM

I am not of India, nor of China, nor of Bulgaria [Bulghar on
   the Volga], nor of Saqsîn,
I am not of the kingdom of 'Irâqain [the two Iraqs], nor of the
   country of Khorâsân.
I am not of this world, nor of the next, nor of Paradise, nor of
   Hell;
I am not of Adam, nor of Eve, nor of Eden and Rizwân.
My place is the Placeless, my trace is the Traceless;
'Tis neither body nor soul, for I belong to the soul of the
   Beloved. (17)

Thank you, Marilyn, for your life, your spark, your support, your loving tolerance, and for taking care of so many of us
so well for so long. We love you and will cherish your example.

Müge Galin
September 5, 1996

That East must ever be East and West must be West is not a belief which is subscribed to by Sufis, who claim that Sufism, in its reality, not necessarily under the name, is continuously in operation in every culture.

—Doris Lessing, "In the World, Not of It"

Contents

Preface

Toward Border-Crossing

There is some quality—a vitality, a yeast—in Sufi work
that affects us in ways not easily explained.
                    —Doris Lessing, Preface to Shah,
                              Seekers after Truth

The treasury of Sufism contains pearls of great value for
both the West and the Islamic world and in fact for all
human beings from whichever clime they happen to hail.
                    —Seyyed Hossein Nasr, Sufi Essays

This book pulls together the fiction of Doris Lessing and the
tradition of Sufism and makes these topics more mutually illu-
minating. It is a study of how Lessing's exposure to a particular
aspect of *tasawwuf*, the classical Sufi Way, has shaped her work.
With very few exceptions, this book deals with the strain of
Sufism popularized in the West by Idries Shah,* because it was
Shah's work that provided the link to the Sufi tradition for
Lessing.[1] Although possibly not the only Sufi influence on
Lessing, Sufi literature as Shah translated and introduced it
to the West has been a major inspiration for Lessing's Sufi
approach, as well as for other aspects of contemporary Western
culture, from literature and the arts to psychology and politics.

---

*As this book was going into press, Idries Shah died on November
23, 1996 in London at the age of 72.

PREFACE

Academic scholars of Islam in the West have in the past created as their object of study something they call "traditional" Islam or "authentic" Sufism, dismissing practitioners such as Idries Shah, who have tailored their message to a Western audience, as not worthy of serious study. However, Edward Said's well-known deconstruction of Orientalism has highlighted the problem of fixing/freezing Eastern culture at one particular point and putting it on a pedestal to be studied (and worshipped or attacked) by those in the West. The traditional Orientalist approach has relegated Sufism to a dying past, as something to be preserved only through the efforts of the Western scholars themselves, as they study classical texts. But in the spirit of Said, I regard Sufism as a living, vital practice that takes many forms, from popular devotion at rural shrines across the Muslim world, to Sufi gatherings in the homes of urban élites throughout the Muslim world and the Muslim diaspora (i.e., Muslims living in places like Great Britain and the United States). In my view, the vitality and relevance of Sufism for the contemporary world cannot be fully appreciated by studying only the forms of *tasawwuf* that evolved up until the moment of the colonial domination of the Muslim world.[2] Lessing wrote in 1973:

> Sufism is not a study of past civilizations—It must be contemporary, or it is nothing. Why is it being offered again in the West now? For the simplest of reasons: Sufism works openly where it can, silently when it must. Even fifty years ago the churches had so strong a hold on thought and morals that the introduction of this ancient way of thinking would have been impossible. But in an open society Sufism can be offered openly. ("Ancient" 78)

It is not the aim of this book to focus on whether the borrowings and variety of Sufism in Lessing's work represent "authentic" Sufism or whether Idries Shah is a "true" Sufi guide. Rather, this book studies the ways in which the strain of

xviii

Sufism, to which we have access as a result of Shah's work, has promoted a degree of familiarity with the longstanding Sufi tradition and has become a Way that some westerners practice or use in their art.[3] Lessing's views on this subject can be summarized in her own words. In a 1981 interview with Christopher Bigsby she said, "I found Sufism as taught by Idries Shah, which claims to be the reintroduction of an ancient teaching, suitable for this time and this place. It is not some regurgitated stuff from the East or watered-down Islam or anything like that" (79).

The term *Sufism*, unlike the term *tasawwuf*, which, in Arabic, Persian, and Turkish, refers to the thoughts and practices of some Muslims who call themselves "Sufis," does not adequately convey the disparate forms of Sufi practice but implies a degree of coherence and systematization that has never been present in the various Sufi traditions. It is not what is understood by scholars of Islam as "Sufism" but is an "ism" created in the West to refer more conveniently to a teaching that originated in the East.[4] Shah writes, "What most people call 'Sufism' is traditionally known in the East as 'being a Sufi,' or 'The Sufiyya,' and the 'ism' part is very typically a Western concept. If we speak of 'Sufism,' it is only for ease of communication" (*Perfumed* 177). In a 1987 interview with Thomas Frick, Lessing commented,

> It's pretty hard to summarize it all, because it's all about what you experience. I want to make a point of that because a lot of people walk around saying "I am a Sufi," probably because they've read a book and it sort of sounds attractive. Which is absolutely against anything that real Sufis would say or do. Some of the great Sufis have actually said, "I would never call myself a Sufi—it's too large a name." (159)

It is said in Sufi Work that when we have received much from the very best, our debt is that much greater: I began to amass debts for this project in 1974, when Tom Flebotte asked me, "What do you know about the Whirling Dervishes, Müge?" I cringed because I knew nothing and set out on a quest. In 1984 when Barbara Rigney challenged her midwestern undergraduate class with news of Sufi mysticism and its influence on Doris Lessing, I was better equipped to begin my research in earnest. I am grateful to Barbara for her support and unwavering vote of confidence that I could write and publish on these two subjects, thereby teaching her West about my East.

Friends and colleagues saw me through various stages of my research and writing process: Dick Davis, Anthony and Nini De Marinis, Katherine P. Ewing, Dana Foote, Luis Miguel Gonzales, Bob Jones, Wally Maurer, Andrew Moyer, Süha Oğuzertem, Barbara Rigney, Marilyn Seymour, and Sara Sviri. I depended on the compassion and firm criticism of Marilyn Waldman, who impressed upon me the necessity to respect the integrity and long-standing tradition of Islam. I received help from scholars I never even met—Katherine Fishburn, Marcia Hermansen, Paul Schlueter, and Eric Ziolkowski— who astonished me with their generosity by closely reading my typescript and offering me invaluable feedback. I was fortunate that Lois Patton kindly offered to consider my research to be published at SUNY Press. Prior to meeting her, I had wished for not necessarily a *publisher* but an *editor* who might understand what Sufis mean by one who is caught trying to sit between two chairs.

The more experts whose path crossed mine, the more complicated my subject became. Orientalist scholarship pulled me in one direction, critical theory in another, Lessing scholarship in another, and contacts with practicing Sufis in yet another. At countless desperate stages, Jim Phelan provided for me a haven: I relied on his ability to tune into a particular pondering where I had gone astray, decipher the knot, and articulate it back to me with precision and added insight. As I was caught repeatedly between East and West, mystics and skeptics, and practitioners and scholars, Jim's gentle care for clarity and his laser-beam focus steadied the violent swings of my pendulum, so that I might write with *some* neutrality.

I know that most of these debts I cannot easily repay.

Between East and West is divided into four parts: (1) Orientations, (2) Consequences, (3) Implications, and (4) Appendixes. Part I orients readers to Lessing, to Sufism, and to the conjunction of the two. It negotiates specific themes present within *tasawwuf* and the variations on these themes that Shah, Lessing, and other westerners offer us today and looks at what happens to the Sufi tradition as Sufism moves "Between East and West." Part II applies Sufi thought to some Lessing novels and studies the manifestations of Sufi influence on Lessing. Various Sufi-like characters and their unconventional life styles are evaluated and explicated for Western readers unfamiliar with Sufism. Part III attempts to re-situate Lessing "Between East and West" and evaluates the role of spirituality in her work. It considers the implications of taking Lessing's Sufism seriously when reading her works or when doing Lessing criticism. It impresses upon the reader the degree to which Lessing is seriously offering her space-fiction utopias as plausible and even necessary alternatives to our present Western ways of life. Part IV discusses *tasawwuf* within the history of Islam and lists scholarship on Lessing's mysticism, some works by Lessing herself, others by Lessing critics.

In the following chapters, I use seven novels by Lessing to illustrate the influence of different aspects of Sufism on Lessing's works. These by no means compose an exhaustive list of Lessing's Sufi-influenced novels. Nor do they reflect a limit to Sufi traces in Lessing's works. They are not necessarily the works that are the most influenced by Sufism. Nevertheless, taken together, they reflect the range of ways in which Lessing manipulates and incorporates Sufi ideas. For instance, *The Golden Notebook* (1962) illustrates Lessing's Sufi-like thoughts even before her introduction to Sufism. *The Four-Gated City* (1969) provides the link between the realistic novel and space fiction, as well as the link between ordinary life on earth and life after an apocalypse and after enlightenment. *The Memoirs of a Survivor* (1974) traces the steps a would-be Sufi takes toward enlightenment. *Re: Colonised Planet 5, Shikasta* (1979) illustrates how things fall apart in the lives of ordinary people who are not on the Sufi Path, while *The Marriages between Zones Three, Four, and Five* (1980) offers a glimpse into the levels of consciousness on the evolutionary ladder. *The Making of the Representative for Planet 8* (1982) shows how things can be different when one "works" on oneself and evolves. *The Diary of a Good Neighbour* (1983) offers parallels between Lessing's teaching stories and Sufi teaching stories. Altogether, these novels allow for an illustration of the major aspects of Sufism: ordinary life contrasted with life on the Sufi Way, the role of the teaching stories on the Sufi Way, life after death, and life as a result of the Sufi Way. They introduce the reader to both masters and disciples, guides and initiates. While the chapter entitled "Lessing's Vision" emphasizes the content of some of these novels, the chapter entitled "Lessing's Teaching Stories" focuses on their style and technique.

As this century and millenium draw to a close, rapid changes in the Eastern Bloc and in the Third World, and larger diasporic movements of populations have resulted in heterogeneity throughout the United States and Western Europe. This cultural diversity appears not only in current literature but also in our classrooms, where the growing presence of minorities needs to be reinforced practically and morally by emphasizing intercultural dialogue involving their experiences and history as equally significant parts of our scholarship and curriculum. For the minority is becoming the majority; what was once "the other" is looking increasingly familiar. As we turn to cross-cultural studies to solve the problems of our times, Doris Lessing seems to be introducing ideas and literature from the world of Islam and challenging us as westerners to consider Islamicate[5] literature and ideology alongside the major influences from other parts of the world.

In this effort I am indebted to Doris Lessing for her part in initiating this discussion. Perhaps it would be much to her chagrin that her novels have made an academic out of this seeker. By endorsing Idries Shah's work in England, she has helped to catapult Sufism into the attention of a broad audience and perhaps even stimulated an interest in Sufism among some of her Muslim readers in the West. I thank her for her inspiration and for giving me the occasion to write about a subject that is dear to me. In turn, I invite Lessing readers to read, or reread, Lessing anew.

Müge Galin

Part I

Orientations

Introduction

Lessing and Sufism
between East and West

People ask, "When did you become interested in Sufism?"
I give an exact reply, but feel the question is really a
statement: "I am surprised that you are the kind of per-
son to become interested in mysticism" . . . I had an incli-
nation towards mysticism (not religion) even when being
political. It is not an uncommon combination . . . If you
are not political, you are reactionary. (If you are not
God's child, you are the devil's.)

—Doris Lessing,
"Learning How to Learn"

Doris Lessing never kept secret her commitment to Sufism, but from the 1960s has persistently and enthusiastically announced her mystical proclivities at every opportunity. Such a frank admission by one of today's most renowned female writers invites and deserves serious attention. While countless works have been written about Lessing, surprisingly few have examined primarily and directly her interest in Sufi ideology.[1] This book is intended to fill that gap and open a new conversation, one that other voices may join; when Lessing's Sufism is taken seriously, her work requires assessment in a new light. Situating Lessing's fiction in the context of the Sufi tradition offers a new view of her work, particularly of her space

3

fiction. At the same time, it contributes to the larger growing conversation "Between East and West."

Sufism seems to have entered Lessing's novels much in the manner demonstrated by the following Sufi tale:[2]

> Time and again Nasrudin passed from Persia to Greece on donkey-back. Each time he had two panniers of straw, and trudged back without them. Every time the guard searched him for contraband. They never found any.
>
> "What are you carrying, Nasrudin?"
>
> "I am a smuggler."
>
> Years later, more and more prosperous in appearance, Nasrudin moved to Egypt. One of the customs men met him there.
>
> "Tell me, Mulla, now that you are out of the jurisdiction of Greece and Persia, living here in such luxury—what was it that you were smuggling when we could never catch you?"
>
> "Donkeys." (Shah, *Exploits* 22)

Lessing has been importing, borrowing, incorporating, and adapting Sufi ideas between East and West and between Sufi literature and the Western novel as openly as Nasrudin was smuggling donkeys. Yet we tend to overlook the obvious when we are confronted with border-crossing challenges. The purposes of this book are to foreground the difference that the Sufi context makes for understanding first, some previously unexplored dimensions of Lessing's fiction, and second, some of the larger issues about East-West connections.

As Lessing readers know, Lessing has been vehemently and consistently opposed to labeling and compartmentalizing under any "ism," and this book does not claim that Sufism is the ultimate key to interpreting her work. At the same time, it would be a mistake to overlook the obvious: Lessing has made use of Sufi ideas to enhance her own perception of human beings on earth and on other planets, in life and in an afterlife. Although there is, of course, much more to Lessing's fiction, the particular focus of this book is to explore in detail the mystical dimension of her oeuvre.

Discussing Sufism requires attention to the implications of Orientalism that threaten all scholars of the Middle East and Islam. Said describes and defines *Orientalism* as the West's distortion of the Orient as an idea without a corresponding reality. Orientalism is a style of thought that distinguishes the East as splendid, cruel, barbaric, sensual, and spiritual, as opposed to the civilized, cultured, rational, and materialistic West. This idea of "us" and "them" encourages one to take for granted Western perceptions of the "superior" West and "exotic but inferior" East; that is, it perpetuates the idea of the world as being made up of two unequal halves (12). Said invites scholars to acknowledge this erroneous assumption and condemns any scholarship that is built on such an unstable premise. The evaluation of Lessing's fiction in *Between East and West* avoids the trap of glamorizing the distant past and the exotic, mystical East. Rather, the Sufism that Lessing encountered is treated here as a vital force that is intimately a part of contemporary Western society. While by Said's definition this book offers only a representation here, that representation stems not from a hope to impose a design on Lessing but rather from an effort to bring out a hitherto neglected design in her corpus. Our recognition of Sufism can enhance our insight into Lessing's works. Therefore, it will be helpful to begin with an explanation of Lessing's Sufism.

Lessing's Connection to Sufism

Around the time when Lessing read Idries Shah's book *The Sufis* (1964), she became a student of Shah,* who writes about and teaches the Sufi Way in the West. She writes:

---

*As this book was going into press, Idries Shah died on November 23, 1996 in London at the age of 72.

I heard about Idries Shah during my inquiries, as a Sufi from Afghanistan with the sort of education that enabled him to be at home both in the East and in the West. I had found what I read about Sufism exotic and not to my taste, but was told that our Western ideas about Sufis tended to be ill-informed and that the situation was being made worse by charlatans claiming to be Sufi teachers. Idries Shah was genuine, in the opinion of my informants who had had experience of cults, sects, and various kinds of teachers. They said he was writing a book. I felt this book might turn out to be what I was looking for. You could say I had a "hunch" about it. It was *The Sufis*. I read it feeling it was for me. I was also amazed at the robustness of its claims. ("Learning" 13)

To a great extent, Shah has been responsible for exposing a Western popular audience to the wealth of Sufi teaching stories finally accessible in English. I use many of his translations to elaborate on my discussion of Sufism in Lessing's novels. He was born in India, lived in Afghanistan, and moved to England in the 1960s. According to Lessing, "it is [Shah's book *The Sufis*] that heralded the arrival of a genuine Sufi teaching in the West" (Preface 629). Shah traces his own lineage to the order of the Naqshbandiyyah in Afghanistan. Today he teaches Sufism not as a tradition of the past but rather as a contemporary body of knowledge, a visible, vital force that has a place in the twentieth-century West.

As "the product of an intensively varied education," Shah has "patented scientific devices; he has been journalist, explorer, traveler; he has studied archeology, geology, economics, politics, writes books on travel, anthropology, magic, Sufism, each unique in its field . . . He corresponds in Arabic, Persian, English, French, Spanish, with experts in a dozen different fields. He is also a husband and a father of four" (Lessing, *Writer's Encounter*, audiocasette). He has collected, translated, and written thousands of Sufi tales about various ancient Sufi orders (*tarîqahs*, lit. "the Way") and has made them available to the Western public through his books and lectures. He also has established and now runs a publishing firm and has founded and runs the Society for Sufi Studies in London.

That Lessing's exposure to Sufism started with Shah's books and his Society for Sufi Studies may be problematic for some scholars and practitioners, who do not appreciate but blame Shah for popularizing and despiritualizing the classical Sufi tradition. However, as Lessing explains, the new and altered form in which we encounter Sufism in the West today is a sign of one of the essential characteristics of Sufism. She writes, "it doesn't do to say that a man, or a book, or an institution is Sufism, which, while it is essentially something always the same, is always taking different forms" ("Ancient" 80). Still, those who are protective of the territory of *tasawwuf* define the classical Sufi Way as "authentic" and the contemporary Western Sufi Way as "pseudo" Sufism.

Elwell-Sutton, for instance, accuses Shah and others, among them G. I. Gurdjieff[3] and P. D. Ouspensky,[4] of playing up to the psychological weaknesses of westerners looking for something to replace their lost family, tradition, or religion in the twentieth century. He refers to the brand of Sufism we encounter in the West as "Pseudo-Sufism," without Islam and without religion, "centered not on God but on man" (*Encounter* 16), "a de-spiritualized accumulation of ritual, superstition, and folklore" (12). According to Elwell-Sutton, the reason behind the Western omission of talk of God from Sufi teachings is "Western individualism and materialism that cannot easily surrender to powers outside the self" (*Islam* 54). Granted, Muslim Sufis would reject the idea that one can be a Sufi without being Muslim; consequently, a boundary will be drawn between Muslim Sufis and any Sufism that does not stress Islam. It seems more appropriate for scholars to *study* this issue of boundary maintenance as a dynamic process than to declare their allegiance to those on one side or the other.[5]

In 1970, Elwell-Sutton reviewed two of Shah's books; this prompted Lessing to write a letter to the editor in Shah's defense. In this letter, Lessing wrote Shah's praises, offering a list of his rich literary achievements. Lessing's argument was centered around the fact that Shah's efforts have been recognized and rewarded by a wide array of institutions and intellectuals (Letter 51).[6] Elwell-Sutton's counterargument, on the other hand, was representative of many critics' objection to the *re*contextualized, Westernized Sufism: that those who endorse and praise it have little knowledge of Islam and therefore are *unqualified* appraisers of the authenticity of the teaching (Letter 51).

Although there has been much controversy surrounding the reception of Shah's movement, the fact remains that Shah has been instrumental in exposing many westerners, who might not have encountered or studied Sufism otherwise, to the wealth of Sufi literature.[7] Lessing has been among those who benefited from Shah's writings and translations, and she frequently incorporates them in her novels, as, for example, she does in the dedication to *The Four-Gated City*, in which she quotes a dervish teaching story from one of Shah's collections. Her space-fiction series, *Canopus in Argos: Archives*, clearly shows the mark of Sufi thought and can even be read as Sufi allegories. Lessing explained her inclination toward Sufi thought: "As for people like myself, unable to admire organized religions of any kind, this philosophy shows where to look for answers to questions put by society and by experience—questions not answered by the official purveyors of knowledge, secular or sacred" ("Ancient" 78).

Lessing's Sufism contains within it some but not all of the features of the classical tradition. Lessing believes in the possibility of individual and world amelioration, and her vision encompasses not only the earth but the whole of the universe. Sufi thought and Sufi teaching stories allow her to demonstrate the Way to transformation. In her novels she frequently introduces the apparently *other* tales in the context of the *familiar* in order to help illuminate the familiar.

8

Introduction

Sufism versus *Tasawwuf*

Reaction among critics to the revisionist resurgence of
Sufism in the West has ranged from (1) across-the-board rejection to (2) tolerance to (3) curiosity as to where it will all lead
to (4) great faith in the possibilities that Western Sufism
promises. Elwell-Sutton writes, "Rejected in the East, and
becoming aware of the mental and spiritual ferment in the
West, with its uncritical search for some new teaching no matter where it is to be found, certain self-styled Sufis have tried
to emulate the fleeting success of the Yogis and the Zen
Buddhists by setting up propaganda centers in Europe and
America" ("Mystic" 36). Nasr, too, has his reservations and
fears that Sufism will degenerate in the hands of the ignorant. But he also concedes that there "can be discerned a more
profound and genuine attraction by both those who wish to
profit from [Sufism's] insights for their spiritual benefit, . . .
and those who are seeking a genuine spiritual path to follow
and are willing to make the necessary sacrifices to become
qualified to follow such a path" (11). In response to the present
attraction the West displays toward Sufism, Bob Summer
witholds judgment. He asks in a *Publisher's Weekly* article,
"So what does the Sufism-in-America curve add up to? Is it
indeed just another 'wave' or New Age ripple? Or is something
deeper with a more enduring potential going on?" (35). Indeed,
we find represented in the West today "the full range of Sufi
approaches, both universalist and Islamic, traditional and
experimental" (Kinney, qtd. in Summer 35). Jay Kinney, the
publisher and editor-in-chief of *Gnosis*, demonstrates great
faith in the future of Western Sufism. He muses,

> If the various orders who now call North America home
> are able to develop in dialogue and clarify the essentials of
> Sufism and the shape they take, the potential exists for a cre-
> ative explosion such as happened in medieval Turkey and
> Andalusia (Moorish Spain), where the mix of Muslim, Christian,

and Jewish cultures helped incubate such great mystics as
[Rûmî, Ibn al 'Arabî,] and Moses de Leon. And that would be
something marvelous to see. (Kinney, qtd. in Summer 35)

Lessing's demonstrable commitment to Sufism places her in
the company of Kinney, Summer, and others who are willing to
"wait and see" what will become of contemporary Sufism in the
West.

Nasr identifies three types of writings on Sufism in the
West today: (1) scholarship or translations, some good and
some bad, done by Orientalists;[8] (2) works by practitioners
who claim an association with a current Sufi movement, all of
which Nasr calls "pseudospirituality inundating the West"
(9);[9] and (3) "authentic expositions" and "genuine teachings."[10]
This last group, according to Nasr, reflects a nonacademic,
profound, and seriously spiritual investigation of Sufism in
the West, an investigation that in turn influences the first
group. Nasr further recognizes the authors of this group as
belonging to traditional Sufi orders established in the West
which, with only a few exceptions, are associated tightly with
Islam.[11] Nasr is very clear and direct on where he stands in
relation to the second and third groups identified above. He
writes, "The spread of authentic Sufism in the West along
with its own literature must not be confused with the continuous propagation of ideas by certain circles that speak in
the name of Sufism but stand outside the traditional Islamic
framework" (9). It is important to note, however, that many
followers of Sufism in Muslim countries, though self-identified
as "Muslim," are also unfamiliar with the "traditional Islamic
framework."

Classical Sufi faith and practices (*tasawwuf*) have been
conveyed to adepts in specialized ways. These "ways" have
been diverse, given the varied circumstances under which individual Sufi masters and members of the Sufi orders or
tarîqahs[12] lived, each corresponding to the inner realities of
its particular time and place. These Sufis in Islam pursued

10

spiritual experience by bodily discipline and a whole different way of life that was in accordance with their particular relationship with God. For them, *tasawwuf*, the belief and practice of humans having direct access to God, was an *experience*, not an ideology. Among Islamicists and Orientalists, these individuals and groups have been variously recognized as "real" Sufis and their thought and practice the substance of "authentic," classical Sufi tradition.[13] At the same time, among Muslims, many Sufis and other "saints" have been periodically dismissed as inauthentic. Consequently, when Western scholars get caught up in making similar criticisms, they are in fact reproducing precisely the kinds of boundary formation in which Sufis and other Muslims have always engaged.[14]

More popular aspects of numerous Sufi orders have been disseminated to the general populace by means of sacred dances, folk tales, love poetry, music, weaving, and all other forms of craftsmanship, literature, and art. These have been preferred and used among members of nonacademic circles to produce a revised and comprehensive system of what Sufis believe, say, and do. As opposed to academics who tend to study Sufi theory and history, members of nonacademic circles have tended to study the Sufi Way in order to practice it, though naturally there are overlaps between these two groups. Some scholars of Sufism have tended to become practitioners also, as some followers of Sufism sometimes also have chosen to study it academically. For some, academic and spiritual interest in Sufism have gone hand-in-hand from the start.

Popular adaptations of *tasawwuf* have focused on some elements of Sufism among *many* practical elements or life styles that tended to characterize Sufis in other places and times.[15] Frequently, the Sufi-influenced works of westerners have shown traces of a filtered version of *tasawwuf*. One of the things usually filtered out in the transfer has been the association between Sufi thought and Sufi practice. As a result, *tasawwuf* has been *re*constructed and *re*conceptualized into the current system of beliefs in the West referred to as

"Sufism," which is a systematic *re*interpretation of a tradition that essentially resists mechanical and literalistic treatment.

Given the variety of circles—academic, nonacademic, Muslim, and non-Muslim—that have been instrumental in propagating Sufi teachings, ideas, stories, and tradition in the West, the meaning of the term *Sufism* has varied greatly and therefore requires careful consideration.[16] In academic circles the word is sometimes used to cover *all* Sufi thought and practice, and in some nonacademic circles it sometimes refers to more practical elements more closely aligned with the word *tasawwuf*. But sometimes in some nonacademic circles, especially among those who practice being a Sufi, the word *Sufism* may tend to foreground systematic Sufi thought not always associated with *tasawwuf*. Sufism that is discussed in this work in reference to Lessing is restricted to the modern *re*conceptualization and consolidation of *tasawwuf* into "Sufism" by *some* practicing Sufis in the West, since Lessing's novels exemplify a *re*construction of *tasawwuf*. For Lessing, Sufism serves as a school of thought comparable to other schools of thought and other "isms" such as Marxism, feminism, Jungianism, Laingianism, or the New Physics, in which she has found a resonance of her own thoughts, a "this is for me" response.[17]

In *tasawwuf*, Sufi practitioners have been Muslims who engaged in certain interrelated modes of piety and thought. One of the points of contention of critics of Sufism as it has disseminated in the West is the absence of an *exclusive* emphasis on God and the dismissal of the practice of the religion of Islam as part and parcel of Sufi practice. The most fundamental concept in *tasawwuf* is the idea of having *direct* access to Allah, an experience that was realized by the prophet Muhammad, who not only is believed to have literally spoken with Allah and recited his words in the form of the Qur'ân but is also believed to have ascended to heaven, where he met Abraham, Moses, Jesus, and many angels and returned back to earth to live out his life as a Muslim. While the prophet Muhammad himself did not claim to be a Sufi, Sufis have made much of these intimate interactions that he had with God; and centuries later, they declared him to have been "the first Sufi."[18] It was this *direct* communion with God that Muslim Sufis contemplated and sought through a variety of special practices. Some dedicated their whole lives to attaining this communion; others engaged in it only occasionally. Most viewed direct experience of God as the only real way to learn and felt that inner transformation could only be experienced, not discussed.

Implicit in the definition of *Islam* is the necessity of being part of the *Ummah*, the Muslim community.[19] Being a Muslim defines not only one's religion but all of one's life, outlook, and conduct from birth to death. All rituals, such as circumcision, marriage, or funeral, and all mundane activities, from proper dress and proper disposal of one's nail clippings to inheritance laws and divorce, are regulated by the *Ummah*, which upholds the models of proper conduct indicated in the Qur'ân and the Hadîth (recordings of what Muhammad said and did). Therefore being a member of the *Ummah* is a prerequisite for being Muslim.

Similarly, implicit in the definition of *tasawwuf* is the necessity of being part of the community of Sufis in a Muslim context, being a member of a particular Sufi order, living communally, and having a guide. *Tasawwuf* stresses the difficulty of following the Path by oneself. It involves a cooperative effort made by all for the good of all. One is unable to grow without the group. Sufi mystics were supposed to aspire to a utopia of awakened beings who were in constant watchfulness of God and who were ecstatically in love with God, the Beloved. However, this was easier said than done. For instance, it is apparent from the poetry of Mawlânâ (Our Master) Jalâluddîn Rûmî (from Rum, 1207–73), the Persian *tasawwuf* poet of thirteenth-century Anatolia, that his attempts at Sufi practice were uncomfortable, disconcerting, and marked with sustained self-questioning. For him, awakening in the Sufi Way was as pleasant as waking up in a dungeon. It was the task of the Sufi guide to see the disciple through the arduous path to awakening. The master became the student's "will" for a time and guided him or her toward becoming a deserving member of the Sufi community. Once the awakening took place, the anguish and suffering turned to elation at having reached God the Beloved, which Rûmî has described as awakening in a rose garden.

What is most distinctive about love for God in *tasawwuf* is that that love is often analogized to romantic love and is *not* generally the equivalent of the *agape* that often characterizes Christian conceptions of love for God. Rûmî did not just worship his God but yearned for and desired him. It was this ecstatic spiritual passion that fueled the fire in his heart. Lessing's characters, though they behave as seekers, do not exhibit this burning desire for God. When we compare Lessing's work to the work of Rûmî, her version of Sufism turns out to be more this-world oriented, even though her space fiction is other-worldly. In contrast, Rûmî *was* the classical Sufi Way. He was the founder of the community of the Whirling Dervishes (the Mawlawiyyah) and he composed poems in which he addressed God and his teacher, Shams. Critics regard his poetry as second only to the Qur'ân. Rûmî was not a cleric. His life was tormented by the loss of his wife and later his spiritual master, Shams, who was murdered by Rûmî's jealous followers, including his son. For instance, when Rûmî wrote the following quatrain, he wrote to his Beloved, God, desiring him as passionately as one desires a romantic lover:

> Come to the orchard in Spring.
> There is light and wine, and sweethearts in the
>   pomegranate flowers.
> If you do not come, these do not matter.
> If you do come, these do not matter.
>   (*Open Secret* 14)

Islamicists insist that the term *Sufism* can be used accurately only when referring to the mystical tradition that developed within Islam. On the other hand, Western practitioners of Sufism from East and West, North and South, from among Muslims and Christians, Jews and Hindus, gnostics and theists, and others, who found something more in Sufism than in the organized religion into which they were born, insist that *tasawwuf* is much older than Islam, that it is timeless and placeless, and that one can hardly assign the origins of Sufism to any one general geographical location in the world. Some even claim that all religions came out of *tasawwuf*. According to some, Sufis do not necessarily have to be Muslims. They do not have to practice Islam, nor need they abandon the religion into which they were born—they are not required to "convert." This outlook has contributed to the critical perception regarding Western Sufis: that they are in pursuit of perfecting themselves and becoming more evolved human beings, rather than aiming to lose themselves in order to become one with God. The focus of the student is perceived to be primarily on him- or herself. Along these lines Lessing writes, "Sufism is not peculiar to Islam, or the property of Islam, though for historic reasons it developed—in the public form—within the Islamic context. The great Sufi teachers in Islam all had innumerable Christian and Jewish pupils. Sufism predated Islam by thousands of years, under many different names, in a hundred different guises" (Preface to Shah, *Seekers* 632).

Indeed, Western contemporary Sufis come from diverse walks of life, countries, and religious traditions.[20] I personally have met "Sufis" in the West from five different nationalities and three separate religions. Furthermore, scholars of *tasawwuf* with varying degrees of spiritual investment in their subject come literally from all over the world. At the conference on Persian Sufism held at George Washington University in Washington, D.C., in the spring of 1992, speakers and attenders represented nations ranging from Switzerland and Norway to Japan and Malaysia, Iran, India, Great Britain, United States, and elsewhere. On a quick glance, one could spot men wearing turbans or women in veils as well as others in suits or jeans, people ranging from undergraduates to professionals to practitioners, including the poet Robert Bly in loose fitting, comfortable street attire, there to recite translations of Sufi poetry to an accompanying Middle Eastern stringed instrument, the *saz*.

In the United States today, there is a robust list of books on Sufism on the market, all of which fall within one of the three major groups identified by Nasr in this chapter. According to *Publishers Weekly* of January 1995, a number of publishers and distributors in the United States specialize in Sufi literature. For instance, Pir Publications sells Sufi books and produces the *Sufi Review / Sufi Book Catalog* quarterly. In 1995, the first copy of the *Divan Books Sufi Catalog* came out, advertising numerous books by and about Sufis.[21] Some of the many sources yearly placing new titles on Sufism in U.S. bookstores include Chicago-based Kazi Publications, Threshold Books in Vermont, Shambala in Boston, Khaniqahi Nimatullahi Publications in New York City, the Fellowship Press in Philadelphia, the State University of New York Press in Albany, the Golden Sufi Center in California, and the International Association of Sufism Publication in California, among others. There also is the Western Spiritual Series, which includes several volumes on Sufism, and an encyclopedia in progress, two volumes of which, entitled *Islamic Spirituality—Foundations* and *Islamic Spirituality—Manifestations* and both by Nasr, deal at length with Sufism (Nasr 7). Furthermore, *Gnosis* devoted its winter 1994 issue to Sufism, and it turned out to be a rather popular issue (Summer 34). The increase in sales of publications on the subject of Sufism, Summer writes, is a "telling indicator of Sufism's appeal" to westerners (33). Among them, Jalâluddîn Rûmî's poetry, for instance, is especially popular, making Rûmî, according to Coleman Barks, a poet and translator of Rûmî's poetry, the "bestselling poet in America" (Summer 33). According to Kabir Helminski, director of Threshold Books, the surge in the popularity of Rûmî's poetry is due to the fact that our current culture is "spiritually wounded" (Summer 34).

There also have been recent events in the United States that had to do with Sufis and Sufism, such as the above-mentioned international conference on Persian Sufism in Washington, D.C., in May of 1992 or the ongoing activities and workshops at the Golden Sufi Center in Inverness, California.[22] In December 1994 in Manhattan, the 750th anniversary of Rûmî's first meeting with his beloved teacher, Shams, was celebrated at an event where poet Robert Bly and dancer Zulaika, among others, appeared. Also in 1994, the Whirling Dervishes of Turkey (the Mawlawiyyah) toured and performed in the United States (Summer 34). In January and February of 1997, the Whirling Dervishes of Turkey toured the United States from New York and Massachusetts to California and Alaska. They were accompanied by a troupe of Turkish classical musicians, the Mevlevî Ensemble of the Mevlâna Culture and Art Foundation. Such performances, as well as lectures, tapes, publications, and retreats organized and presented by Pir Vilayat Inayat Khan at various locations in the United States or the Threshold Society's 99-Day Program developed by Kabir Helminski typify the forms that Sufism has taken in the West today.

Naturally, there are stark differences between these contemporary activities in the West and their Muslim-based counterparts in the East or West. For instance, a whirling ritual of the Jalaliyyah order in İstanbul, Turkey, takes place every Monday at midnight at a *tekke* (a Sufi retreat) in Fatih, the district of İstanbul where many fundamentalist Muslims live. The whirling is accompanied by prayers, in which the observers also are expected to participate. The observers are mainly pious Muslims, many of them Sufis. Before they enter the *tekke*, they remove their shoes as one would at a mosque, since one is entering "God's territory." Female visitors who do not think or know to bring a headcover (more frequently true for non-

17

Muslims) are asked to borrow or buy a scarf that is provided at the entrance; if their clothing is in any way immodest, they are given a large sheet with which to cover their whole bodies. Men and women sit on the floor in segregated quarters. During the ritual, both the observers and the participating Jalalis assume a supplicant prayer posture, holding up their hands to God while internally reciting prayers. A group of the Jalalis sings and prays while another group begins to go through the motions of whirling after receiving the blessings of the master, who remains at the center throughout the ceremony. At the end of the ceremony, one of the members invites the observers to partake of tea with them in an adjacent room, where the master offers to answer any questions the visitors may have. By this point, it is midnight, but they are insistent that the visitors not leave without sharing tea, fruits, and sweets with them and having their questions answered. It is unclear whether this is a form of missionizing or an earnest interest in informing the public, or both.

In contrast, a performance of the Whirling Dervishes in the United States usually takes place in an auditorium at a college campus, where the audience is seated in mixed company. In this context, the performance is treated as one equal in value to any dance concert or play. It is for a limited time only, as the performers tour the country and then leave. For the Muslim audience in the ritual described above, it would be sacrilegious to talk or to leave for the toilet, as it also would be, during mass at church. At the auditorium, however, the audience observes the etiquette that one would at *any* dance concert. In both the Muslim and the Western settings, the performers are all males. In the former, the performance is free. In the Western setting, tickets cost as much as twenty dollars or more. When watching, the audience is not expected to participate in any prayers whatsoever, nor is it invited to meet with and talk to the performers. This is also true of the yearly performances of the Mawlawis in Konya, Turkey, where Rûmî lived, taught, and is buried. These take place every December in a gymnasium and are intended for the general public, mainly for foreign tourists. They are motivated by tourism and the revenue that they bring in.

As a result of the variety of occasions that have allowed Sufism to make its way in the modern world, Sufism has exploded in countless ways and has undergone numerous interpretations. The manner in which Sufism has adapted to the new times and places is in fact a sign of its vitality, breadth, and flexibility. Since Lessing's connection is to Sufism in the West, her novels reflect the departures of Western Sufism from *tasawwuf*. For instance, most Western Sufis, who do not live in a Sufi community, *cannot* practice *tasawwuf* as it was originally intended: as an ongoing part of their lives. They live their individual lives in their respective homes and gather to discuss Sufi concepts in theory, in workshops and seminars, usually at retreats that last a limited length of time. Furthermore, such retreats cost a significant amount of money, giving one the impression that the "Sufis" in charge are running a business.

It seems that when Lessing absorbed Sufism originally through Shah's books and lectures in London, she encountered much more of Sufi thought than she did of Sufi practice or of a Sufi community. When she began to study Sufism under Shah's tutelage, Lessing did not have to abandon her Western socialization and move into a community of Sufis to worship God. As a novelist firmly rooted in the Western tradition, she is able to read and think about classical Sufi practices without having to assume the passionate language of the Sufis or their lifestyle. For the most part, her characters do not have a relational identity—they suffer and seek alone. There is very little group effort, and hardly a community spirit. Some of her characters seem to find the utopia that they are seeking, but not in a Sufi brotherhood. Nor do they partake of spiritual journeys in groups, except perhaps in *The Making of the Representative for Planet 8*, in which they work as one to save their planet from freezing, though even there the relationships are less committed and less intense than that exacted in a Sufi brotherhood.

ORIENTATIONS

Lessing Criticism

Whether critics have accepted Lessing's mysticism or not, response to her works has been overwhelming. In their overview of Lessing criticism, Kaplan and Rose sum up the attention Lessing has received: "From 1971, when Paul Schlueter dared to propose an MLA seminar on the 'popular novelist' Doris Lessing to 1986 when the MLA officially recognized *The Golden Notebook* (1962) as a 'Masterpiece of World Literature,' Lessing scholarship has taken a giant step, comparable to Lessing's own leap from Africa to Argos and beyond" (37).[23] Greene writes, "the move from history to myth takes Lessing back to the oldest knowledge of the race, to those ancient repositories of wisdom, the Bible, the [Qur'ân], and Sufic lore" (*Poetics* 26). When Sprague and Tiger bring up the issue of Lessing's Sufism, they note "That [Lessing] has turned to mystic themes of madness as spiritual release is no minor aberration: she herself converted to Sufism under Idries Shah" (2). At the same time they add, "Lessing remains highly rational. In Margaret Drabble's words, 'she is prophetic, but not in a vague, exhortatory, passionate mode'" (2). This book makes a similar distinction about Lessing's work in chapter 1, where it compares Lessing's novels to the passionate love poetry of Mawlânâ Jalâluddîn Rûmî to show how Lessing's Sufism is inevitably tempered by her Western outlook.

In 1978, Paul Schlueter commented that "most Lessing criticism thus far has been thematic in nature, with such fairly recent excursions as Sufi or Jungian or Laingian influences, or the like, still new enough not to have impressed themselves into our collective critical estimation" ("Schlueter" 6). Two decades later, this is still somewhat true of Sufism. In a 1992 article Perrakis points out that "in the very act of 'marrying' Eastern and Western thought [Lessing] is offering a model for cooperation and interchange between nations" (119). Addressing critics who have faulted Lessing for having become irrational and religious (12), Fahim defends Lessing's turn to

Sufism as her way of "deepening her understanding" of the world and of humanity. This stand facilitates further discussion of the place of Sufism in Lessing's life and work. While Fahim's book elaborates on the Sufi equilibrium in Lessing's novels "between the rational and non-rational modes of consciousness" (13), this book evaluates the influence of Sufism as Lessing encountered it in the West with an eye on not only how Lessing's novels are affected by Sufism but how Sufism itself is altered and adapted in Lessing's Western context.

In her annotated bibliography, Fishburn acknowledges that "It is widely agreed among scholars that most if not all of Lessing's fiction qualifies as a kind of Sufi teaching story, intended to have profound and lasting influence on the way her readers think" (15). Hardin confirms the same in Lessing's personal life: "Lessing herself has been involved with Sufism for a number of years and she is one of the better-known students of Idries Shah" ("Sufi Teaching" 317). Bazin adds, "Lessing's ideas have been nourished and clarified through her interest in Sufism, the name in Western languages for Islamic mysticism" ("Evolution" 159). The implications of such a consensus demand that we interpret Lessing with Sufism in mind. Fishburn adds, "If readers had been somewhat taken aback when they first encountered *Briefing* and *Memoirs*, they were stunned by the appearance of *Shikasta* and the disappearance of 'their' Lessing. . . . And as the next four novels appeared in swift succession . . . we found we simply had to rethink our critical position on Lessing" (22). Such rethinking is the purpose of this study, which offers a new dimension to Lessing scholarship. It does not reject previous scholarship but builds on it.

Lessing's Western readers who were not familiar with Sufism were disconcerted when, to their dismay, Lessing appeared to abandon her usual rational worldview. But had we considered her Sufism with less resistance, perhaps she might not have surprised us to the extent that she did. Her move into Sufi studies is not a sign of abandonment of her earlier political, psychological, or social stands. Rather, Lessing uses complementary motifs in all of her novels; and "at the root of all these diverse trends is an interest in the individual and the means of fulfilling his potential in relation to his community" (Fahim 5).

Part of what we were unwilling to see in Lessing's earlier works was the way in which there were hints of Sufism in *Landlocked* (1965), *The Four-Gated City* (1969), *Briefing for a Descent into Hell* (1971), and *The Memoirs of a Survivor* (1974). We also did not give serious consideration to the apparent connection between Lessing's novels and her frank discussions of Sufism both in public lectures and in writing. Part of the argument in this book will be that some of what Lessing was doing in her earlier fiction was introducing Sufi ideas and building up to a fuller exploration of those ideas in the *Canopus in Argos: Archives* (1979–83) series. Lessing returned to writing more realistic novels after the *Canopus* series, but some critics still were not happy with her. She still seemed offbeat, and Janna Somers's experiences were somehow too ordinary. She was not quite a radical Anna Wulf, who made a political statement by refusing the traditional role for women and who sought psychotherapy to find her new identity. Nor was she so outrageous as Martha Quest, who abandoned even her own daughter to "find herself."

Feminist critics felt particularly let down when Lessing refused to be the feminist cult figure for whom they had so desperately yearned to see them through the 1960s and 1970s. After all, *The Golden Notebook* had been, according to early feminist critics, "a document in the history of [women's] liberation" (Margaret Drabble qtd. in Greene, *Changing* 108) and "a nearly pure expression of feminine consciousness . . . honestly reflecting the truths of feminine experience" (Elayne Antler Rapping qtd. in Greene, *Changing* 108), even though initially women had accused Lessing of betraying the female sex by exposing all of women's "secrets" as well as for depicting women as victims. The letdown that followed was mutual. On this, Lessing said in an interview in 1992, "The feminists claimed me for one of theirs, which made me very angry because I don't like this separation off into sheep and goats. And I've never written specifically either for men or women" (Upchurch 224). However, while Lessing refused to become a feminist cult figure, she had become, according to Bazin, a writer whose vision of saving the world is accomplished by *women's* (not men's) psychic powers.[24]

All along, Lessing had refused to conform to the expectation that she serve as a static role model. While sympathetic critics finally realized she was indeed not going to speak for women alone, but had other interests that included outer space and mysticism, many others lost their patience and decided Lessing had gone too far. She was not the same author who wrote *The Golden Notebook*, and many sulked—*not* because Lessing had erred, but because they could not follow where she was going. This unease may have something to do with the kind of relationship that Lessing wanted to create with her readers.

In *The Company We Keep*, Booth argues that novels are like friends we make, that the act of reading is analogous to entering to varying degrees into a relationship with the novel, its characters, its narrator, and its author. A novel, then, succeeds to the degree that that relationship is in some way fulfilling for the reader. Consequently, when readers' relationships with Lessing no longer satisfied them, some declared her novels "unsuccessful." Gayle Greene writes, "reviewers do show amazing unimaginativeness in approaching her works, a reluctance, a refusal, to grant her her premises" (*Poetics* 31). What some critics failed to see was that Lessing was trying to establish a different kind of relationship with them. Rather than the comfortable friend of many novels, they found in her a nagging friend who always wanted them to question themselves, change, and do *more*. Hardin writes, "Just as Sufi teaching stories are intended to make the listener uncomfortable, so also do the Lessing stories" ("Sufi Teaching" 318). But most do not want friends like Lessing's character Johor, the emissary from mainland Canopus, to disturb their peace; nor do they want friends like Lessing herself, those who point out their shortcomings as a human society—at least not quite so overtly. Consequently, "more than one reader has expressed the sense of having lost a friend with Lessing's abandonment of earthlings" (Knapp 130). To quote John Leonard, "I, and rational discourse, have lost a friend . . . in a smog of mystifications" (qtd. in Hazleton 21). Greene adds, "it is not only [Lessing's] mysticism that puts people off: so too does her realism" (*Poetics* 31).

Sufism, as she came to know it in the West, accommodated Lessing's various questions regarding higher powers and life on other planets. Space fiction enabled Lessing to explore these questions from the point of view of Sufi ideology. Still, readers became impatient with Lessing, because she neglected to sugarcoat her prophecy of doom and rebirth. We in the West have come to mistrust sermons; our tolerance for them has long worn off. Stone expresses this sentiment best: "There was a time when I could tolerate didactic work if it sent a piece of closeted knowledge into the world, but that period is past. I need artists who pay as much attention to expression as to history and their inner lives" (29). Rubenstein complements this with her opening remark in her review of Lessing's *Prisons We Choose to Live Inside* (1987): "There has always been a side of Doris Lessing that likes the soapbox" (7). Rubenstein is so irritated by Lessing's *Prisons*, she continues: "Hearing her voice directly from the podium rather than indirectly through her characters, I feel grateful that Lessing years ago chose fiction as the primary medium of her message and that, since these lectures, she has stepped down from her soapbox to write another novel" (7). Despite this displeasure at Lessing's didacticism, it is widely accepted that Lessing writes about "the mind discovering, interpreting and ultimately shaping its own reality" (Rubenstein, *Novelistic* 7). Kaplan and Rose call Lessing "an alchemical writer" because "[m]ore than any other major twentieth-century writer—excepting, possibly, D. H. Lawrence—Lessing challenges her readers and changes them; alters their consciousnesses" (5).

Wilson compares Lessing's tendency to raise human consciousness to de Beauvoir's contribution to feminism. She describes both writers as Cassandras who loomed in the 1960s. Both women share the romantic pessimism of the post–Second World War period. They also share the honesty of expression about women's sexuality as an irrational force, a response to love for men (65).[25] Both de Beauvoir and Lessing are convinced that desertion by men and broken hearts can undo women. But while Lessing sees madness as potentially liberating, de Beauvoir does not. On this point Lessing takes the road of R. D. Laing, while de Beauvoir trusts the rational choice that existentialism offers, a choice that overly privileges the Cartesian conscious agent and the Western idea of freedom. Both writers give voice to many women, but neither represents the collective concerns of all women. As a result, they anger their readers who mistakenly feel misrepresented.[26]

Paying attention to Sufism will not only complicate our understanding of Lessing's work but also reshape our assessments of its quality. If part of the purpose of literature is to entertain, Lessing pays little attention to that. If literature ought to be aesthetically pleasing, Lessing ignores that goal to a great extent, as well. She foregrounds the didactic and concerns herself very little with the sugarcoating that can aid readers to swallow the bitter pill of her "sermons." In Booth's terms, Lessing deliberately chooses to be the irritating friend. While this choice does not exactly fit our dominant aesthetic standards that privilege thematic indirection and subtlety, it fits another one—in which aesthetics and ethics are more closely intertwined. In that case the didactic does not necessarily become a flaw, the question of sugarcoating is not quite that relevant, and we have Lessing's writings that are deliberately designed to get under our skin. In fact, the more Lessing succeeds at getting under our skin, the better it is. When and if we are ever able to leave aside our automatic rejection of her moralistic style, we can appreciate her courageous insistence on traveling the road not taken by most westerners and the groundbreaking boldness with which she privileges the value system of another tradition.

When we question prevailing views on Lessing's works, especially on her *Canopus* series, that overlook or downplay Sufi elements in her work, we find that attending to those elements significantly alters our understanding of Lessing's work. Lessing herself encourages a spiritual reading of her novels whenever she remarks on her own writing. In a 1984 lecture in New York she told her audience, "I hold some very old-fashioned views, very different from what I thought any age up to forty. I think that we are here for a purpose—to learn—and that there is a God: I don't think that we are purposeless. Forgive me for that old-fashioned and ridiculous view" (Tiger, "Candid" 6). In *The Memoirs of a Survivor*, for instance, Lessing expresses her narrator's awareness of God or a higher power as the sensation of "being held in the hollow of a great hand" (101); in *The Four-Gated City* Martha is involved in what she calls her "work." By trusting that "great hand" and through "work" on the self, the Sufi believes in the possibility of achieving a higher state of being—not higher as in "superior," but higher in the sense of becoming more than what one already is.

This book follows in the spirit of Ann Scott, who has written about Lessing's mysticism. When Scott recalls the introduction that Lessing wrote to Olive Schreiner's *The Story of an African Farm* (1976), she explains the parallel that Lessing draws between Schreiner's allegory of "The Hunter" and the Sufi poet Farîduddîn 'Attâr's (d. 1220) *The Conference of the Birds* (1177). In both stories there is a search for a famous "Bird of Truth," or God. Scott points out that Lessing's use of religious language is rather liberal and diluted. It is her personal version rather than a clone of other Sufi artists and writers. Scott focuses on Lessing's use of "meta-language . . . which by definition secularizes 'mysticism' in putting it to work as one of the materials of a text" (165). But even as she asserts a formalist reading, Scott allows for the "possibility that Sufism, along with other religious narratives and symbols . . . , does also represent itself and the ultimate unexplainability of things to which Lessing considers we all must yield" (165). This study argues along similar lines as it attempts at a comprehensive understanding of the corpus of Lessing's novels and of the way of life that Lessing prescribes.

More frequently, the tendency in Lessing criticism has been to focus more on Lessing's changed technique and language as a result of Sufism and not enough on the changes in her themes and content, her characters' resolutions and expectations. Mysticism in Lessing's fiction has inspired many to discuss "defamiliarization, a writer's attempt to make use of a form of language, a way of looking at narrative, or an interpretative framework" (Scott 167). Fahim, for instance, focuses on Lessing as an artist and aesthetic creator between the years 1950 and 1983. She refers to Sufi methods of writing to explain and to trace some of the changes in Lessing's style, among them, the change (though not total) from realism to fantasy. She is interested in explaining Lessing by placing her between Eastern and Western modes of writing. *Between East and West* focuses more on Lessing's characters' spiritual quests on the Sufi Path and looks at how that spirituality requires a different fictive technique for its expression. It assumes no prior knowledge of Sufism on the part of readers and discusses Sufi ideas that have circulated in the West.

The Scope of Lessing's Work

As Western critics, we are often troubled by either/or categories rather than both/and. Sufis are both political *and* spiritual. They are by definition anything but one-dimensional. They are neither only this-worldly nor only other-worldly. Lessing's preference for Sufism has much to do with this flexibility of Sufism and with its resistance to pigeonholing. In an interview with Susan Stamberg on National Public Radio

Lessing exclaimed, "Why do you make it 'or, or, or?' It could be 'and, and, and' . . . either/or [has] very little to do with how things really are." In defense of Lessing's use of the "and, and, and" mind-set, Kaplan and Rose discuss the Sufi "scatter technique" which refers to "fragmented ideas that recur and demand a new perspective, a new understanding, therefore always resist[ing] final analysis" (4).

Fishburn recognizes Lessing's conflicting realities in the *Canopus* series through which she wants to shake our present worldview. She sees a parallel to these unstable truths and paradoxes in modern physics (123). Indeed, the New Physics helps us to read Lessing, for much of modern physics approaches Eastern mysticism and vice versa (Capra). Modern physics, among other influences, has shaped Lessing's thinking, and it helps us in following the lessons that Lessing communicates to her readers. There is value, however, in acknowledging Lessing's mysticism as well as her scientific bend. In particular, the didactic style with which Lessing anxiously delivers her lessons appears to have been enhanced by Sufism that has permeated her life and mind. When we read *The Making of the Representative for Planet 8*, for instance, we cannot overlook the Sufi context in the lessons that Johor teaches Doeg and Lessing teaches us. The relationships Lessing establishes in *The Representative* distinctively follow the Sufi hierrarchy, such as that of Johor to Doeg, Doeg to the community, or Lessing to her readers. In every case there is a transmission of knowledge from a higher level to a lower, from guide to initiate.

In passages such as the following, Lessing blurs the boundaries between science and spirituality and seems to invite critics to use both physics *and* mysticism to interpret her fiction: "the atoms and the molecules were losing their associations with each other, and were melding with the substance of the mountain" (*Representative* 118). This also brings to mind many *tasawwuf* poets who make references to the physical world, as does the better-known Western mystic and poet, William Blake, who sees

Introduction

> A World in a Grain of Sand
> . . . a Heaven in a Wild Flower,
> Hold Infinity in the palm of your hand
> And Eternity in an hour. ("Auguries")

The fourteenth-century Sufi sage Sa'd ud Dîn Mahmûd Shabistarî sounds just like Blake or Lessing in his use of the physical environment to discuss the spiritual realm. Lessing quotes part of Shabistarî's poem, *The Secret Garden*, in her opening to *Briefing for a Descent into Hell* (1971):

> If yonder raindrop should its heart disclose,
> Behold therein a hundred seas displayed.
> In every atom, if thou gaze aright,
> Thousands of reasoning beings are contained.
> . . . .
> Upon one little spot within the heart
> Resteth the Lord and Master of the worlds.
> Therein two worlds commingled may be seen . . . (1)

Similarly, Rûmî wrote that one could cut an atom and find a miniature solar system in it. Consider also the following lines from Yunus Emre, a thirteenth-century Turkish mystic and poet of the Bektashiyyah Sufi order:

> I am the kingfisher of love, admired of the sea.
> The sea is but a droplet within me, its atoms an
> overflowing infinity. (Öztürk 64)

As these examples from Lessing, Blake, Shabistarî, Rûmî, and Yunus demonstrate, the fascination with the realm of atoms and particles is not reserved only to scientists. Yet, unlike the scientist, the Sufi does not stop at the miniscule world of atoms but proceeds into God's territory.

Lessing follows the above quote with one from a scientific passage by Rachel Carson: "a world in which the micro-droplet

29

of water separating one grain of sand from another is like a vast, dark sea" (*Briefing* 1). With this, Lessing implies and invites a dual reading, one that acknowledges the effects of both science and mysticism on her thinking. She suggests dual readings also in *The Four-Gated City* (1969) when she quotes from both scientific and spiritual sources in the opening epigraphs to each chapter. Hardin writes that Lessing's "novels and her short stories partake of the two worlds—of real life on the one hand and of mental processes on the other. The secret is that Lessing, like the Sufis, does not see the two as separate" ("Sufi Way" 571). Fahim adds, "the dialectic between [science and spirituality] propels the argument for equilibrium" (141).[27] Lessing in fact has commented in a 1980 interview with Nissa Torrents that "[t]he best scientists, those on the highest levels, always come closer and closer to the mystical. Much of what Einstein said could have been said by a Christian mystic, St. Augustine, for example" (66).

The Sufi tradition influenced not only Lessing's choice of subject matter but also her literary style. In fact, her turn to Sufi content in her novels may have instigated her choice of space fiction as an appropriate medium through which to communicate a different worldview. The new outlook that Sufism provided for Lessing complemented her inclinations to the ideas of Marx, Jung, Laing, and the New Physics rather than displaced them. In what she prefers to call *space fiction* (rather than *science fiction*),[28] Lessing seems to have found a welcome outlet through which to explore the realm of the human soul. It would be unlikely that she would talk and write about Sufism without also assimilating it into her psyche. Sufis frequently liken their way to the nature of garlic. When a clove of garlic cooks in a pot with other foods it gradually permeates the whole of the dish until it loses its flavor and becomes a part of the whole. The same is true of the action of Sufism in those it touches—it does not remain only in one's library or one's lectures but pervades one's total reality, imagination, and psyche. Those whom Sufism touches are expected to become like the clove of garlic—potent, yet willing to give of themselves freely until they dissolve and merge with their environment. Lessing's space-fiction novels inevitably display this action of Sufism operating in them in various obvious and subtle ways. At the same time, Lessing is not necessarily interested in converting us to Sufism. Her primary concern seems to be social, not religious education. As Ann Scott puts it, Lessing's is "a critique of contemporary society rather than a call to piety or withdrawal from the world" (175). That is, after all, the Way of the Sufi. Sufis prefer to remain firmly in the world, even as they strive not to be completely "of" it.[29]

Lessing does not relent in offering novels as potential catalysts that might provoke an epiphany for her readers. "We are, she warns in that quiet, persuasive voice, running out of time. We have much to overcome before we can break out and away from contemporary conditioning" (Hardin, "Sufi Teaching" 324). Lessing speaks to all of humankind and implores us to shake ourselves out of our lethargy. In the Preface to *The Sirian Experiments: The Report by Ambien II of the Five* (1980), she asks us to entertain the possibility "that this earth [may have] been used for the purposes of experiment by more advanced creatures . . . [and] the human race [might have] a future planned for it more glorious than we can imagine" (viii). To this potential end, she writes.

Lessing's urgent prophecy involves mobilizing her readers into conscious "work" in order to manifest their full potentials and thereby fulfill their destinies.[30] As she stated in a 1973 lecture on Sufism, "man is woefully underused and undervalued, and he doesn't know his own capacities" ("Ancient" 78). In fact, Lessing has acknowledged that what attracted her to a serious study of the Sufi Way was precisely this idea of developing one's potentials, which is central to Sufism. Moreover, like the Sufis, while Lessing is concerned about humankind, her real interest lies in the larger scheme where the whole universe is what matters, and individuals are important only to the degree of their contribution to the big picture. She believes that "the petty fates of planets, let alone individuals, are only aspects of cosmic evolution" (Hazleton 25), which belief she advocates in the *Canopus* series. Lessing asserted in a 1972 interview with Josephine Hendin that it is necessary for humanity to "look at itself as a whole, and to face its problems as a whole" (43).

Humanity is a big word; however, we have to take Lessing's understanding of the concept seriously. What matters to Lessing as a student of Sufism is the biggest picture possible, like the large Oriental carpet—or the cosmos—in *The Memoirs* (1974). An individual's only real task is to find his or her color and design or destiny in life on that carpet and to fill it in. Similarly, Lessing insists on including all of humanity in a larger plan in which a person is both unique and individual and also completely subordinate to the whole, as a finger is to the hand—that is, we are both ourselves and subjects who surrender to serve the needs of the greater community of humankind. Nowhere does Lessing prescribe a particular method for acquiring this balance, however, beyond demanding that we pay attention to our unique place in the universe. She puts no restrictions on us but appears to believe in the essential ingredient of time to be one's best teacher. Perhaps as a result of her insights into Sufi teachings that encourage perpetual self-study and growth and that do not recognize achievement of any goals as an end in itself, Lessing often carries her characters through to the end of their lives. Most of the protagonists in her lengthy novels not only grow old in the process of their lives' "work," but also die.

In addition to her fictional characters who "work" to rise to a higher level of being for the sake of a greater common cause, Lessing also speaks in her prefaces, afterwords, essays, and lectures about actual, nonfictional persons such as Edward Wilson, explorer and scientist, or Idries Shah, writer and businessman. What these men share with each other and with Lessing's characters is their ways of learning by living through "crammed and thoughtful" times (Lessing, "Ancient

Way" 81). Lessing expects us to look upon her characters as
fully mimetic role models, persons who have truly fulfilled
their destinies and found their place and duty in the Big
Picture. She offers us countless testimonials, real and fictional:
Wilson's journey after penguin eggs in the South Pole, Anna's
struggle to overcome her writer's block, Martha's search for
harmony, Emily's courageous maturing process, Al·Ith's sacrifice for the sake of educating those below her, Doeg's prolonged
suffering and death, or Janna's struggles with herself and
with Maudie.

It is irrelevant that Martha Quest's island or the black
iron egg out of which the new humanity is born are only
Lessing's vision or that we cannot locate Shikasta, the plains of
Al·Ith's territory, or Planet 8 on a map. Lessing concentrates on
mapping out precisely the inner worlds of her characters, and
she does this especially carefully in her space fiction. When we
feel disappointed that she is exploring spaces which are not
familiar to us, we need to stop and consider whether these foreign territories do not in fact correspond to the lands which
we know in our dreams and the places which we experience
in our minds.[31] And if so, then Lessing deserves our gratitude
and applause for her part in familiarizing us with these plains
and for finally mapping out the twilight zones for us. For we
have much to learn about the art of inner "work" from the
examples of Anna Wulf, Saul Green, Martha Quest, Emily,
Al·Ith, Johor, Doeg, Maudie, or Janna, who compose Lessing's
team of boulder pushers. Through their individual struggles
within and through "work" on themselves, they persevere and
bear the cross of our moral and spiritual education.

The Scope of This Book

This study takes advantage of the opportunities that Lessing's
appropriation of Sufi ideology has presented. As a prominent
Western writer, Lessing naturally draws the attention of a

wide, international audience, and westerners who are inclined to read criticism about her should be willing to learn about Sufi communities, mysticism, and teaching tales from the Muslim world and in the West. This book aims to offer to these readers a deeper understanding of Sufi ideas and stories as well as of Lessing and many of her protagonists as aspiring Western Sufis, for as citizens of the global village, we *must* know our neighbors—in this case, the Sufi masters of old and new, whose ideas and teaching tales have found their way into Lessing's novels.

The effort to illuminate the relation between Lessing and Sufism necessarily entails an investigation of elements of the East that are for the most part only dimly known in the West. Popular stereotypes of Sufi mystics in both the East and the West are of ones who chant and dance with fervor, or of veiled women who inspire pitying scorn among their more "liberated" Western counterparts. Muslim forms such as Sufism seem exotic because we encounter them more rarely, even though there are almost as many Muslims in the world as Catholics.[32] If it were not for the appalling death warrant on Salman Rushdie for his *Satanic Verses*, or the "ethnic cleansing" of Muslims and mass rapes of Bosnian women in the former Yugoslavia, we in the West would be even less aware of matters "Muslim" than we are now. Of the three Abrahamic traditions—Judaism, Christianity, and Islam—the Islamicate tradition is the least known and most mistrusted in the West. This unfamiliarity with Islam may have something to do with its traditionally having had far less of an American presence than has been the case with the other two Abrahamic religions.[33] Along similar lines Lessing bemoans the European ignorance of Islam in her Preface to Shah's *Seekers after Truth*:

> Two great religions have influenced Europe, we say: Christianity and Judaism, but we scarcely mention Islam, which has been the third. We are the heirs, we claim proudly, of Greece and Rome, but seldom think of the Arabs, the Persians,

the Moors, who, through Spain, fed culture into a Europe that was considered a poor and backward place, with a culture far below the dazzling civilizations of the cities of North Africa, Spain, the Middle East, India. It is being recognized that these blocks have caused a pitiful imbalance in our view of ourselves as Europeans. We Europeans are Euro-centered. We know it; we say so; but we are only beginning to understand how much we are, and to what extent it has impoverished us. (629)

This book takes up one strand of Islam from among the many different traditions that fall under the rubric of Islam—Sunnî, Shî'î, Bâtinî, Khârijî, Ja'farî, Wahhabi, Mu'tazilî, Ismâ'îlî, Hanafî, Mâlikî, Shâfi'î, Hanbalî, or Sufi, and more. In an effort to introduce some concepts taught in the Sufi tradition, it is concerned with Islamicate folk tales, which have served as teaching tales in the Sufi tradition, as they are told orally or found in written form in Islamdom[34] and as they are *re*told by Idries Shah.

Many of Lessing's readers could not get through the first few pages of her space-fiction novels both because they felt they no longer "knew" her and because they found very little in them with which they could engage. For skeptical readers, part I of this book makes terms like *tasawwuf* and *Sufi* less foreign. Familiarity with these terms helps in understanding the succeeding chapters, which seek to illuminate the enigma which Lessing has become for some of her readers. For the most curious and inquisitive readers, appendix A will provide a historical background to *tasawwuf*, from which Western Sufis draw their inspiration.

This book argues, on the one hand, that many of Lessing's subtleties will remain eclipsed unless her critics make a concerted effort to understand Sufism. On the other hand, it examines the extent to which Lessing remains a rational Western writer despite her more mystical side that acknowledges Sufism as well as telepathy, ESP, the possibility of lives on other planets, or the spiritual potential of all humans.[35]

35

The difference between Lessing's fiction and the passionate testimonies of a classical Sufi poet such as Rûmî to God, the Beloved cannot lessen our high esteem for Lessing's boldness and imagination that allow her to experiment with new subject matters and new styles, among them, space fiction. Lessing's message to mobilize whole societies to "work" to awaken and to save themselves from impending annihilation is not easy to hear because it requires *active* participation. However, she must be commended for being our difficult friend who is always nagging us to change. Her relentless didacticism and her insistence to stand her ground despite our rather considerable resistance to her "experiments," as she calls her own novels, is admirable.

One

Sufism in Lessing's Work

*People ask, "How can you, a feminist, have anything to
do with an Islam-based study?" First, the real Sufis will
say that Sufism is not more Muslim than Christian, that
it predated Islam and Christianity because it has always
been in the world under one name or another or none
and cannot be equated with the temporary phase of any
culture, though it found a home within conventional
Islam for a time. Secondly, it is not enough for us to be
concerned with the situation of women; it is the situation
of humankind that should be our concern.*

—*Doris Lessing,*
"Learning How to Learn"

This chapter first defines Sufism as represented in nonacademic circles in the West. Second, it exemplifies the distinction between *tasawwuf* and Sufism by studying a poem by the thirteenth-century Persian *tasawwuf* poet and master of the Whirling Dervishes (the Mawlawiyyah), Mawlânâ Jalâluddîn Rûmî (1207–73), and a popularized, Westernized version of the same poem translated today, seven centuries later. Third, the chapter compares and contrasts the ecstatic message in Rûmî's original, longer poem with the optimistic message in Lessing's fiction.

For proponents of the Sufi Way in the West, Sufism falls somewhere between philosophy and religion—it is more a way

37

of seeing. It stresses attuning oneself to the needs of the human race and of the cosmos. A practicing Sufi in a Muslim society might say that a Sufi is a particularly good Muslim. A practicing Sufi in the West might say that a Sufi is a Sufi and that Sufism supercedes the lines of religion. In either case, it goes against the Sufis' grain to be pigeonholed. Just as nothing that we might be told about a rose can give us the smell of the rose, Sufis believe that "it is only those who taste who can know" (Lessing, *Writer's Encounter*, audiocasette). Mystical experience, like taste or smell, is something that is intimately inside us and can only be felt, not defined or explained. It "is as incommunicable to those insensitive to it as is musical experience to those deaf from birth" (Hodgson 1: 395). In this particular sense, Sufis share much with Jewish or Christian mystics.[1] As Arberry defines it, mysticism is "a constant and unvarying phenomenon of the universal yearning of the human spirit for personal communion with God" (11). Hodgson compares classic instances of the mystical experience to moments of apoplectic anger or climactic orgasm but says they are "more overpowering and intense . . . yet at the same time much calmer and deeper" (1: 396). He adds,

> the whole range of mystical experience, both ecstatic and everyday, is the commonplace experience of arriving at relative personal clarity: the clarity that comes when the elements of a problem finally fit together, or when one has shaken away the haziness after waking suddenly, or perhaps most especially, when a surge of anger has died down and one can look at the situation realistically and with a measure of generosity. . . . At best, in such moments (as many have discovered), one can face the loss of anything one has most desired, and even recognize one's worst traits, without either anxiety or self-pity, and can find the courage to try to be the best one can imagine being. (397–98)

Such serenity approximates what a Sufi may experience on the mystical path.

The word *Sufi* has many meanings. We do not know the word's total etymology, but in Arabic, *soof* means "wool," which could refer to the coarse woolen garments which the wandering mendicants or dervishes wore. *Sufi* also may have been derived from *ashab-i Suffa* in Arabic, meaning "the People of the Bench," referring to the inner circle of worshippers who gathered around Muhammad's mosque. The word *suffa* in this case refers to the *sofa* or bench on which the worshippers sat. Or *Sufi* may have been derived from the Arabic root *sfw*, meaning "to be pure." This root also constitutes the word *tasawwuf*, meaning "purity" (Arberry, *Sufism* 78). Sufis believe: "He that is purified by love is *safi*, or 'pure,' and he who is purified by the Beloved is a *Sufi*" (Bennett, *Gurdjieff* 47).

Idries Shah teaches that the Sufi Path is called "the Path of Love," referring to the search for God or one's Higher Self, with whom the Sufi mystic enters a love relationship. A passage from the Qur'ân, "He loveth them and they love Him" (5.59), supports the Sufi doctrine of love and authorizes "the idea of a trinity of Lover, Loved, and Love" (Arberry, *Sufism* 21). This is the reason why most classical Sufi poetry is written in the form of love poetry in which the poet addresses, beseeches, and longs for the Beloved (God), which is depicted as an ecstatic, even erotic love, not a Platonic liaison. In the case of the Sufis throughout history, the Christian term *agape* is supplanted by a less abstract, more direct desire for the Beloved Allah.

As understood in the West, Sufism loosely covers a wide range of ideas and practices that, when followed and carried out with careful attention to all of one's self, can lead to the transformation of individuals and to the betterment of humankind. This is at the heart of Lessing's Sufi message: for Sufis the child's slow progress into adulthood figures as only a developmental stage, "for which the dynamic force is love, not either asceticism or the intellect" ("Ancient" 76). According to Sufis, all of humanity can be induced to grow harmoniously in this fashion if individuals take upon themselves the task of following the Sufi Path while remaining in life and at work, in the world, but not of it.

According to Shah, Sufis have taught and led in varying manners that were appropriate to their times, circumstances, and geography. Shah quotes Ahmad al-Badawî: "Sufi schools are like waves which break upon rocks: [they are] from the same sea, in different forms, for the same purpose" (*Way* 269). Sufis characterize fake cults or imitations as a fur coat that one wears only in winter and has no need for in warm weather or good times. In contrast, they encourage a way of living and a way of interpreting the world that one maintains always and everywhere. Dervishes have been "kings, soldiers, poets, astronomers, educators, advisers, and sages" in the past. And today, a "Sufi can be a scientist, a politician, a poet, a housewife, the usherette in the cinema, and may never be known as one, since Sufism may have nothing to do with outward appearance and behavior. It is in operation all the time, all over the world, in every country, sometimes openly, sometimes not. The people offering it can be well known, as it were, beating a drum to say, 'We are here.' Or they may teach secretly" (Lessing, "Ancient" 75). In short, Sufis and their activities are only as supernatural and out of the ordinary as our lives are.

The Sufi approach to knowledge is a practical one. Sufis feel that although books have their place in one's development, true knowledge cannot be attained through books. They are more interested in immediate knowledge that comes from experience. Sufi education favors a holistic approach to learning in which the seeker is asked to see and understand with the heart and with all of one's being, not the mind alone, or the body alone. Rûmî says, "If you grasp knowledge through the heart, it is a friend. If you limit it to the 'body' alone, it is a snake" (Friedlander 58). Similarly, Sufis shun a purely academic approach to learning. The paradox, however, is that Sufis in history who have condemned book learning have been at the same time the most productive, prolific writers of theoretical books in Islamic history.[2]

Shah does not advocate that Sufis abandon their worldly duties. On the contrary, he argues that the treasure which a would-be disciple seeks should derive from one's work in the world. He calls for a commitment to the evolution of all of humankind through the struggles that an everyday living provides. Practical work is considered to be the means through which the seeker can do self-"work," whereby one becomes perfected. In Lessing's *Four-Gated City*, we see an instance of this self-"work" in what goes on in the basement apartment, which Lessing calls "work," also. Throughout history, too, Sufis have followed ordinary professions to earn their livelihoods through which they "worked" on themselves. Their surnames point to these professions: *saqatî* (huckster), *hallâj* (cotton carder), *nassâj* (weaver), *warrâq* (bookseller or copyist), *qawârîrî* (glassmaker), *haddâd* (blacksmith), and *bannâ'* (mason) (Schimmel 84).

Rûmî warns both the academician and the theologian: "When will you cease to worship and to love the pitcher? When will you begin to look for the water? . . . Know the difference between the color of the wine and the color of the glass" (Shah, *Sufis* 138). In other words, if confused and incomplete people make money or become professional successes by worshipping the pitcher, they still remain incomplete. Life merely has happened to them, their behavior continually changing with their mood, state of health, the weather, or other external stimuli. Lessing speaks of an old Sufi, the Lord of the Skies, who said that Sufis find strange the belief that one can progress only by improvement, for they realize that "man is just as much in need of stripping off rigid accretions to reveal the knowing essence as he is of adding anything. Those who are really the wise know that the teaching may be carried out also by exclusion of those things which make man blind and deaf" ("Ancient" 81).

In the 1971 introduction that she wrote to *The Golden Notebook* Lessing calls the present system of education in the West "indoctrination," and she believes that "[w]e have not yet evolved a system of education that is not a system of indoctrination" (xvii). She feels that we still teach the current prejudices of our particular time and culture, and we mold and pattern people to fit the needs of our particular society. She adds, "I am sure that the manifold talents, creativity, inventiveness of young children—who can sing and dance and draw and tell tales and make verses and whose view of life is so very clear and direct—could go into adult life and not disappear, as tends to happen in our system of education" ("Ancient" 78). The Sufi aim, therefore, is to encourage balanced and creative beings with properly working minds, hearts, and bodies. Ultimately, as Lessing said in an interview, what she "would like to be able to say . . . is that someone who has just read a book of mine is incited to ask questions" (Rousseau 154).

An important aspect of Sufism that especially disturbs the individualist westerner is the idea that in order to follow the difficult Sufi Path, one must have a guide (*shaikh* or *murshid*), and must have absolute trust in that guide. Without a guide, one can read all the books of instruction for a thousand years, but can achieve nothing (Schimmel 103).[3] Lessing says, "Every person comes to a point when the need is felt for further inner growth. Then it is wise to look for the guide, the teacher, the exemplar, that figure central to Sufism who shows others what is possible. This person, the product of a certain kind of varied and intensive education, will be master not of one trade but of a dozen, learned through pressures of necessity, created by the people by whom he has been surrounded from birth, people whose duty it is to see that he fulfills all his capacities" ("Ancient" 79).

The image of the guide or master in *tasawwuf* has been identified by Sufis with the true Beloved who cures the lover's heart (Schimmel 104).[4] The master's task is to open the eyes of the adept (*murîd*) to act as a physician of the soul. Shah promotes himself as such a guide to members of his institute in London, among whom Lessing figures as an active participant. About the role of the teacher Lessing says, "God is love can be the highest experience one can have, or it can just be some words scrawled on a poster carried by some poor old tramp. In between these two are a thousand levels of experience. How to guide the student from one level to the next is the knowledge of a [Sufi] teacher" (Lessing, *Writer's Encounter*, audiocassette). Lessing adds in her preface to Shah's *Seekers after Truth* that the Sufi teacher is far from "the father figure (the priest) of tradition" (631). She recommends, "if you want to study Sufism, then what a Teacher is *not*, is what you first of all have to study" (631).

A primary technique that Sufi teachers use is to cause discomfort in students by challenging their patience and sense of reality. They do this in order to eliminate curiosity seekers who will quit after a brief frustration and to reveal to their adherents that different people have different and everchanging perspectives of the truth. Mulla Nasrudin (or Nasreddin Hodja) makes fun of the gatekeeper's conception of truth in the following tale: A king orders that any liar passing through the city gates be executed. After several victims, it is Nasrudin's turn. Like the others, he is asked where he is going, and what his business is. Nasrudin answers, "I am on my way to be hanged." And when the guards challenge his statement he replies, "Then hang me if I'm lying!" (Shah, *Sufis* 68).

Concepts of wholeness and indeterminacy are among the building blocks of Sufism.[5] Students on the Path know that they are infinitesimal though still significant parts of the whole universe and that when they approach a Sufi master they can make no provisions to determine the outcome of their discipleship. There are an infinite number of Sufi stories that illustrate this lesson. In the case involving Mulla Nasrudin, "A woman brought her small son to the Mulla's school. 'Please frighten him a little,' she said, 'because he is rather beyond my control.' Nasrudin turned up his eyeballs, started to puff and pant, danced up and down and beat his fists on the table until the horrified woman fainted. Then he rushed out of the room. When he returned and the woman had recovered consciousness, she said to him, 'I asked you to frighten the boy, not me!' 'Madam,' said the Mulla, 'danger has no favorites. I even frightened myself, as you saw. When danger threatens, it threatens all equally'" (Shah, *Sufis* 85). As Shah explains this tale, "the Sufi teacher cannot supply his disciple with only a small quantity of Sufism. Sufism is the whole, and carries with it the implications of completeness" (85).[6] These concepts are so much a reality in Sufism that recognizing their parallels in Lessing can help us to understand her better. Her cosmologies in the various space-fiction novels depict different manifestations of Sufi teaching environments—from the plains in *The Marriages between Zones Three, Four, and Five* to the ice in *The Making of the Representative for Planet 8*.

In the Sufi experience, it is natural for a teacher to cloak his teaching intentionally under various disguises as the need arises. This is called *taqiyyah*, which in Arabic refers to the "pious dissimulation of one's true opinions" (Hodgson 1: 381). The reasons behind concealment are many. The truth must be protected from the ignorant. It is unsuitable to expose it to those who cannot yet understand it. Those who are not properly prepared to receive the truth must be protected until they can absorb it. And the bearers of truth must be protected against persecution. Scientists as well as spiritual and political leaders have been persecuted for publicly sharing their discoveries or insights at various points in time, and one need only look at history to see cases in which the practice of *taqiyyah* has been justified. One of the most popular cases in the history of *tasawwuf* is that of Mansur al-Hallâj, who neglected practicing *taqiyyah* or dissimulation, and who publicly declared himself to be one with God. His ecstatic exclamation, "I am the Absolute Truth," or "I am God," was so threatening to the 'Abbâsid caliphate that he was tortured and put to death in 922 C.E. He was stoned, his hands and feet were cut off, and he was left hanging on the gallows overnight before he was decapitated and burned. In his agony he is said to have "expressed his delight that he was suffering so for God's sake, but acknowledged that his judges were as right to condemn him, so as to safeguard the community life, as he was right to express paradoxes so as to proclaim the love of God" (Hodgson 1: 409).

Figures in the West with similar fates include Socrates, Jesus, Gandhi, and Martin Luther King, Jr., to name only a few. Persecution was never limited directly to the spiritual realm. Others, such as Leonardo da Vinci or Galileo, were not executed but were severely opposed. A paranoid da Vinci resorted to writing the results of his multifarious inventions in great detail on pages no larger than a man's hand, in mirror image so as not to be read by his contemporaries. As a result, although he observed that the pendulum might be used to make a clock keep equal time, today we credit Galileo for "discovering" the pendulum one hundred years after da Vinci. Galileo himself threatened the religious authorities of his time with his declaration that the earth revolves around the sun. The following Mulla Nasrudin anecdote illustrates the human tendency to persecute the bearers of truth: "Nasrudin entered the Land of Fools. 'O people,' he cried, 'sin and evil are hateful!' He did the same thing every day for some weeks. One day as he was about to start his lecture, he saw a group of Foolslanders standing with folded arms. 'What are you doing?' 'We have just decided what to do about all this sin and evil you have been talking about all the time.' 'So you have decided to shun it?' 'No, we have decided to shun *you*'" (Shah, *Subtleties* 90).

In response to persecution, coupled by the outlawing of Sufi activities in some countries at the end of the nineteenth century, some Sufi groups have operated underground and they intentionally have obscured their teachings. However, "hidden" does not mean "extinct." Shah quotes Saa'di of Shiraz, the thirteenth-century Persian Sufi poet:

> If a gem falls into mud it is still valuable.
> [But if] dust ascends to heaven, it remains
> valueless. (*Way* 83)

45

According to Shah, the truth is kept within because Sufis believe that it is not right to explain the experiences of the heart with words formulated by the intellect. The only proper form of communicating anything real is carried out from heart to heart, without words. This is why the Sufi Path is called "the Path of Love" and the aspirant a "lover" for whom explanations and apologies not only are considered unnecessary but are to be avoided lest they interfere with the exercising of true communion with the Beloved. If judged by the Sufi principle of *taqiyyah*, this book will prove to represent just what Sufis conclude one must avoid doing. Nonetheless, an analysis and clarification of Sufi tendencies in Lessing's novels may facilitate an understanding of Sufism as a vital and natural force in Lessing's work.

Following is a popularized translation of a *tasawwuf* poem by Rûmî. It takes advantage of the subject matter of the original poem, which addresses God the Beloved. As is typical of *tasawwuf* literature, the Beloved, or Allah, is depicted, incarnated, and cloaked in the language, form, and garb of a romantic lover. This depiction is foregrounded in the following poem at the expense of the original poem's spiritual message.

> I want to say words that flame
> as I say them, but I keep quiet and don't try
> to make both worlds fit in one mouthful.
>
> I keep secret in myself an Egypt
> that doesn't exist. [*Mesr-e 'adam*]
> Is that good or bad? I don't know.
>
> For years I gave away sexual love
> with my eyes. Now I don't.
> I'm not in any one place. I don't have a name
> for what I give away. Whatever Shams[7]
> gave, that you can have from me.
>> (trans. Barks, *Open Secret* 43)

46

In *Open Secret* translators Coleman Barks and John Moyne explain that this was a collaborative effort. It is a reworking by Barks of a more literally faithful English translation done by the late Orientalist A. J. Arberry. Furthermore, when we refer to Arberry's *Mystical Poems of Rûmî* we learn that Arberry's translation was completed when his health was failing and that his publication was prepared posthumously by Hasan Javadi and Ehsan Yarshater, who had to decipher Arberry's handwriting. Consequently the poem we have is not only twice removed but possibly three or four times removed from the original in the *Divan-e Shams-e Tabrîzî* by Rûmî. In the process it has lost quite a bit, not only in length but especially in depth.

More often, it is reworkings like this poem that circulate in the general populace in the West because they catch the reader's attention with their mystery and romantic lure, although they have very little to do with the original poem. Such popularizations are faithful to the flavor and spirit of the Sufi poem, but they unwittingly reduce to a secularized fancy the intensity of spiritual passion and the force of mystical insight that fueled the original poet's imagination more than seven hundred years ago. Many translators do disservice to the Sufi tradition by shifting the context of the poetry from the realm of God to the level of the mundane. The figurative lover who is really God in the Persian poem becomes a literal sexual lover in the translation that remains devoid of the smoldering spiritual core of the original.

One wants westerners to become interested in *tasawwuf* and its literature; however, the only access for people who cannot read the original languages is through translations of *tasawwuf* poetry. The dilemma of present-day Sufis in the East and West, who have direct access to *tasawwuf* literature in Arabic, Turkish, or Persian, is that they *want* to encourage westerners to tap the wealth of classical Sufi material, while they cannot help but bemoan the loss in translation of what they feel to be the authentic Sufi message. However, even popularized translations at least fulfill the role of attracting westerners to Sufism.

Barks, in an introduction to a collection of his translations, sensitively distinguishes between Rûmî's originals and
his own adaptations. He tells the story of an Ocean-Frog's visit
to a pond-frog who lives in a pond three feet by four feet by two
feet deep: "The pond-frog is very eager and proud to show off
the dimensions of his habitat, which in the story signify the
limits of mind and desire. He dives down two feet to the bottom and comes up and asks, 'Did you ever see water this deep?
What is it like where you live?' [to which the Ocean-Frog's
answer is,] 'One day I'll take you there, and you can swim in
it.'" Barks admits, "I am very much the pond-frog before
[Rûmî's poetry, which is] a sacred text that invites one to
drown in it. I don't claim to have done that" (Rûmî, *Longing*
ix). This is clear when the reader compares Barks's poem on
page 46 to the literal translation from the Persian original,
which comparison demonstrates the degree to which the
authentic Sufi message is compromised in at least this
instance. The Ocean in which Barks, Lessing, and I flounder is
the limitless Ocean of Divine Wisdom, the flavor of which is
preserved in the following literal translation by Dick Davis.[8]

> I have a fire in my mouth for you [Shams]
> > But I have a hundred seals on my tongue.
> These flames that I have in hiding
> > will make the two worlds into a fine morsel
> > [i.e., will burn the two worlds into something
> > edible].
> If all the world should pass away
> > I have, without the world, the wealth of a
> > hundred worlds.
> The caravans loaded with sugar
> > I have coming from the Egypt of extinction
> > [*Mesr-e 'adam*].
> From the drunkenness of love I have become
> > ignorant
> > Whether I profit or lose from it.

The eyes of my body wept pearls for love
    Until now, when my soul weeps pearls.
I am not confined to the house [body or world], for
    like Jesus
    I have a home in the fourth heaven.[9]
Thanks be to Him whose soul gives up the body.
    If the soul goes I have the soul of the soul.
That which Shams-e Tabrîzî gave to me
    Seek that from me, for that's what I have [to offer
    you]. (trans. Davis)[10]

Although the work of a thirteenth-century *tasawwuf* poet
is a far cry from twentieth-century British literature, the two
versions of Rûmî (on pages 46 and 48–9) are apt examples
with which to launch my discussion of the works of Lessing,
because a comparison of the two poems illustrates the ways in
which Western Sufism is both similar to and different from
the practice of *tasawwuf*. Furthermore, the central image in
both poems, "Egypt of extinction" (*Mesr-e 'adam* or *Mesr-e
fanâ'*), offers an ideal point of reference for the imagined spiritual spaces or the "Unreal Cities"[11] to which Lessing takes us
in her novels, *The Four-Gated City*, *The Memoirs of a Survivor*,
or the *Canopus in Argos: Archives* series.

In Rûmî's poem whether Egypt has a physical locale or
not, it is an ideal, abstract model of nothingness, or *fanâ'*,
analogous to Nirvana in Buddhism, which is the Sufi's ultimate goal: to burn his ego and his individual soul until they
are extinguished, at which point they attain "the soul of the
soul" and become one with God. When the word *fanâ'* is combined with the word *Mesr* (Egypt) which has a geographically
concrete location and a historical connotation of prosperity
and fertility, the "Egypt of *fanâ'*" represents a paradox, for it is
both nonexistence and ultimate reality, both extinction and
verdant fertility. It is a cultivated, immaterial place within,
one that has no external locale. The literal translation of the
whole line is, "I have caravans of sugar [or wonderful mystical

49

insights] coming from the Egypt of extinction [or the place of the soul, the place of truth, the place of wealth]." Hence, this poem is about the interiorization of space, as are many of Lessing's novels. In the last stanza, "Shams" refers to the poet's beloved friend and teacher on the Sufi Path, Shams-e Tabrîzî, who guides Rûmî to his ultimate Beloved or God. The only things of value Rûmî feels he has are the words he received from Shams, which he in turn offers to us in the form of this poem.

Unlike Rûmî's narrator, who feels whole and able to offer his love, Lessing's narrators depict characters who feel spiritually disconnected from God, from Nature, from the universe, and from other humans. In Rûmî's poem the narrator speaks of one kind of an Unreal (or most real) City, that is, the heart in love and at peace. On the other hand, Lessing's novels are more akin to those of her British and American predecessors and contemporaries. The following passage from *Shikasta* has strong affinities with such well-known representations of the urban landscape as those in Fitzgerald's *Great Gatsby*, Orwell's *1984*, or Burgess's *Clockwork Orange*. The ashheaps in Fitzgerald's Long Island or the desolate trash-strewn streets in Orwell's London resemble Eliot's Waste Land,[12] and Lessing has not fallen short of adopting the same subject matter: the barren and troubled heart:

> All the old supports going, gone, this man reaches out a hand to steady himself on a ledge of rough brick that is warm in the sun: his hand feeds him messages of solidity, but his mind messages of destruction, for this breathing substance, made of earth, will be a dance of atoms, he knows it, his intelligence tells him so: there will soon be war, he is in the middle of war, where he stands will be a waste, mounds of rubble, and this solid earthy substance will be a film of dust on ruins. (198)

Lessing's London after the Blitz or Planet 8 during The Ice or Zone Four at war represents desolate corners of the heart suffering an external apocalypse and internal annihilation that are already here, suggesting that modern "Unreal Cities" are not necessarily cities of the future but are the real spaces that we inhabit today. Gayle Greene sees direct similarities between *Landlocked* and *The Waste Land*: both works "[register] the aftershocks of a world war and the reduction of Western civilization to 'a heap of broken images'" (*Poetics* 60) and both are concerned with rebirth to varying degrees. Greene also studies the image of the ruined city in *Martha Quest* and *The Four-Gated City* and she traces the increase in "Lessing's sense of cataclysmic destruction" in succeeding novels (70).

In the movie *The Wizard of Oz* Dorothy exclaims, "I have a feeling we're not in Kansas any more," and we watch her with delight, knowing that she is *not* in Kansas any more. In those works of modern and post-modern literature concerned with metaphorising contemporary society, when we encounter Oz and places that are even more outlandish and hallucinatory, we have to remind ourselves that we are unfortunately and unmistakably in "Kansas," which is always a wasted, surreal landscape, unlike Rûmî's hypothetical thirteenth-century Egypt of fluorescence, greenness, and prosperity. Only in Lessing's case, the standard pessimism of twentieth-century apocalyptic literature is mitigated, given her knowledge of Sufism. Greene, too, finds "Lessing's energy and feistiness, her passionate plea for imaginative sympathy and the unexamined life anything but depressing" (*Poetics* 33). Greene insists that Lessing's novels "allow the confidence that things make a kind of sense; they offer . . . a kind of faith" (33).

Although the resolutions in Lessing's novels may not be as positive or as satisfying as the messages in *tasawwuf* poetry written by devout Muslims who practiced the Sufi Way, the influence of Sufism has made Lessing's work more optimistic and more constructive than it might have been, and definitely more promising of a future than are the works of most other canonical modern Western poets and writers.[13] Greene sees in

Landlocked, for instance, both the bleakness of twentieth-century novels and the new light of hope shining through: "Imagery relating to landlock, on the one hand—desert landscapes, ruined cities, nightmare houses—and to the regenerative forces of water and light, on the other" (*Poetics* 58).[14]

Lessing shows us desolation in the guise of "Unreal Cities" in much the same way that we distance intimate corners of our hearts by casting them in foreign and surreal images in our dreams. She writes persistently of the collapse of the old society and of an apocalypse triggered by various catastrophes: freezing temperatures, pollution, bombs, radioactive spills, or nuclear war. Assuming the role of prophet in *Shikasta*, she writes in desperation about the ignorant inhabitants of the unreal planet:[15] "But there the young are, in their hordes, their gangs, their groups, their cults, their political parties, their sects, shouting slogans, infinitely divided, antagonistic to each other, always in the right, jostling for command. There they are—the future, and it is self-condemned" (174).

Here the narrator expects no "caravans of sugar" to arrive from a spiritual Egypt, and the characters are not "drunk with love"[16] but with egoism and its downfall. Likewise in *The Memoirs* the slow and mysterious disintegration of society as we know it is chronicled in an effort to frighten and awaken readers. *The Memoirs* reflects the breakdown of the old order on the level of government as well as on the level of society and individuals. People who undergo this breakdown revert to a primitive state of barbarism and terror. The narrator/protagonist refers to the immediate threat of destruction as "it" that cannot be averted: "'It' is a force, a power . . . pestilence, a war, the alteration of climate, a tyranny that twists men's minds" (153). She concludes that "'It', in short, is the word for helpless ignorance, or of helpless awareness" (154). She also observes how, as a result of "it," people are forced to move out of the city in tribes, and those who remain behind resort to stealing and killing, growing their own food, and building air filters.

Against this background Lessing introduces Emily, the fourteen-year-old from the world behind the wall who must be prepared [in the Sufi Way] for her future role as leader of the new and evolved society. Emily's case is at least more hopeful than the plight of her counterparts in apocalyptic literature by other twentieth-century writers, even if her destiny does not measure up to the joy of Rûmî's narrator, whose "mouth is on fire" to speak words of love and whose "soul weeps pearls" or poems full of wonderful mystical insights. As Emily develops, we witness the growth in her inner world. Her guardian describes the nonexistent place behind the wall, a "place" which is really an abstract spiritual state: "a few rotting planks lying about on earth [were] putting out shoots of green. I pulled the planks away, exposing clean earth and insects that were vigorously at their work of re-creation" (101). Emily is accompanied by her lover Gerald, the savage street-children, the cat-like dog Hugo, and a female presence as she transcends the destruction of civilization. She cannot quite say, like Rûmî's protagonist, "If all the world should pass away, I have, without the world, the wealth of a hundred worlds." However, she *is* transformed and she *does* survive the apocalypse in *The Memoirs*, even if the reality of her inner life lacks the richness and cultivation of the lush lower Nile valley that nourishes the land of Egypt—the physical place Rûmî uses as an external manifestation of a positive spiritual state.[17]

Lessing's *The Four-Gated City* also opens with a war-torn city, in this case London in the 1950s and the scenes of bomb-sites; and the novel closes with the end of civilization when a mysterious accident contaminates the atmosphere with toxic fumes. There are rumors that the pollution is caused by the wrecking of a submarine carrying radioactive missiles, or by the crashing of a plane carrying lethal nuclear devices. Survivors escape to different islands around England, and many years later, a new race of special children comes into being in the aftermath of the apocalypse, who are trained as "gardeners" or nurturers of the new society. They are gifted with powers of telepathy, foresight, benevolence, a knowledge of history, and the ability to transcend it. That is, sixth, seventh, and more senses, or new organs of perception, have manifested in them.

Ultimately, it is these special survivors with whom Lessing would like her readers to be concerned. Unlike most modern writers, she is able to conceive of a way out of the surreal realms of chaos and destruction, given her knowledge of Sufism. On the other hand, there is an even more satisfying solution available to the *tasawwuf* poet Rûmî's narrator, who exclaims that even "If the soul goes I have the soul of the soul" (in the longer translation, by Dick Davis, quoted earlier in this chapter). Rûmî's poem was produced as a result of his heightened spiritual state, and Rûmî expressed his endless faith in something beyond all materiality, even beyond heaven. In fact, Sufi mystics rejected both worlds because they believed one must not love God for fear of hell or hope of heaven. Hence, Rûmî speaks of giving up his soul as well as his body, and of not being "confined to the body, for like Jesus I have a house in the fourth heaven." There is *something* in Lessing's message that strongly parallels this kind of declaration of faith. At the same time, although some of Lessing's fiction is suggestive of spiritual themes and mystical solutions, its positive message has a very different flavor than the pure faith in Rûmî's poetry. Lessing often has said that she is resistant to the idea of speaking about "religious faith" and prefers to speak about "optimism" instead (Bigsby 85). In a 1990 interview with Jean-Maurice de Montremy she said, "I am absolutely, childishly, allergic to religions—even though I have the greatest respect for our nature, which is profoundly religious" (de Montremy 199).

The outcome of parallels to Sufism in Lessing's novels is a slightly mitigated destruction, or *shikasta* in Persian—a word that even has become the title of, and provided the theme for, one of Lessing's novels. Many of Lessing's other titles also reflect this destruction. Words in the titles of her novels such as *survivor, representative, diary, memoir,* or *notebook* suggest that only a single person or limited records are left behind to report the end of the world; and words such as *hell, dark, storm, violence,* or *descent* in various titles forewarn the reader that the end is near, and that it will be grim. Still, in all the grimness, what is distinctive about Lessing is her optimism *in spite of* the signs of destruction. In a 1980 interview with Christopher Bigsby, Lessing elaborated on her optimism:

> Since the history of man began, has there been anything else but disaster, plagues, miseries, wars? Yet something has survived of it. Now our view is, of course, that we're onwards and upwards all the time. I just have an open mind about all that. But I do think that if we have survived so much in the past we are survirors, if nothing else, and if nothing else we are extremely prolific. (85)

'Attâr, a classical Sufi author, likens the state of humans to a branch that has been freshly cut from the tree. It is full of sap and happy, because it is unaware of its own demise. But, says 'Attâr, "it will know in due time. Meanwhile you cannot reason with it. This severance, this ignorance, these are the state of man" (Shah, *Way* 72). 'Attâr uses the metaphor of this healthy yet already severed branch to describe the tragedy of humankind. Like the branch, humans do not know that they have been already dealt the fateful blow. They are, in Sufi terminology, asleep and therefore unaware of their compromised condition in relation to eternity and to God.

Insofar as Lessing perceives human lives to be headed toward annihilation, she resembles many twentieth-century Western writers. However, unlike a majority of Western writers who urge their readers to take heed in some fashion but who offer no solutions, Lessing has the vantage point of Sufism from which also to offer hope. She can conceive of an evolved society or the evolution of the whole cosmos based on her Sufi faith in spiritual growth and mystical transformation even under the worst of circumstances. For this reason, she unceasingly urges her readers to prepare themselves for the end in the same way that she prepares her characters for the various inevitable catastrophes that never fail to fulfill her predictions.

Because of her insight into Sufism, Lessing writes not only about the time preceding an apocalypse but also about its aftermath with the promise of a potentially positive outcome. We also see positive outcomes in the works of other post-apocalyptic female science-fiction writers, such as Suzy McKee Charnas or Sally Miller Gearhart. However, the similarity stops there. The difference between Lessing's space fiction and, for instance, Sally Gearhart's *The Wanderground* is that Lessing's solutions are transferable to (and from) real life. Their message is applicable to the readers' lives literally, not only hypothetically.[18] In *The Wanderground*, on the other hand, there is a utopia in the abstract, but no models that one can use in daily life.

Lessing conveys the sense that breakdown is breakthrough, which means the breakdown of a society or an individual and the breakthrough to a higher, more advanced society or a higher personal and spiritual understanding. Her works that followed her exposure to Sufism hold out a hope rarely found in modern and postmodern literature; these works invite us to go past the "stuffy old room" to see the sunshine and new growth, and to come somewhat closer to the fountain of love that Rûmî was able to offer in his poetry once, a long time ago.

Rûmî is certain and secure in the embrace and light of his Beloved and is sure of the existence of the riches of a spiritual Egypt. In contrast, even when Lessing disguises the earth as a far-away planet or zone, the spiritual clarity and conviction that is characteristic of Rûmî's poetry is elusive in her fiction, because she writes about humans *on earth*, a wretched place according to many Sufi poets. Still, like Rûmî but to a lesser degree, Lessing draws on the assurance and optimism of Sufism, which she communicates to her readers. Given her

Sufi point of view, Lessing promises a flame of hope for the future, which is considerably more than the promises her contemporaries typically make. Insofar as she is able to carry her characters beyond death to the safety of Canopus, to the Presence of the One, or onto an uncontaminated island where evolved beings can be born, Lessing is able to establish a rare twentieth-century facsimile of the medieval Sufi mystic's "Egypt," that immaterial but most real city of nothingness containing "the wealth of a hundred worlds," where dwells the Beloved.

Part II

Consequences

Two

Lessing's Vision

*I would not be at all surprised to find out that this earth
had been used for the purposes of experiment by more
advanced creatures . . . that the dimensions for buildings
affect us in ways we don't guess and that there might
have been a science in the past which we have
forgotten . . . that we may be enslaved in ways we know
nothing about, befriended in ways we know nothing
about . . . that our personal feeling about our situation in
time, seldom in accordance with fact, so that we are
always taken by surprise by "ageing," may be an indica-
tion for a different lifespan, in the past—but that this
past, in biological terms, is quite recent, and so we have
not come to terms with it psychologically . . . that arti-
facts of all kinds might have had (perhaps do have) functions we do not suspect . . . that the human race has a
future planned for it more glorious than we can now
imagine . . .*

—Doris Lessing,
Sirian Experiments

Lessing offered us her views on Communism, feminism, mysticism, human relationships, politics, and life in general, and
she took us to outer space when the earth proved too small
for her visions. Drabble describes her as a writer who "changes
tense, tone, place, . . . skips decades, moves from the past to

the future, documents, speculates, describes, with relentless urgency" (52). She appears to remain enigmatic and diverse, perhaps because she prefers ambiguity to the traditional labels with which we like to classify our writers. Yet her work *is* of a piece, when evaluated from a Sufi point of view, and not so radically different over the years.[1] In fact, even works written before Lessing began to explore Sufi ideas reveal her natural inclination for Sufi thought and demonstrate ways in which she was already working through processes of self-study and development. Lessing expresses this inclination in a letter to Roberta Rubenstein: "When I read [*The Sufis*] I found that it answered many questions that I had learned—I feel too belatedly—to ask of life. Though that book was only the beginning of a different approach" (Rubenstein, *Novelistic* 121). The very core of Lessing's insights has been the same—that is, the need for perpetual evolution on all levels: individual, national, worldwide, and universal, and this concern in evolution has been as much biological as it is spiritual.[2]

Fahim has remarked on the progress of Lessing's style in the body of her work. For instance she writes, "While *The Grass is Singing* and *The Golden Notebook* dramatize the need for personal equilibrium and *The Memoirs of a Survivor* enlarges on the theme of personal and collective equilibrium, *Canopus in Argos: Archives* comprehends and complements the earlier works" (136). Fahim explains the search for equilibrium in the space-fiction series as the dynamic force and the drive of the action in the individual novels (137). Sprague and Tiger recognize a change from *The Children of Violence* series and African novels to *Briefing for a Descent into Hell*, *The Summer before the Dark*, and *The Memoirs of a Survivor*. In the latter three works, they see hints of the upcoming galactic voyages of the *Canopus* series, which they call "a kind of secular triptych" (13). Draine recognizes Lessing's tendency to commit to the role of prophet who will move the reader to a desirable state of consciousness. She also recognizes allegory and teaching stories in Lessing's fiction and addresses Lessing's tendency to preach "whenever she feels the burden of evil to be just too heavy to be borne in silence" (*Substance* 167). Later, Lessing preaches also because she wants to educate us about the Sufis.[3]

Sufi thought has confirmed Lessing's insights and validated what she had suspected all along: the possibility of individual and world amelioration. Variations of this belief in evolution are echoed in all of Lessing's works under one guise or another, as the following two passages from novels written twenty years apart demonstrate: Doeg, the protagonist in *The Making of the Representative for Planet 8* (1982), a product of Lessing's so-called space-fiction era in the early 1980s, says, "Do not sleep in all day in your dark rooms, but rouse yourselves, work, do anything—no, bear the burden of your consciousness, your knowledge, do not lose it in sleep" (49). These words recall Saul Green's words to Anna Wulf in *The Golden Notebook*: "We will use all our energies, all our talents, into pushing that boulder another inch up the mountain . . . and that is why we are not useless after all" (618). Both of these passages signal a positive outlook. As Fahim notes, Lessing alters the myth of Sisyphus in her retelling of it. The rock described by Saul Green does not roll back all the way but ends a few inches higher than where it started, every time. In other words, there is progress and evolution in Lessing's vision of the world, which does *not* align with Camus's heroism of the absurd (Fahim 76).

The Golden Notebook and
The Memoirs of a Survivor

In various interviews, Lessing has maintained that her seeming change of vision from utopian politics to spirituality or mysticism is not really so radical and that both areas deal with a psychological understanding of people, groups, and social developments. Furthermore, Lessing claims in a 1982 letter to Mona Knapp that *The Golden Notebook* (1962), written *before* she encountered Sufism, is her "most 'Sufi' book" (13). In the same letter she says, "I became interested in the Sufi way of thought because I was already thinking like that, before I had heard of Sufis or Sufism" (13). This is in fact the case when one evaluates *The Golden Notebook*, fragmented necessarily to reflect the many aspects of Anna Wulf's life from the Sufi point of view.[4] Even though *The Golden Notebook* was written without Lessing's prior knowledge of Sufism, it anticipates her turn to Sufism, while later novels, such as *The Memoirs of a Survivor* (1974),[5] build upon that turn. Reading *The Golden Notebook* and *The Memoirs* in light of Sufism allows on the one hand a useful additional way of reading some of the events in *The Golden Notebook*, and on the other hand provides a *necessary* way of reading some of the events in *The Memoirs*. Sufism accounts for the difference in Lessing's vision between these two novels.

In *The Golden Notebook* London of the 1950s provides Anna, a single parent, only married men as potential lovers in a society that shuns women who choose to be "free" from the traditional roles intended for them. The novel is imbued with Anna's sense of emptiness and despair, her self-searching and struggle.[6] She is frequently described as an "empty shell" or an "empty paper bag": "She became a shell. She stood there, looking at words like love, friendship, duty, responsibility, and knew them to be all lies. She felt herself shrug" (514). Anna becomes an expert at observing herself during such states of intense nothingness, and she usually emerges from them feeling at least more honest and more whole than before. She also observes the emptiness of those around her and the meaninglessness of their emotions. For instance when she confronts De Silva, a potential lover, and tells him he doesn't really care whether he sleeps with her or not, he responds by almost throwing a temper tantrum. Manifestations of hollowness in herself and in others drive Anna to the point where she can no longer write for publication, having lost faith in her ability to feel or write anything authentic. Instead, she spends long hours with her therapist Mrs. Marks, discussing her self-imposed writer's block. When "the world is so chaotic, art [feels] irrelevant" (42), she says, and she finds writing degrading when it is merely an outlet for indulging in one's own emotions. Furthermore, when she is asked to authorize the creation of a television version of her earlier novel, she is mortified and refuses to prostitute her mind to television. She fears, as Lessing also must, the possibility that television could take over and demean the noble act of teaching.

It is possible to understand Lessing's switch from Communism to Sufism here. Communist art, according to one of Anna's comrades, is "joyful, communal, [and] unselfish" (350). Anna's and Lessing's original reasons for becoming Communists had included the hope of saving the world through teaching and conversion. And their reasons for breaking away from Communism are again the same: to save the spiritual lives of people through teaching them how to learn. A comparison can be made here to Graham Greene, who remained torn between Communism and Catholicism. For Lessing, Sufism appears to have presented not a conflict of allegiances but a new layer of knowledge to add onto her earlier commitments. One of the basic differences between the two ideologies, one political, the other spiritual, is that in their later choice Anna and Lessing teach and fight their battles alone, not in a group effort. They have realized that their primary responsibility is to themselves and that without first becoming whole within themselves, it is useless to try to save the world through any "ism" or novel. Mrs. Marks accuses Anna of dissipating all of her creativity in her dreams; she urges her to start writing again, for the simple reason that it is her calling, and she owes it to herself to write. If dreams are, as in Mrs. Marks's and the Sufis' understanding, the result of unused creative energies, then it becomes clear why Anna dreams so very much during her inert period as a writer. Nonetheless, she is too conscious of her own spiritual emptiness to have the audacity to write. She feels she has nothing worthwhile to say, except to emphasize the chaos and nothingness with which she has become so finely in tune.

Following her immersion in Sufi study in the early 1960s, Lessing became more didactic in her novels in which analogies to Sufi experience were more overtly suggested and more clearly applicable. In contrast to Anna Wulf in *The Golden Notebook*, the narrator in *The Memoirs*—a novel written twelve years later—was taken much further in the protagonist's self-discovery, which suggests that perhaps Lessing later knew (and did not only *intuit*) that there was a further place to which one could go. While Lessing could not have pushed Anna in *her* context any further, she was able to carry the narrator of *The Memoirs* into new worlds which she created and which she later explored at greater length in her space fiction. The space behind the wall in *The Memoirs*, for instance, is clearly a metaphor for the narrator's inner life, which, like the infinite rooms behind the wall, daily unfolds into a rich tapestry of experience and self-discovery. It is also noteworthy that Lessing introduces the carpet imagery in *The Memoirs*, the weaving of carpets being one of many basic teaching tools in Sufism: the narrator sees a roomful of people gathered around a faded carpet, colors and patterns of which emerge brightly in patches as individuals find their particular piece in the carpet and place it on the faded material—that is, as they fulfill their destiny.[7]

Like a Sufi tale, *The Memoirs* is written to be read on different levels. As one peels the layers, one moves deeper along a spectrum from the political and rhetorical readings at one end, to the psychological and spiritual at the other.[8] Given Lessing's Sufi knowledge, it is justifiable to suggest a mystical reading of *The Memoirs* without dismissing other readings. This has been the intent of Sufi teaching tales, as well: to offer many lessons to many audiences at many levels. In turn, *Between East and West* aims to provoke further discussion on all sides, not to foreclose it.

Sufism makes a noticeable difference in Lessing's vision as Lessing moves from *The Golden Notebook* to *The Memoirs*.[9]

Like Anna, Emily and her guardian are aware of chaos, too, as it unfolds daily around them; but for them, Lessing can draw on the Sufi Path to self development and transformation—a remedy that was not yet part of her vision when she wrote *The Golden Notebook*. In *The Memoirs*, political and economic calamities prompt people to band together in tribes and move out of the cities, while those who remain behind resort to stealing, killing, growing their own food, and building air filters to survive. During this time Emily is left with the narrator who records the events and mood of the times: "Inside it was all chaos: the feeling one is taken over by, at the times in one's life when everything is in change, movement, destruction—or reconstruction" (81). In light of Sufism, this guardian, who remains unnamed in the novel, could represent the mature Emily.[10] She shares Emily's identity, especially during the times when she pays frequent mysterious visits to a space through and beyond the faded designs of the old wallpaper, where she is confronted with rooms in shambles.[11] In the Sufi context, this imaginary space serves as a metaphor for Emily's inner life and childhood, and the guardian is the adult part of Emily who has committed herself to working on reconciling her inner and outer worlds, or her essence and personality, as well as her past and present. My interpretation here is consistent with that of Jeanne Murray Walker, who also reads Emily's childhood scenes as necessary steps for learning about her past. She is aware that the past influences the present, as in the connection between baby Emily's frigid white nursery and teenager Emily's present sense of deprivation and isolation (106).[12]

At the heart of Sufi thought is the necessity for individual and cosmic evolution and the idea that men and women do not know themselves, nor their potentials. This corresponds comfortably to Lessing's natural inclinations, so that Idries Shah's representation of Sufism reinforces Lessing's own belief in an evolution of a more whole society. As a result, Lessing readily incorporates Sufi perceptions of human beings in her very involved and lengthy novels. Anna in *The Golden Notebook* writes in her diary, "I came home thinking that somewhere at the back of my mind when I joined the [Communist] Party, was a need for wholeness, for an end to the split, divided, unsatisfactory way we all live" (161). Sufis see human beings as incomplete and expect them to transcend their merely human state of incompletion through "work" in the Sufi Way. This is not only the situation of humanity and its potential in most of Lessing's novels, but is also intentionally emphasized in the lives of her characters.

In *The Golden Notebook* and *The Memoirs* Lessing's vision encompasses the discomfort her protagonists feel when faced with social and ideological corruption and fragmentation, their own and that of the rest of the world. When *The Golden Notebook* is considered against the backdrop of Sufism, it will lend itself to an additional reading: spiritual destitution. Ella, Anna's fictional double, thinks to herself, "probably they were all like this, all in fragments, not one of them a whole, reflecting a whole life, a whole human being; or, for that matter, a whole family" (222). And echoing Ella, Anna says, "I don't know anyone who isn't incomplete and tormented and fighting, the best one can say of anyone is that they fight" (522). This despair is echoed in *The Memoirs*, which reminds DuPlessis of an abstract *Four-Gated City* because in both novels Lessing repeats similar arguments regarding the end of the world and spiritual transformation ("Feminist" 4).

Teenager Emily in *The Memoirs* feels "a hunger, a need, a pure thing, which [makes] her face lose its hard brightness, her eyes their defensiveness. She [is] a passion of longing" (34). Here, the Sufi context offers not only an additional reading, as in *The Golden Notebook*, but provides the crucial key to understanding *The Memoirs*. Lessing does not define what Emily longs for, but the novel as a whole invites an allegorical reading. Through "working" on herself and fighting her battles, Emily has the chance to transform herself and thereby satisfy her longing. Walker calls *The Memoirs* "an allegory of psychological integration" but also more literally a story of two "human beings painstakingly forming a social bond" (95).[13] As its dust jacket describes it, *The Memoirs* is "an attempt at autobiography," which claim Lessing confirms in *Under My Skin*.[14] Greene adds, "That Lessing's mother and grandmother were both named Emily suggests why *autobiography* is a relevant term" (*Poetics* 149). Lessing had only recently encountered Sufism when she wrote *The Memoirs*, and the narrator's trips behind the wall can be read easily as Lessing's own allegorical quests for her "self."[15] When evaluated in light of Sufism, the world behind the wall in *The Memoirs* emerges as the only real world, while the reality of daily life on the pavement pales in contrast. The classical Sufi poet Omar Khayyam (d.1132) describes the human being as a lantern of imaginings inside a lamp: one's petty and mundane experiences are the lantern of imaginings trapped within the brightness of the only real world (Shah, *Way* 60).

Sandra Lott likens Lessing's variations on sex stereotypes in *The Memoirs* to those in Lewis Carroll's *Alice in Wonderland* and *Through the Looking-Glass* and notes that Lessing may have been influenced by Carroll. Both authors depict a female protagonist conditioned to behave by her culture's rules. It is only when Emily and Alice look beneath the roles imposed upon them that they begin to grow. This, of course, happens when both delve into fantasy. Lott notes how for Emily, unlike Alice, this newfound freedom in another world is satisfying enough that she stays there for good. In other words, in Sufi terms Emily's turn to another reality is a permanent transformative move, whereas for Alice, it is transitory and artificial.[16]

Both Anna in *The Golden Notebook* and to a greater extent Emily in *The Memoirs* live during a time of "death and destruction" which, to Anna, seems "stronger than life" (235). Both women live under the pressures of the dead and dying Western civilization, fighting in their own ways to escape death. If read in light of the Sufi tradition, *The Golden Notebook* gains more meaning and *The Memoirs* becomes a more satisfying novel, one that offers more than a mere futuristic ghost story.[17]

CONSEQUENCES

During her earlier visits behind the wall, the guardian always finds discord and turmoil, as any would-be seeker does at the outset of his or her "work." "To make the [rooms] inhabitable, what work needed to be done!" (14) she tells us, in direct correlation with Sufi thinking that we are incomplete and need years of hard work to complete ourselves. The guardian adds, "I stood there marking fallen plaster, the corner of a ceiling stained with damp, dirty, or damaged walls . . . The exiled inhabitant: for surely she could not live, never could have lived, in that chill empty shell full of dirty and stale air?" (14). From a Sufi perspective, the rightful inhabitant exiled from this place would be Emily's perfected self who may not return until Emily is properly prepared to receive her. However, for the time being, the incomplete Emily hides behind a cold, impervious, hard, and enameled presence (16).

Throughout the course of the novel her guardian tries to get past or around Emily's defenses, and the closest she gets to the Emily who is in hiding is when she walks through the old wallpaper into Emily's inner world. However, the two worlds on either side of the wall still remain disconnected, "one life exclud[ing] the other" (25). The guardian recognizes this impasse that is so sharply pronounced in Emily and comments on the prison in which we all live and the difficulty we have in allowing anyone to come close to us (31). This idea later led to the title Lessing chose for her book of essays, *Prisons We Choose to Live Inside* (1987).

As the novel progresses, more and more of the influence of the world behind this allegorical wall remains with the guardian when she returns to the external world. These memories help the guardian to protect Emily during the present disharmony. In fact, the trips behind the wall become such an obsession and an obligation that she experiences a sense of fear and of lowered vitality whenever she is about to cross over again, for what she finds there is chaos and turmoil as if savages and soldiers had been there (40). She finds chairs and sofas slashed with their stuffing spewing out, curtains ripped off, and feathers and blood

70

everywhere. She works hard to clean and reorder, scrubs the walls with buckets of hot water, and airs out the rooms with the sun and wind. However, she tells us, "whenever I re-entered the rooms after a spell away in my real life, all had to be done again. It was like what one reads of a poltergeist's tricks" (64).[18]

In Sufism, the necessary step for attaining harmony and perfection to replace chaos is self knowledge. Not knowing oneself, one appears to be not one, but many, for one is unaware of the body's needs, the spirit's wishes, and the mind's intentions. There is not only one "I" but many, who either desire or repel, love or hate, are curious or uninterested. In Sufi understanding, the manifestations of schizophrenia or multiple personalities can be regarded as a sign of one's incomplete state and one's need to work on oneself. This "work" is done by relentless self observation. A retrospective look at *The Golden Notebook* through Sufi lenses discloses Anna and Ella frequently engaged in self observation: "At this point, Ella detached herself from Ella, and stood to one side, watching and marveling" (323). Anna further observes the phenomenon of multiple personalities emerging in herself in the form of Saul, her psychological double, or animus, and notes her impressions in the notebook which she lets Saul read:[19] "I was thinking how, in any conversation, he can be five or six different people; I even waited for the responsible person to come back . . . Literally, I saw him come out of the personality he had been . . . The person speaking then was the good person (20–21). Saul may totally agree with Anna, and then thoroughly disagree with her a few minutes later. Anna well understands this inconsistency in the human psyche. She writes, "All self knowledge is knowing, on deeper and deeper levels, what one knew before" (239), again anticipating the Sufi context. While Saul accepts and rejects truths about himself, he still retains what Anna tells him, and he even learns a portion of it; when he learns something more about himself, it isn't new information, but a deeper understanding of what was already registered in his mind.

71

CONSEQUENCES

The apparent result of being out of touch with one's inner self is a spiritual sterility, which Anna describes as a drying up of the well. This dried up state leaves behind a mere machine that is efficiently in control, but lifeless.[20] "She saw the dry well, a cracked opening into the earth that was all dust . . . Anna knew she had to cross the desert . . . There was no water anywhere" (407). Emily, too, suffers from a similar experience of longing for meaning. Only in her case, this longing is more deliberately fashioned by Lessing, given the Sufi context that can now accommodate such thirst and that can enrich Lessing's vision. Emily has felt deprived of fertile surroundings since she was a baby, and she still knows very little about the world behind the wall. Before she can grow out of her stifled existence, it is necessary for her to know this world thoroughly. Just as Anna's contact with Saul, her mad animus, is necessary for her growth, the guardian's contact with the world behind the wall is necessary for Emily's growth.

In both novels, Lessing has set up less than ideal surroundings to provide her protagonists with the friction against which they must work. Anna, who has sought Mrs. Marks's help in order to work her way through the dark alleys of her psyche, tells Mrs. Marks, "you've given me back feeling, and it's too painful" (544). She bemoans the "glass wall certain kinds of Americans live behind" because they are afraid of being touched, afraid of feeling (485). This defense mechanism is not used against other people as much as it is used against one's own inner world. Emily in *The Memoirs* retains her glass wall almost to the end of her stay with her guardian and only rarely allows parts of herself to show through.[21] Anna, who is older than Emily, is conscious of her own defenses, but she has realized that without outside help from Mrs. Marks, she cannot break through her glass wall.

The Sufi hopes to reach the essence within and to help it grow into maturity. One's inner world needs to keep up with, or catch up with, one's external development in everyday life. Of course, a mind that could possibly begin to think creatively about its own improvement is one which is uncluttered. In order to reach one's essence, one is expected to undo the "useless superstition, habits, convention, irrelevant assumptions, and expectations" which one has been fed, so that the mind can see what is really there (Courtland 86). "To follow Sufism is to die gradually to oneself and to become oneSelf, to be born anew and to become aware of what one has always been from eternity (*azal*) without one's having realized it until the necessary transformation has come about" (Nasr 17). On this subject the thirteenth-century Sufi poet Sa'd ud Dîn Mahmûd Shabistarî writes in *The Secret Garden*:

> Go sweep out the chamber of your heart.
> Make it ready to be the dwelling place of the
>   Beloved.
> When you depart out. He will enter it.
> In you, void of yourself, will He display His
>   beauties. (Friedlander 23)

The process of voiding oneself is an essential step toward acquiring real self knowledge.[22] But of course, this nothingness brings with it hopelessness and despair. Saul says to Anna: "We are comforting each other. What for, I wonder? . . . We've got to remember that people with our kind of experience are bound to be depressed and unhopeful . . . Or perhaps it's precisely people with our kind of experience who are most likely to know the truth?" (567). Despite her depression, Anna knows that she is closer to knowing the truth in her present state than she was as a successful career woman and writer. In her dream of being in the desert she sees herself "a long way from the springs," and she wakes up knowing that "if she [is] to cross the desert she must shed burdens" (408). This jettisoning of burdens is reminiscent of the experiences of Christian in Bunyan's *The Pilgrim's Progress* who must abandon his worldly attachments to enable him to proceed on his way. As in the case of Christian, Anna's choice to shed burdens and thereby become a whole person demands that she pay a high price. The analogy of a full glass of water is often used in Sufi teachings: just as a full glass can only overflow if one tries to pour more water into it, neither can a cluttered mind admit fresh knowledge.

In *The Memoirs*, the guardian frantically scrubs and cleans out the area behind the wall, trying to make it inhabitable for "the other" Emily. She also does her best in the apartment in her "real" life in order to accommodate Emily's growing life; or, in the Sufi context, the grown up Emily's personality accommodates the essence of Emily that is still in embryo. It is important to note also that Emily's room in her guardian's apartment is no larger than a closet space and that she shares even this space with her closest friend, the cat/dog-like beast, Hugo. This narrow space is symbolic of the underdeveloped state of Emily's essence. She remains stifled literally as well as figuratively until that time when her inner and outer worlds join in harmony. Meanwhile, the process of purification continues behind the wall.[23] The guardian describes how she scrubs and paints the walls until the sheets of dust have been replaced by clean and clear whiteness like "new snow or fine china" (66).

Just as the guardian literally works in the grimy areas of that other world, self-work in the Sufi Way is carried out in the problem areas of Emily's psyche. In the Sufi context, this choice of concentrating on the hurdles in life, or deliberately engaging in conscious labor and intentional suffering, is essential for real transformation to take place. A retrospective look at *The Golden Notebook* through Sufi lenses reveals that Anna, too, often chooses this kind of suffering, which illustrates the inclination toward Sufism that has been part of Lessing's vision. Anna writes, "if what we feel is pain, then we must feel it, acknowledging that the alternative is death. Better anything than the shrewd, the calculated, the non-committal, the refusal of giving" (545–46). Anna recalls times in her past when she used to concentrate on her difficulties, but she is now able to distinguish the ordinary suffering of those days from the conscious suffering of the present time. In the past, she enjoyed indulging in her pain and had even made it profitable in the form of a novel. Having advanced in her personal growth, she now looks back at her publishing days and confesses to Mrs. Marks: "there's pleasure in pain . . . that sad nostalgic pain that makes me cry is the same emotion I wrote that damned book out of" (239).

It is essential to recognize the difference that emerges in Anna's experience between ordinary and intentional suffering. In Sufism ordinary suffering is an indulgence in one's negative emotions, whereas intentional suffering always produces a new person. Ordinary suffering is self-pity grown out of self-importance, vanity, sloth, fear, jealousy, or greed; and the Sufi aspires to convert such suffering into a conscious act. The manner in which Ella waits for Paul night after night against her own better judgement displays ordinary suffering: "She could see herself standing there, and said to herself: 'This is madness. This is being mad. Being mad is not being able to stop yourself doing something that you know to be irrational'" (227). Intentional suffering, on the other hand, is impressively and deliberately demonstrated in *The Memoirs*. Each of the guardian's journeys behind the wall into young Emily's disturbing world is an example of intentional suffering. At the end of these journeys, the guardian's and Emily's lives are changed. Every journey contributes to balancing the aspects of Emily's character within a unified person and to bringing her closer to completion and (psychological and spiritual) rebirth. Often the guardian witnesses Emily trying futilely to bring order into her life behind the wall. A poignant image depicts Emily trying to amass fallen leaves into heaps. But as she sweeps and makes piles, the leaves fly about in the wind. Emily/the guardian works faster and faster, trying to empty a whole house full of leaves to no successful end, while "The world was being submerged in dead leaves, smothered in them" (137). Emily continues her frantic and desperate fight even against nature—in this case, her own nature. And while going through this process of self purification, she appears discouraged and maddened with the seeming futility of her task: "Her stare, fixed, wide, horrified . . . She saw only the fragments of the walls that could not shelter her, nor keep out the sibilant drift" (137), and she vanishes among the rustling leaves and decaying world.

Both Anna in *The Golden Notebook* and the guardian in *The Memoirs* learn that unless one makes an effort, one gains nothing real. In the Sufi tradition, only conscious efforts without expectation of rewards lead one to true liberation. This message is inherent in *The Golden Notebook* and more overt in *The Memoirs*.

Anna contains her fragments by keeping four different colored notebooks (as Carl Jung did in real life). In these, she compartmentalizes different aspects of her experiences, irreconcilable in any other way. The black notebook contains records of her financial success as a published novelist as well as reflecting her loss of faith in art; the red notebook is a record of her political involvements and her loss of faith in the Communist party; the yellow notebook is a fictionalized version of her personal life and reflects her loss of faith in love; and the blue notebook is her current diary. She purchases a fifth notebook, which she calls the "Golden Notebook," and starts writing in it only after she emerges from her descent into madness and feels whole. In her conversation with Saul, Anna decides to write again, this time having something real to say. Saul reminds her that after all, they are not the failures they think they are: "We spend our lives fighting to get people very slightly less stupid than we are to accept truths that the great men have always known" (618). Such conversations with Saul eventually lead to the thawing of Anna's emotions and, along with that, to a free flow of her creativity, at which point Saul is no longer necessary.[24]

In *The Memoirs*, as Emily develops further, her guardian begins to remember more and more of the world behind the wall. This symbolically implies that Emily is becoming more and more successful in her self-remembering and that her essence is becoming increasingly empowered to assert itself over her personality. At first, this self-remembering manifests itself in the form of the guardian's ability to hear a child crying faintly in the distance, miserable, lost, and weighed down with incomprehension. Yet, whenever the guardian asks anyone else about hearing this sound she discovers that it is only she who hears it. Emily cannot hear the cries. Sometimes the sobbing is almost inaudible and the guardian has to strain her ears to hear it. At other times, she "twist[s] and turn[s] inwardly not to hear that miserable sound" (148).

This attempt not to hear the crying is the natural human response to one's own pain. The fact that Emily's guardian can hear the crying even when she is on the ordinary side of the wall signals the break Emily has made through her personality to her essence, or the breakthrough the adult Emily has made to the young Emily. "Sema [our prayer] is an awakening," says Rûmî. "But he who awakens in a dungeon of course does not wish to wake up. However, he who has fallen asleep in the rose gardens . . . If he wakes up, his joy increases, and perhaps he is spared from fearful dreams" (Araz 239, my translation). In Emily's case, her inner world that used to be in shambles, worn out, pained, dark, mossy, smelly, tortured, and stifled, begins to be lifted out of Rûmî's dungeons into the rose gardens. At least Emily is now awake enough to hear herself cry, her glimpses of truth stretching into periods of consciousness.

Both Anna and Emily take pains to get to know themselves and to arrive at that new person in themselves who is capable of growing. However, Anna does not go any further in her self-searching, perhaps because *The Golden Notebook* was written prior to Lessing's exposure to Sufism. Anna lacks the further development which Emily experiences in *The Memoirs*, written twelve years later.[25] Anna only experiences a temporary madness and depression from which she is restored to a healthier and more whole person, while Emily undergoes a permanent transformation. Emily's experiences can be read

77

as a self-work manual which illustrates how one can transform one's self. As Emily awakens, there is new life behind the wall, "a few rotting planks lying about on earth that was putting out shoots of green . . . clean earth and insects that were vigorously at their work of re-creation . . . The smell of growth came up strong from the stuffy old room" (101). The work Emily's guardian has to do is not completed yet; but after this breakthrough, her task becomes easier and more rewarding. She now has new creation and not the moss and the shambles with which to contend. Greene recognizes the same theme in *Landlocked*, in which "creation of the new requires the destruction of the old." She also sees that this new creation "is based on intuitive rather than logical faculties, the first step toward which is a radical disorientation" (*Poetics* 59). This is similar to the disorientation that Emily experiences in *The Memoirs* until she gains some strength and balance.

Lessing points out that the guardian's journeys and activities behind the wall were never really her choice, but her duty. The narrator/guardian remarks, "Very strong was the feeling that I did as I was bid and as I must. I was being taken, was being led, was being shown, was held always in the hollow of a great hand which enclosed my life" (101). This is reminiscent of the greater evolutionary cause of the Sufis. If an individual's personal growth can help to raise the level of the whole of humanity even a very slight degree, this is considered a success. Emily's guardian feels "too much beetle or earthworm to understand" (101) the greater purpose behind her own actions, but she still feels compelled to walk into that "other" world in order to explore and unearth the "real" Emily. In this role, she is, according to Greene, a female Christ figure or cosmic mother, as are other saviors in Lessing's oeuvre, such as Al·Ith or Martha Quest. Greene sees these protagonists as Christian, rather than Sufi seekers and saviors (*Poetics* 26).

After the disaster in the unnamed city in *The Memoirs*, the guardian is able to share her vision with Emily, Emily's lover Gerald, and her pet Hugo, feeling confident that the world behind the wall is now strong enough to withstand intrusion from outside. And together, they witness the following vision as it unfolds: "a bright green lawn under thunderous and glaring clouds, and on the lawn a giant black egg of pockmarked iron but polished and glossy (216). Lessing could have chosen a real egg, or a crystal egg for the occasion of Emily's rebirth; however, an iron egg by nature is difficult to break open, and this in itself provides the symbolic meaning of the difficulty of one's task in the Sufi Way.[26] Romance and glory are not qualities sought after by Sufis. Rather, rebirth is possible only after hard work and a strong presence of being that results from self-remembering.

As Emily and her entourage stand looking at the iron egg, it breaks open "by the force of their being there" (216), revealing the apparition for whom the guardian had been waiting throughout the novel. Following this Being is Emily, but the new, transmuted Emily and her beast Hugo, followed by Gerald and the savage children of the ordinary world. When all of Emily's family crosses into that new order, "the last walls dissolve" (217).[27] In a Sufi light the dissolving of the walls marks Emily's death and rebirth; it is only when the walls of the old rooms are demolished that Emily can move on to become her new, enlightened self. As a point of comparison, a classical Sufi account of renewal, as it was experienced by Rûmî seven hundred years ago, is related by Ira Shems Friedlander below:

> Like the Prophet before him, the angels descended to earth, cut open his breast, and removed the thin shell that remained over his heart. They removed the last bit of ego that remained within him and filled his heart with Love. Then they made his breast as it was before. As this was happening, [Mawlânâ Rûmî] was in his garden lost in deep meditation, in a state of disassociation from his body, experiencing the highest initiation he would know until his 'wedding day' . . . He was now ready to reenter the world. (Friedlander 55)

CONSEQUENCES

The "wedding day" refers to death, which is celebrated as a union with God, the Beloved, and marks one's rebirth. Aspiring Sufis must remember at all times that their purpose is to rise on the vertical ladder of enlightenment and share the fate of the legendary phoenix, the beautiful, graceful white bird that is reborn out of its own ashes after burning itself on a fire kindled with a hundred trees. With its final breath the phoenix sings a most beautiful song from the depths of its soul, sounding a plaintive cry as it dies to its old self (Friedlander 153). In Gerald's efforts to build a new family structure, Gayle Greene recognizes the necessity for destruction that can make new creation possible: "Human beings produced by the prison of the family are incapable of making a free society, and the ruined garden of Gerald's commune represents the impossibility of making anything new from existing social conditions: you can't get there from here" (*Poetics* 150).

It is required of all humans and beasts to protect the phoenix, the emblem of immortality, between each of its deaths and rebirths. Similarly, students of Sufism are asked to work hard to preserve themselves, something that can be possible only through a lifetime of harmonious development, which involves the induced growth of the essence to an equal proportion with the personality. In support of self-preservation and transformation, which in turn contribute to the preservation and evolution of the human race, Lessing has remarked in an interview, "Maybe out of destruction will be born some new creature. I don't mean physically. What interests me more than anything is how our minds are changing, how our ways of perceiving reality are changing" (Raskin 66). Lessing, like the Sufis, expects that humanity will continue to participate in cosmic evolution. Beyond this, Sufis make no provisions; nor do they argue about whether every individual has the potential to share the lot of the phoenix. Gurdjieff, for instance, speaks of the acorns that do not all become oak trees. Most serve as fertilizer while very few take root and develop into an oak.

As for Lessing's vision, Emily in *The Memoirs* is clearly delivered into a new sphere in which the limitations upon her can be lifted. Anna of *The Golden Notebook*, on the other hand, does not have the added horizon that the Sufi context allows Emily. Anna can be rescued from the ordinary world and its madness only to the extent that a psychiatrist can deliver her. While Emily's search for herself is presented to us as a spiritual quest, similar in many ways to the Sufi Way, Anna's search has to suffice as a psychological soul-searching that necessarily must come to its resolution in the ordinary realm of existence. The closest Lessing comes to a different kind of solution for Anna is to suggest that there might be "a crack in [some people's] personality like a gap in a dam, and through that gap the future might pour in a different shape—terrible perhaps, or marvellous, but something new" (473). Yet this idea is only suggested and dropped during a conversation between Anna and Mrs. Marks: "But sometimes," says Anna, "I meet people, and it seems to me the fact they are cracked across, they're split, means they are keeping themselves open for something" (473). In *The Memoirs*, Lessing is able to develop this idea further, because she is able to reinforce her perceptions with Sufi truths.

Suvin's concept of cognitive estrangement helps us to read Lessing's "other worlds" in which she first makes the familiar unrecognizable and strange so that later it is even more memorable when recognized.[28] As a student of Sufism, Lessing not only paints this world in new colors and strokes, but she would like us to believe in the mimetic dimension of the other world, as well. For example, the breakthrough to the other world at the end of *The Memoirs* is not only metaphorical. The guardian and Emily are finally able to join forces in earnest, share the same vision, purpose, and future because of the guardian's preceding Sufi "work" behind the wall to make their union possible. No matter what the external circumstances, they are now one whole individual, who is able to withstand the challenges of daily life even at a time of war and destruction. Such a character is not only important in her thematic and synthetic dimensions but is equally important in her mimetic dimension. She is not a freak in the novel to be read only for the ideas she represents, but a plausible human being who is seeking something more than ordinary life. Any supernatural phenomena in Lessing's later novels really belong to the same world that we experience daily. However, as Lessing points out, only the so-called mad ones in her novels know and believe this to be true.

Two things become very clear from our comparison of *The Golden Notebook* and *The Memoirs*, written before and after Lessing's exposure to Sufism: one, that Lessing was naturally inclined to promote "work" on oneself; and two, that the Sufi tradition has offered her a very welcome pathway to explore beyond the limitations of psychology, psychiatry, politics, Communism, Jungianism, or any other "ism" to which she had appealed prior to her study of Sufism.

Re: Colonised Planet 5, Shikasta and The Making of the Representative for Planet 8

As a whole, the surrealism of Lessing's space-fiction series disturbed many who preferred her earlier realism. At the same time, critics made an effort to understand why Lessing used the space-fiction genre.[29] When we fully acknowledge Lessing's Sufism, it becomes necessary to evaluate her space fiction also as spiritual tracts that map out ways to transformation which resemble the Sufi Way to enlightenment. The remainder of this chapter shall draw parallels between the Sufi Way and Lessing's "Way" in order to demonstrate that Lessing's space fiction involves much more than a rhetorical construct.

As each of the characters in the *Canopus* series grows to varying degrees of completion in the Sufi Way, we witness their deaths and afterlives, unlike Anna Wulf's life story—written before Lessing's exposure to Sufism—which stopped short of Anna's old age or death. Furthermore, Anna had a last name indicative of her mimetic identity, while some protagonists in *The Memoirs* and the *Canopus* series do not even have first names, let alone last names. Consider, for instance, the case of *The Memoirs'* narrator, who remains nameless, or the cases of Doeg, Klin, Marl, Pedug, or Masson in *The Representative* (1982), who have interchangeable names depending on their roles in the community. When faced with the freezing of Planet 8, Doeg asks in desperation, "If we are not channels for the future, and if this future is not to be better than the present, then what are we?" (39)—a question that drives Lessing herself to write these and other novels narrating the fates of nations and planets confronted with a holocaust of one kind or another.

Sufi thought appears to have required a new style and subject matter in Lessing's novels, one that could offer a *fresh* look at the world. When Lessing defamiliarizes physical reality, she seems to suggest an alternate reality and alternate myths that can actually aid spiritual awakening through the Sufi Way.[30] In the context of Sufism, a character such as Johor (George Sherban) in *Shikasta* (1979) and in *The Representative* can be read as a potential Sufi master. Although his name is not spelled *Jawhar*, it could be that Lessing intentionally gave him a name that sounds like the Persian, Arabic, and Turkish word *jawhar*, meaning "jewel or jewelry, something precious"; Johor is indeed a valuable asset in Lessing's cosmology.

Bazin discusses Lessing's Sufi envoys: "The Sufi functions as a kind of emissary of the gods to remind individuals that they must humble themselves and accept the higher truth that all is One. Lessing has fictionalized two such emissaries of the gods in Charles Watkins . . . and Johor/George Sherban" ("Evolution" 159). Bazin adds that Lessing must see herself "as such an emissary" (159), a point argued here throughout. For instance, as our emissary here to warn us, Lessing has picked the Persian word *shikasta* for her title of the first book in the space-fiction series. In Persian the word *shikasta* has two meanings, both of which are relevant to Lessing's apocalyptic vision in the *Canopus* series.[31] On the one hand, it means "weighed down, broken down in health, destroyed, doleful, sad, decrepit, infirm, weakened," all of which describe the state of the planet Shikasta; on the other hand, it also means "breakable, that may or *must* be broken," which is how those on the mainland Canopus regard the planet Shikasta. The planet is crumbling and already broken down because of its inhabitants' wicked ways—as is our own planet, earth. Lessing then concludes that it may or must be broken down, precisely because of its wicked state: nothing new or fresh can come from corruption until all are destroyed so that, like the legendary phoenix, something new can be born out of the ashes. Spiritual rebirth is the goal of the Sufis, which goal Lessing seems to have adopted here without reservation.[32]

Lessing not only creates fictional Sufi characters, but she also frequently refers to actual living persons from our times who live exemplary lives. For instance, in the afterword to *The Representative* Lessing mentions the team of British explorers who traveled to the South Pole and manifested the will to withstand painful and impossible circumstances simply in pursuit of knowledge. Edward Wilson, a scientist on the 1910–13 British expedition to the South Pole led by Robert Falcon Scott (his first expedition was in 1901–4), is one of these explorers who risked his life to gather penguin eggs to further scientific knowledge. Lessing suggests to her readers that so long as people such as Wilson and his coseekers succeed in their endeavors, the possibility exists for all humans to use all, not only a part, of the potential with which they were born. Lessing's prophetic call to action is not only supernatural or metaphysical. When she praises Wilson for his courage to break out of his ordinary possibilities, which she calls "the cage we live in that is made of our habits, upbringing, circumstances, and which shows itself so small and tight and tyrannical when we do try to break out" (134), she does so with the belief that people could do anything if they shook themselves out of their atrophied existences, and worked at something, anything, not even necessarily a spiritual path.

In *Shikasta* Johor reports, "every child has the capacity to be everything. A child was a miracle, a wonder! A child held all the history of the human race, that stretched back, back, further than they could imagine . . . Just as a loaf of bread holds in it all the substance of all the wheat grains that have gone into it . . . so this child was kneaded together by, and contained, all the harvest of mankind" (167). In as much a practical sense as a spiritual one, Lessing implores her readers, and demands of her characters, to work to the limits of their strength and capacities and no less. "Man is woefully underused and undervalued," she says, offering the analogy of children born in a circus who become acrobats. "Is this because these children have 'acrobats' genes' or because they are expected to be acrobats?" When we answer this question for ourselves, we have to agree with Lessing that our ordinary education is geared toward narrowing us and creating only "a tinker or a tailor, but not both." Meanwhile, the few multifaceted persons appear so unusual to us that we congratulate them on their versatility as though they were superhuman ("Ancient" 78–79).

Lessing appears to demonstrate the Sufi Way of creating whole persons when she portrays a people challenged by and coping with the worst of circumstances in *The Representative.*[33] Throughout the tale the characters who are urged to remain awake and fight are offered no rewards for their suffering. In the context of Cherry Garrard's biography of Edward Wilson, which Lessing quotes in the afterword to her novel, the survivors are not the "shopkeepers," who, Garrard considers, populate England and who cannot respect research unless it promises financial gain. And in Garrard's opinion Edward Wilson is of those few whom we congratulate for marching on his winter journeys alone simply for the sake of securing penguin eggs while expecting no monetary rewards (*The Representative* 137). Just as, upon his return to England, Wilson is not greeted with fanfares, neither are the inhabitants of Planet 8 rewarded outwardly for their suffering and endurance. What matters is not Wilson's visible worldly accomplishments but the fact that he survived a violent inner conflict and a "high drama that results from such tensions" (*The Representative* 140).

　　Shikasta, when interpreted in the Sufi context, seems to teach the means to develop oneself.[34] Its action spans the time immediately before a holocaust and the time immediately after it. The book consists of a series of reports by Johor, the emissary from mainland Canopus, on the condition of the Shikastans. Johor's reports specify that this holocaust is a result of a war between Canopus and Shammat, the enemy colony. At the end of the war the Shikastans suffer from radioactive-like destructive emanations and an illness which is both physical and mental. To this planet, Johor brings the Signature representing Canopean Law, tries to remind the inhabitants of their Canopean origins, and warns them of their doom. His wish is to relocate them in Canopus. Lessing invented the word *SOWF*, an acronym for "The-Substance-of-We-Feeling," pronounced quite similarly to the word *Sufi*.[35] According to Arberry (*Sufism* 78), the Arabic root *sfw* means "to be pure" and lends itself to *tasawwuf*, which means "purity." Lessing may have created a cognate of her own, *sowf*, which she defines as the spiritual nourishment the Shikastans receive from Canopus. It is due to a lack of this nourishment that the Shikastans are asleep and cannot hear Johor's warnings. They have the "degenerative disease" discussed throughout the novel. Allegorically, this disease causes a gradual loss of faith, which results in spiritual death.[36]

　　If we interpret the *Canopus* series as Sufi allegories, then Lessing could be implying that Canopus is the place where all enlightened beings reside and whence the rest of the inhabitants of Shikasta and Planet 8 originated—what was called "heaven" in the old order. In other words, in a Sufi reading of the series, Canopus functions not as a political power that is separate and removed from Shikasta or Planet 8, but as the spiritual powerhouse, the beginning and the end of all life on Shikasta, Planet 8, or any other planet. If so, then Johor from Canopus could be the Christ figure, sent from heaven to save the lost souls.[37] The various holocausts Lessing imagines, whether they take the form of nuclear war or an ice storm, could symbolize complete spiritual death or complete senility involving the forgetting of the nature and even the existence of Canopus on the part of the inhabitants of Shikasta, or of Planet 8, both metaphors for earth. For example, as long as the inhabitants of Planet 8 remember their connection to the mother planet Canopus, they can find the courage within to withstand the ice and the snow. Those who are numb and indifferent to the idea of Canopus/heaven are the ones who eventually freeze and disintegrate under their protective hides.

In *The Representative* we meet both those inhabitants who eventually die (the acorns which become fertilizer in Sufi symbolism) and the inhabitants for whom quitting is not even a choice (the acorns which evolve into oak trees). While everybody dies physically in the long run, those who have evolved have the chance to survive their bodily death. In the context of Sufism not all persons can evolve, but all beings at all levels are useful for the balance of nature and the cosmos. Johor, the messenger from Canopus, and Doeg, as well as the other representatives for Planet 8, can be seen as the few acorns in Sufi allegory that evolve into oak trees, as opposed to the thousands of acorns that simply rot. Likewise, Wilson in the non-fictional world evolves in Lessing's eyes.

In *Shikasta*, too, there are the rulers and the ruled, the rulers being the spiritual teachers who can guide the ruled in their ascent on the ladder of consciousness. Lessing also refers to them as "The Guardians" at the end of *The Four-Gated City*, or "The Providers" in *The Marriages*. Johor and Doeg, in this case, are the Providers and the Guardians of Lessing's fiction, and it is their level of being to which Lessing urges her characters, as well as her readers, to aspire. Commitment and wholeheartedness in Lessing's fiction are at the core of all meaningful endeavors that bring her characters closer to perfection. She quotes from Edward Wilson's diary: "It is amazing and most puzzling when one tries to think what is the object of our short life on earth—a mere visit—and how desperately this must represent our effect on the little part of the world with which we come into contact" (*The Representative* 143).

The protagonists' purpose in both *Shikasta* and *The Representative* is to reconnect with Canopus. In the Sufi context, Lessing describes the atmosphere of Shikasta as contaminated, and she renders Planet 8 uninhabitable to provide her characters with situations that force them to decide whether they will fight and earn the right to live in Canopus, that is, become the acorns that grow into oak trees, or give in to the hardships and die to become the acorns that disintegrate into fertilizer. Doeg, who is a potential Representative for Planet 8, tells us in the opening pages, "We knew that we had ceased to understand. We had understood—or believed we had—what Canopus wanted for us, and from us: we had been taking part, under their provision, in a long, slow progress upwards in civilization" (5). Doeg feels that he and his companions may be forgetting why they have to suffer so intensely since they know they are going to die anyway, with or without the struggle. In the Sufi tradition such suffering results in spiritual evolution, whereas ordinary suffering results in nothing positive. Lessing offers many elaborate descriptions of the conditions of life on Planet 8: "the winds screamed over us and sometimes came sucking and driving down where we were, and we shivered and we shrank, and knew that we had not begun to imagine what we had, all of us, to face" (*The Representative* 13).

Suffering this intensely, Doeg and his companions are humbled and are drawn closer together to share their warmth against the blizzard, and inner strength against their fate. Their situation makes them acutely aware of their vulnerability under Canopean Law and of their place in the hierarchy of levels of being. In the Sufi tradition, a disciple looks up to his or her master, as Doeg does to Johor, and the master in turn aspires to become like his saint. Likewise, Doeg and the others with him are aware that there are other beings above and below themselves; they feel they are being watched by other creatures which they cannot see, just as they themselves keep watch over their surroundings for signs of edible vegetation or animals that they can see—this makes them realize their place in the greater scheme of things: "We each took a watch, and all felt that a watch was being kept on us—we had a sense of being stared at" (28). These beings belong to various levels of consciousness, which levels in turn correspond to various steps on the Sufi ladder toward enlightenment. On this ladder, both those higher up on the ladder and those further down need one another to pull, or to push up, to feed, or to be fed. Doeg tells us, "Both kinds of us, the people of Planet 8, the represented and the Representative—endured. The thought in our minds was that they were being changed by what we were forced to do; that we were being changed by their being made to stay alive" (101–2). This joint effort toward the same purpose recalls the carpet imagery in *The Memoirs*.

In *The Memoirs*, *The Representative*, and *Shikasta*, Lessing portrays a breaking and broken (*shikasta*) people who are alive under the worst possible circumstances. In the case of *The Representative*, the people are broken to the point of not even caring about their own children, the inheritors of their civilization, their potential future: "A child died, and we all knew we might be thinking secretly: So much the better; what horrors is it going to be spared" (39). The Shikastans, too, are in pain and in need of help, but at the same time they reject Johor's warnings and his offers to help. They are so detached from their origin in Canopus that they cannot recall it or trust it. Johor says, "some were already mad. One of them would shake and shake a pain-filled head . . . and then let out howls of pain and start running, rushing everywhere, howling as if pain were something he could leave behind" (53). In this state, the Shikastans do not heed Johor's pleas, and they continue to stay in their doomed but nevertheless familiar surroundings. A Sufi interpretation would be that in order to grow and become enlightened, persons must be able to give up what they possess—their egos, their outer shells, and their habitual ways of being, with the faith that in essence, they will lose nothing. Johor's efforts to awaken the Shikastans' memory, however, are in vain: "Everywhere ideas, sets of mind, beliefs that have supported people for centuries are fraying away, dissolving, going. What is there left?" (197).

In *The Representative* we observe similarly trying circumstances. The starvation and subzero temperatures on Planet 8 continue to strain people's nerves and compassion, causing that "inner friction" which is so necessary for Sufi "work." Sufis often use the metaphor of thorns and roses; thorns without, they say, account for roses within, and vice versa. In the same vein, they demand to know whether it is easier to push a wheelbarrow uphill or downhill. Without resistance, there is no work, and without work, one's mind, heart, and muscles will atrophy. While Doeg and the other workers finally shovel up sparse loads of sea creatures out of the boats, their will is challenged: they must abstain from eating the food in order to carry it to those who are half unconscious deep in their caves. And in this toil of will more than of muscle, they are offered the opportunity to evolve.

As the cold weather and starvation continue on Planet 8, those who do not have enough self-control turn to crime and murder. Doeg remembers that not long ago they used to have only one Representative for the Law, whereas now there are several, because the tensions and difficulties make people quarrel more readily. He reports, "It had been, before The Ice, a rare thing to have a killing. Now we expected murder" (21). Doeg remembers the purpose of this catastrophe and accepts the cross he has to bear. While the wars and arguments among his countrymen leave him alone in his mission, he quietly knows that "argument does not teach children or

90

the immature. Only time and experience does that (21) . . . We were learning, we old ones, that in times when a species, a race, is under threat, drives and necessities built into the very substance of our flesh speak out in ways that we need never have known about if extremities had not come to squeeze these truths out of us" (24).

Doeg knows that what happens to the people and the rest of the creatures on Planet 8 is not really important, but how they cope with this dilemma will make a significant difference in their future existence in another form and another place. What matters is not that they will die, but how they live until they die. However, only Doeg and the other Representatives seem to understand this, while most of the inhabitants begin to give in to the freezing of their bodies and the numbing of their minds. In between occasional bursts of rebellion and refusal to go on, Doeg works hard to keep the others alive. He knows that whatever fate Planet 8 is experiencing is in fact proper and even necessary for its development and for its ultimate purpose in the universe. He says, "The hardest thing for any one of us to realize—everyone of us, no matter how high in the levels of functioning—is that we are all subject to an overall plan. A general Necessity" (16), which expresses a central thought in Sufism.

Accepting this "general Necessity," Doeg works, as more and more inhabitants simply give in to the freezing temperatures and resign themselves to die. At times he finds himself longing to go to sleep as much as the rest, feeling unable to withstand the intense physical pain of cold and hunger. Along with the other Representatives, Doeg's daily activity consists of going from cave to cave, striding about among the half dead, still "trying to impress on them that vigorous movement [is] indeed still possible" (46). And at such times of forgetfulness and despair, Doeg asks Johor *why* they must prolong their death. In his misery, he goes in and out of sleeping and waking states where sometimes he knows the meaning of Johor's words and sometimes he cannot comprehend them. Johor's answers are as vague as always: "You will be rescued from this freezing death when you earn it (59) . . . there is more than one way of dying" (64).

The Sufis' purpose in asking the inhabitants of Planet 8 to remain alive for as long as they can would be that a new self (roses) could be born out of inner friction (thorns). Johor, possibly a Sufi master, tries to impress upon Doeg and the others that they belong to a shared pool of thoughts and dreams and that they cannot be wrong in sensing that a day will come when the snows will melt. How else could anyone even dream of such a day if it weren't a truth already offered by Canopus? he asks. This truth, which is hard to imagine in the midst of suffering, angers Doeg. He reproaches Johor saying, "You will say, Johor, that this charm, this delightfulness, will vanish here and reappear elsewhere—on some place or planet that we have never heard of . . . yes, they will be gone soon, the little creatures will be dead, all of them, all—but we are not to mourn them, no, for their qualities will be reborn—somewhere" (80). Yet by these very words Doeg admits that he partially understands the idea which he appears to reject so violently.

Canopus's attitude toward annihilation recalls the Sufi parable about the river that must give itself up to the sands in order to cross the desert, while in essence it remains the same as it comes down in the form of rain on the other side of the desert and forms another river (Shah, *Tales* 23).[38] Thus Johor continues to encourage people to remain awake, despite the fact that the wall built for protection against the ice falls down, and it is clear that there simply is no protection against the cold and deep sleep.[39]

The Shikastans experience a similar fate: "All the old supports going, gone, this man reaches out a hand to steady himself on a ledge of rough brick that is warm in the sun: his hand feeds him messages of solidity, but his mind messages of destruction, for this breathing substance, made of earth, will be a dance of atoms, he knows it, his intelligence tells him so: there will soon be war, he is in the middle of war" (198). And again, Johor works with the help of a handful of enlightened Shikastans in his mission against atrophy. One of the techniques he uses to awaken people is the "Signature" from Canopus which he carries with him on a tablet.[40] When he shows it to the people, he observes that "They were remembering a little of what they had been: the Signature induced this in them. Nothing much, but they did remember something splendid and right" (13). He also uses chants which he orders the Shikastans to repeat to themselves like a prayer: "Canopus says we must not waste or spoil, / Canopus tells us not to use violence on each other"(73).

Lessing gives us a closer look at Taufiq, an individual who is struggling to wake up. Taufiq's name in Arabic and Persian, when spelled *Tawfiq*, means "grace, divine favor, success, and good luck," suggesting Lessing's faith in the salvation of the Shikastans, despite their broken down (*shikasta*) state. In a passage reminiscent of the Sufis' metaphorical account of awakening in the dungeons as opposed to waking in the rose gardens, Lessing's narrator in *Shikasta* demonstrates what torture it is for Taufiq to accept his own faults, to recognize his own pathetic situation, and in short, to confront his embarrassing obliviousness to his incompletion. A Canopean reincarnated as a Shikastan, he experiences the pain of self-remembering—the necessary step to enlightenment: "He smiled as he slept. He wept, tears soaking his face, as he walked and talked in his dream with us, with himself" (82). Exasperated by his observations of hopeless people like Taufiq, Johor concludes that these people are self-condemned—that they are in fact given a chance to help themselves, yet they choose sleep. If Johor were to be read as a Christ figure, his impatience with the people might recall Christ's fury at and intolerance of the money lenders at the temple. Johor maintains only a detached compassion for the inhabitants of Shikasta and, in the long run, is able to resign himself to the fact that he cannot save everyone: "I have known more than once what it is to accept the failure, final and irreversible, of an effort or experiment to do with creatures who have within themselves the potential of

development dreamed of, planned for . . . and then—Finis! The
end! The drum pattering out into silence" (3). And having done
everything he can to save as many as he can, he resigns himself
to the destruction of the rest of the multitudes.

Similar circumstances find a sad and rebellious Doeg in
The Representative asking, "But what for? In our hearts now
we all knew, everyone, that they would be roused and stimulated . . . to no end . . . most showed signs of wanting to stum-
ble back under the snow into their sleep again. How strong is
that deep, dark drive towards sleep, towards death, towards
annihilation" (98–99). Yet he works despite his reluctance.
When the people are awakened, he instructs them to build
shelters out of snowhuts with piles of hides inside for warmth
and stores of dried meats for sustenance. In each such house,
four or five people are sheltered, alive and safe for a time. And
out of these people, one is chosen to remain awake and to
make sure the others do not slide back into lethargy.[41]

The act of building these huts is allegorical, recalling the
idea behind the Masonic order, or "the builders," said to be
associated with Sufism: "[one must] detach from fixed ideas
and preconceptions, and face what is to be [his] lot" (Shah,
Sufis 205). *This* is what Doeg and the others must do: accept
their lot and build a new system which can accommodate the
new circumstances, slowly giving up the old ways of being and
behaving. Lessing uses the word *mason* (or "builder"), which
she spells *Masson*, as both a proper name and as a title for
someone who has achieved a higher level of being.

When Doeg recalls how he happened to become a
Representative, he remembers having been apprenticed to
Masson as a child to dig out the earth for the foundation of the
protective wall. He remembers the series of chances that caused
him eventually to become Memory Maker, Keeper of Records,
and Representative, while he considers that he could have been
called "Masson" instead of "Doeg" by still another series of
chance events. He tells us, "when we three came back from
Planet 10, we were all Doeg" (54). As soon as one takes on a

different occupation in the community, one's name, too, changes to reflect one's new social function on the planet. Thus there is Masson, the builder; Zdanye, who shelters and protects; Bratch, the physician; Klin, the fruit maker; or Marl, keeper of herds, among others.[42] As with all names, the name *Doeg* is both a proper name and a title. Doeg explains, "I have remained Doeg nearly all the time, though Klin and Marl have not. Though I have been Klin and Marl and Pedug and Masson, when needed. But Doeg is my nature, I suppose" (55). As a result of the act of building against atrophy and death, Doeg becomes conscious of a newness in himself and in the other representatives: "we were being changed, molecule by molecule, atom by atom" (101).

A similar saving of souls also takes place in *Shikasta*, in which, after millions are destroyed at the end of the "Great War," Lessing establishes a new cosmology where the one percent who survived live by following orders from Canopus. They no longer have selves, individuality, or will, as did Anna Wulf or Martha Quest, but are in fact freer and more responsible for their actions. The new cosmology operates through an intergalactic exchange between Canopus and its various colonies, which, in Lessing's words, furthers "the prime object and aim of the galaxy . . . —the creation of ever-evolving Sons and Daughters of the Purpose" (35). In the Sufi tradition this "Purpose" would imply evolution and enlightenment through "work" on the self. Kassim Sherban is one of the survivors of Shikasta who has completed this "work." Now an enlightened being in Lessing's new cosmology, he recalls the not-so-distant past with great curiosity and asks, "How did we live then? How did we bear it? . . . not knowing anything, fumbling and stumbling and longing for something different but not knowing what had happened to [us] or what [we] longed for" (364).

On Planet 8, too, the joint effort of the Representatives and the represented result in the death of those who had made no efforts to awaken and evolve and the rebirth of the Representatives who struggled to rise above their ordinary states of being. Lessing offers their experience to her readers as successful results of Sufi "work" on the self. In *Shikasta* Kassim Sherban writes to two other survivors: "And this will go on for us, as if we were slowly being lifted and filled and washed by a soft singing wind that clears our sad muddled minds and holds us safe and heals us and feeds us with lessons we never imagined" (364). Similarly in *The Representative* Doeg reports how "for the last time with our old eyes, we sat close and looked into each other's faces, until, one after another, our faces shuttered themselves in death, and our bundles of bones settled inside the heaps of our shag-skin coats . . . we slid away from that scene, and saw it with eyes we had not known we possessed" (116). The Representatives' and the Shikastans' efforts to survive the catastrophe on their planet do not save them from physical death but rescue them from spiritual death, transforming them into higher beings. When these two novels are read as allegories, the snow/ice and the blasting of cities by space-fleets represent spiritual crisis and depravity.

Evaluated in a Sufi context, this ending is appropriately Sufi, as is Lessing's urge to awaken her readers. The Sufi's task is to prepare for death by living with death every minute. Likewise, Lessing's impulse to reform in *Shikasta* and *The Representative* is directed not toward averting and avoiding death but toward improving the quality of life on earth, thereby securing the survival of an essence that will live beyond death. Sufis take death for granted and look at life as the practicing grounds for it. Therefore, from a Sufi point of view, both Lessing's consolation at the end of *The Representative* and her threats and pleas throughout the novel are impulses that complement each other, rather than one making the other unnecessary.

Conclusion: Lessing's Vision

For Lessing, as for the Sufis, famine, war, plague, or other catastrophes are unavoidable aspects of life, necessary for keeping the balance of nature, much as forest fires ignited by natural causes must be allowed to burn. Always interested in the larger scheme, Lessing is more concerned with the fact that the human race as a species has survived all calamities thus far in spite of the millions of individuals who have been annihilated. She concludes, "We [the human race] can survive anything you care to mention. We are supremely equipped to survive, to adapt and even in the long run to start thinking" (Hazleton 26). She believes, as do Sufis, that mankind evolves through stress. Because of this belief, Lessing accepts even the threat of nuclear war or another ice age as an opportunity for humans to evolve.

When we stand back and look at Lessing's works as a whole, Lessing's vision expands to encompass more than the planet earth and its inhabitants. She believes with certainty that there are worlds beyond that which we can see, and she wants her readers at least to entertain the mimetic possibility of these worlds and of other living beings whose existence deserves our consideration and acknowledgment. In order to communicate even the slightest hint of these worlds in her novels, it was necessary for Lessing to break out of the conventional fictional modes and to experiment with styles and genres more conducive to giving free reign to her expanding vision. Appropriately, in the afterword to *The Representative* Lessing writes, "It seems to me . . . that we do not often enough wonder if our lives, or some events and times in our lives, may not be analogues or metaphors or echoes of evolvements and happenings going on in other people?—or animals?—even forests or oceans or rocks? . . . even in worlds or dimensions elsewhere" (145). Knowing her direct interest in and knowledge of Sufism, we can conclude that Lessing did not utter these words merely as a shot in the dark, that she not only wonders but is *convinced* of the reality of other potentials in other dimensions. Accordingly, she incarnates them in her teaching stories for us to recognize and, perhaps, to accept and emulate.

Three

Lessing's Teaching Stories

An illiterate came to Nasrudin, and asked him to write a letter for him.
"I can't," said the Mulla, "because I have burned my foot."
"What has that got to do with writing a letter?"
"Since nobody can read my handwriting, I am bound to have to travel somewhere to interpret the letter. And my foot is sore; so there is no point in writing the letter, is there?"

—*Idries Shah,* Exploits of the Incomparable Mulla Nasrudin

As chapter 2 has demonstrated, the contents of Lessing's novels written after her introduction to Sufi mysticism naturally lend themselves to Sufi interpretation; the current chapter focuses on the way in which this is done. How does Lessing invite a Sufi reading of her novels? Are there direct signs or changes in her choices of genre, mode, and style that suggest a new vision and a changed worldview? Like the whimsical Nasrudin quoted above, whose burnt foot prevents him from interpreting the letters he writes, Lessing leaves her readers to their own devices where her narratives are concerned. She even said as much in her 1971 introduction written for the third printing of *The Golden Notebook*: "why don't you read what I have written and make up your own mind about what you think, testing it against your own life, your own experience. Never mind about Professors White and Black" (xvii).

A significant change in Lessing's fictive technique in her post-Sufi novels is her use of teaching stories. A teaching story is an example of one of the many ways in which Sufi elements are transmitted, and it has been one of the main tools with which Idries Shah has taught Sufism in the West. Lessing does not only directly employ Sufi teaching stories in the dedication to, for instance, *The Four-Gated City*, but she also attributes Sufi or Sufi-like anecdotes to her characters in *The Four-Gated City* and in *The Diary of a Good Neighbour*, among other novels.[1] She also structures many of her narratives in the form of tall tales and fables; this is the case in *The Memoirs*, *The Marriages*, *The Representative*, and *The Fifth Child*, each of which offers enigmatic lessons that make sense in the Sufi context. These narratives have the flavor of a fairy tale: "We all remember that time," begins *The Memoirs*; "You ask how the Canopean Agents seemed to us in the times of The Ice" (3), begins the narrator in the opening of *The Representative*; and *The Fifth Child* all but opens with Once Upon a Time: "Harriet and David met each other at an office party (3) . . . The first baby, Luke, was born in the big bed" (17).

In her preface to Shah's *Seekers after Truth* Lessing writes, "It was they who developed, [Sufis] claim, the teaching story, an artifact created specifically for influencing the deepest and most hidden part of a human being—a part not accessible to any other approach" (634). Lessing has been closely involved in the dissemination of these stories in the West by way of giving public readings of Sufi stories and announcing the publication of collections by Shah, as well as by writing introductions and prefaces to collections of teaching stories such as *Seekers after Truth* and *Learning How to Learn* by Idries Shah, *The Tale of the Four Dervishes* by Amina Shah, and *Kalila and Dimna* by Ramsay Wood. Lessing adds in her preface to Shah's *Seekers after Truth* that "[t]he teaching story is not to be considered as a parable, which the Sufis use, too;

for the parable has a more limited aim, such as the inculcation of a moral, or ethics, or to transmit information" (635). To facilitate our understanding of Lessing's teaching stories, this chapter will first study the Sufi teaching story, which is a minute portion of the enigma that is Sufism, and which Shah uses as a teaching tool in transmitting Sufism to his readers and followers in the West.

The Sufi Teaching Story

There exist innumerable Sufi teaching stories that originally were told orally and later were written down for the main purpose of transmitting Sufi faith and practice to future generations. In the Middle East, where these stories are told and retold, they are not considered to be for children only; rather, they are said to contain several layers of meaning which render them suitable for people of all ages. Shah likens the Sufi story to a peach: "A person may be emotionally stirred by the exterior as if the peach were lent to you. You can eat the peach and taste a further delight . . . You can throw away the stone— or crack it and find a delicious kernel within. This is the hidden depth" (*Sufis* 88). It is in this manner that Shah invites his audience to receive the Sufi story. If one does not seek to uncover the kernel, one will have accomplished nothing more than looking at the peach or regarding the story as merely amusing and superficial, while others may internalize the tale and allow it to touch them.[2]

In addition to the intentional layering in its content and structure, the Sufi teaching story also acquires embellishments of many more layers as it undergoes the natural transformation of traveling across time and space. Hence every story also becomes a new story in the retelling, acquiring new twists and mysteries depending on the idiosyncrasies of the particular storyteller and the context in which the story is being told. Lessing likens these longer tales to a ball of magic thread which "You unwind and unwind, going back and back, to long before the birth of Islam, and then still farther back, and you find yourself thousands of years away, and still the thread is unwinding, with no end in sight" (Amina Shah xi). One story leads the way to another and another, stories unfolding like Chinese boxes until the audience is lost in the maze. Finally no one cares about the very first king who had abandoned his kingdom in search of wisdom, and who had met four dervishes, each of whom had told a different story which had unfolded into many more stories. At that point of abandonment, the lesson is quietly learned, sometimes unbeknownst to the hearer. The most important purpose of enchanting the audience with this ball of magic thread, in addition to entertaining, is to blur the black-and-white distinctions between right and wrong, good and bad, cause and effect, villain and saint, guilty and innocent. Actions do not necessarily provoke the reactions one is conditioned to expect, the future is not always shaped by one's plans, and one's life and behavior are not as independently governed by the self as one would like to believe. Everything is infinitely interconnected, even if through bizarre and unexpected ties.

The Sufi tales translated and revised by Idries Shah frequently do not fit the above description of the longer Sufi stories. Rather, Shah eliminates many embellishments which characterize the original tales, thus considerably shortening them. He makes sure that the kernel of the stories is not completely obscured by centuries of accretions and tall tales. Thus, for instance, stories about Mulla Nasrudin are frequently only a few sentences long in Shah's translations. In contrast, the same stories might be several pages long in a translation by Alice Geer Kelsey, who narrates the stories primarily in order to delight. Sometimes, Shah's renderings consist almost only of the moral itself, narrated to make its intent more accessible to the Western ear unaccustomed to search for Sufi wisdom amid layers of narrative. In her introduction to Amina Shah's collection Lessing explains the difference between the short and long stories: "One is precise and sharp, with instructions for students in a certain phase of study (as well as other dimensions, of course), and in a form appropriate for its existence for that phase; the second has the charm and the affability" (xiii).

On the whole, whether condensed or not, Sufi teaching stories sufficiently disorient the reader's rational faculties so that a potential channel for discerning the story's wisdom can be established. Lessing does this in many of her later narratives, including *The Memoirs of a Survivor*, *Briefing for a Descent into Hell*, and *Re: Colonised Planet 5, Shikasta*. Perhaps in order to disorient her readers and to break mechanical thought processes, she does not provide clear markers in these novels. Assuming she emulates Sufi teaching stories, it has to be her hope that readers will relinquish their usual thought patterns and will allow the story to guide them to a fresh space, time, and understanding.[3] Gayle Greene's reading of *Shikasta* is similar to my own. She sees that Lessing writes to justify the ways of man to God, as Milton did to justify the ways of God to man (*Poetics* 162).

The Sufi teaching story aims to shake the audience's existing worldview to such a point that one stops looking at the world through any single lens. The story allows for no fixed points of reference, daring its audience to transcend rational boundaries. It aims gently to remove blinders, to show a greater picture of reality. The expected logical result is eliminated by the change in the frame that shakes the participating party in the tale and the audience out of their habitual thought patterns.[4] "These stories guide the reader along unfamiliar paths; some contain a pattern of activity so that the reader can become familiarized with the unusual, and some are intended as 'shock'—a fresh stimulus to the mind to upset the normal paths of thought and consciousness" (Ornstein 376).

The Sufi teaching story is meant to serve as a tool for growth and enlightenment. As Lessing writes in her introduction to Amina Shah's collection, "in whatever form it appears, whatever the kind of language, each tale has its place, its kind of pleasure; and each will appeal to the people who, for that time, are right for it, as it is right for them" (xiv). The Sufi teacher knows that the depth to which a story succeeds in touching its hearer and the degree to which the story is decoded depends upon the hearer's level of being. Hence at any one telling, only the received portion of the tale can be considered the "real" story. The transmitter of Sufi stories is aware that for every single telling, there emerge as many "real" tales as the number of hearers in the audience. Knowing this, the Sufi teacher does not only expect multiple interpretations but intentionally creates teaching stories so as to evoke them. This is also what happens in Lessing's works. A Sufi reading of Lessing's fiction enhances, complements, and complicates other, non-Sufi analyses of her work.

A sample protagonist of Sufi teaching stories is the popular folk figure known as Nasreddin Hodja in Turkey, as Mulla Nasrudin in Iran, as Joha in North Africa, and by other names in other parts of the world. He is also well known in Greece and the former Soviet Union, where Muslims do not predominate. Stories and jokes about him have been made available to English speakers by many translators, including Shah. He is frequently referred to as simply "the Hodja" or "the Mulla," meaning "spiritual teacher." He is known and enjoyed by all in the Middle East as a spiritual teacher, a fool, a joker, a judge, and a trickster, as well as a victim; his witty stories are still told in the teahouses, coffehouses, and homes throughout North Africa, the Middle East, and Central Asia. It is debatable whether the Hodja really lived or whether he is only legendary; however, according to popular lore, he lived in Central Anatolia in the thirteenth century during the reign of the Anatolian Seljuks, attended a Muslim theological school (*medrese*) in Sivrihisar, Turkey, worked as a prayer leader (*imam*) in the mosque, taught in a *medrese*, and was a government official. There is even a grave on a hilltop in Akşehir, Turkey, in Central Anatolia, to indicate that he *did* live. There is no question about the Hodja's popularity: he and his patient, long-eared best friend—his donkey—are like family to every Turk.

Many westerners who are not familiar with the Nasreddin Hodja stories find them silly. When read with an awareness of the Sufi tradition, however, the silliness becomes part of the point. The humorous joke is the first level on which we are invited to respond. Knowing the stories of Nasreddin Hodja, we both smile and look beneath the surface. Lessing's direct quotes and simulation of them in her novels would suggest that she takes them seriously and gives them her full attention, in turn requiring our full attention and effort at understanding her own stories that resemble Nasrudin's in spirit. As Dee Seligman explains, "Sufi jokes mock the ultimate inadequacy of logic" (199), as does the Zen Koan.[5] For example, the Hodja demonstrates the interconnectedness in life when, while walking along a deserted street in the night, he sees a troop of horsemen coming toward him. Frightened out of his wits, he jumps over a wall and finds himself in a graveyard. The horsemen follow him and see the Hodja cowering with fear. "What are you doing there?" they ask him, and the Hodja replies, "It is more complicated than you assume! You see, *I* am here because of you; and you, *you* are here because of *me*." (Shah, *Sufis* 81).

On the surface, this is a great joke and its message is obvious. We can take the Hodja at his word. On further examination, the story also illustrates the inevitable interconnectedness of human life—that one can do nothing without affecting others and that one's actions open up infinite new possibilities and have unlimited consequences and repercussions like rings in a pond. Still deeper is embedded the fundamental understanding between the Sufi master and the disciple: the former needs the latter as much as the disciple needs the master to move up the evolutionary Sufi ladder. They are interdependent. Yet another layer might be that until the disciple appears, the master is not yet a teacher; and until one recognizes the teacher, one does not know what one is seeking, or what one is meant to do. The story sets up a simple, humorous circumstance under which the master and disciple can recog-

105

nize, then in turn identify, one another: *I* am here because of you, and *you* are here because of *me*! Perhaps a deeper layer would disclose the disbelieving novice on the path who fears, rather than loves, God and yet who cannot escape God's presence on a deserted street or in a graveyard, in life or after death.

This chapter refers both to the tales that Lessing quotes from the wealth of Sufi literature and to the tales that she herself has created. The latter are of two kinds: shorter anecdotes within a novel and an entire novel acting as a teaching tale from beginning to end. Hardin writes in "The Sufi Teaching Story," "[o]ne will discover that the Lessing story contains the same components as the Sufi story [for in both,] moments of wakeful insights" are the focus (319). In her article, "Humor and Survival," Stitzel remarks that the Nasrudin jokes provide one form of relief from the usual sober context of Lessing's novels. Stitzel acknowledges the jokes' methodology of breaking conditioned thought processes and actions. This chapter studies four teaching stories by Lessing: *The Four-Gated City* (1969); *The Diary of a Good Neighbour* (1983); *The Marriages between Zones Three, Four, and Five* (1980); and *The Making of the Representative for Planet 8* (1982). These novels communicate the Sufi message through the direct use of quotations from Sufi literature as well as through the use of characters as constructs, role models, and potential Sufis. They by no means exhaust the ways in which Sufism has permeated Lessing's works. The analyses in this chapter also can be applied to other novels by Lessing where she emulates Sufi teaching stories.[6]

Lessing's Characters as Potential Sufis

Regardless of whether Lessing strictly follows and advocates Sufism, she manifests a strong sense of duty to teach and to demonstrate the development of consciousness through daily struggle and much suffering. To this end, she subordinates her characters to her message in her teaching stories. She appears to be only secondarily interested in a protagonist as a well-rounded person and as a character in her own right. For instance we get to know Anna Wulf in choppy, kaleidoscopic segments and Martha Quest, named after her occupation, the quest for herself, in the fragmented pieces of a mosaic. With the introduction of the narrator in *The Memoirs*, Lessing's characters carry fewer mimetic responsibilities and function more on synthetic and thematic levels to serve as vehicles in Lessing's teaching stories. At the same time the readers' full acceptance of their mimetic reality always remains crucial for understanding Lessing's message.

Lessing's development of characters who are under varying degrees of Sufi influence can be understood better along the lines that James Phelan draws among the three dimensions of character—namely, the mimetic, synthetic, and thematic.[7] For Phelan, the mimetic dimension reminds us that characters are images of possible, growing people with traits such as beauty, maleness, or shyness. The way and degree to which these traits coalesce to create a plausible person results in the mimetic function (11). The synthetic dimension is the artificially constructed component that remains covert in realistic texts, although all characters are fundamentally synthetic constructs. As such, they serve as devices that behave as protagonist, antagonist, or minor character who carry out various roles to further the plot. Whenever characters perform their plot functions, they are carrying out their synthetic function. Usually, the more we become aware of the synthetic component, the more the reality of a character as mimetic diminishes, and vice versa. Finally, the thematic dimension of characters refers to their ideational component and representativeness of a class, such as bigots, revolutionaries, or individualists. Phelan argues that there is no fixed relationship among the components of character that all narratives share. Instead, he claims that progression of any narrative establishes the particular relation among components for that text.[8]

CONSEQUENCES

Using these terms helps to identify the different uses Lessing makes of her characters to communicate Sufi ideas. For example in *The Representative* when we identify envoys such as Johor and Doeg as Sufi masters and disciples on the Sufi Path we invite readers to consider them to be *more* than literary tools used by Lessing to translate the alien world to us. In this light, they become not only synthetic characters designed to communicate Lessing's ideas, nor only thematic characters designed to embody those ideas, but also mimetic models designed to invite us to experience vicariously some of what it means to live and suffer the lives of actual Sufi mystics: Johor is a plausible Sufi master; Doeg is a believable disciple on the Sufi Path. Taking for granted that Lessing wants us to accept the reality of another world, her characters must be understood not just as rhetorical devices to be "read past" as we seek her ideas but also as plausible characters whose ways of being are crucial for our understanding of Lessing's ideas. And at the same time, as true Sufi mystics, their individual mimetic existences and egos do not matter in themselves but are significant only insofar as they contribute to the greater evolution of all human life.[9] Paradoxically, then, our awareness of the relative insignificance of their *individual* identities depends precisely upon our recognition of those identities.

Moving further into the realm of space fiction in the *Canopus* series, Lessing reduces even more of the mimetic dimension of her protagonists.[10] They mainly serve as tools to demonstrate an allegory in which Lessing articulates her view of humankind and history. Therefore it becomes more difficult for us to identify with the characters, for they are only more important because of the ideas that they represent. Yet their mimetic dimensions and functions provide the key to Lessing's message to her readers. In the life, suffering, and death of characters such as Doeg or Al·Ith, rather than in their raison d'être as constructs, can the reader find exemplary models worth imitating.

In the preface to *Shikasta* Lessing writes by way of explanation, "It is by now commonplace to say that novelists everywhere are breaking the bonds of the realistic novel because what we all see around us becomes daily wilder, more fantastic, incredible [and] . . . fact can be counted on to match our wildest inventions" (ix). Having exhausted the possibilities in the existing, visible world, Lessing creatively appropriates the world of fantasy in which she can show what is possible. She writes in the preface to *The Sirian Experiments*, "It has been said that everything man is capable of imagining has its counterpart somewhere else, in a different level of reality" (xiii). Therefore, space fiction serves Lessing as the appropriate genre through which she can express her insights into human consciousness. It illustrates Lessing's conviction that human beings must learn to expand their minds to new ways of seeing, thinking, and being if they wish to survive.

In *The Representative*, written as a tall tale, characters cannot even keep the same name for long but change their names as their nature and roles on the planet change. For instance, anyone involved in building is named "Masson" for the stretch of time that he remains a builder.[11] The effect of the subordination of characters to Lessing's teaching is that we are hardly interested in them as heroes and heroines but rather in their allegorical role in the planet's evolution.[12] Likewise, Lessing is interested not directly in the plight of individual human beings but in their roles in the evolution of the *whole* of the human race within the expanse of the universe. In her preface to *The Sirian Experiments* she adds, "I would so like it if reviewers and readers could see this series, *Canopus in Argos: Archives*, as a framework that enables me to tell (I hope) a beguiling tale or two; to put questions, both to myself and to others; to explore ideas and sociological possibility" (ix). In her preface to *Shikasta* Lessing shares her "exhilaration that comes from being set free into a larger scope, with more capacious possibilities and themes . . . It was clear I had made—or found—a new world for myself, a realm where the petty fates of planets, let alone individuals, are only aspects of cosmic evolution expressed in the rivalries and interactions of great galactic Empires: Canopus, Sirius . . ." (ix). Lessing's concerns do not stop at the level of individuals on earth but go beyond the visible world; she wants her protagonists to make efforts on a cosmic level where they will contribute to a universal growth and the survival of humanity, and her overall message supports this common cause.

The Four-Gated City

For Lessing, the introduction of Sufi material into her work is almost a reflex. Having read and ingested Sufi thought in earnest, she brings in fragments of Sufism intermittently and most naturally, just as she writes about Africa and the African or British points of view. Furthermore, it is said that when a student of Sufism achieves a certain level of understanding, he or she can begin to make up Sufi anecdotes similar to those about Nasrudin. This definitely appears to be the case with Lessing. Traces of Sufism emerge in different forms in different novels, sometimes subtly, at other times quite overtly. Sufi materials that seem "other" to a Western audience help Lessing to reinterpret the familiar. *The Four-Gated City* and *The Diary of a Good Neighbour* illustrate how Sufi ideas have worked their way into Lessing's texts and how they have infiltrated her works in many large and small ways, claiming new ground for themselves as transplants within modern Western narratives where they can take fresh new root.

 The Four-Gated City and *The Diary of a Good Neighbour* include some remnants of Sufi material, while at the same time they are not so radically different in mode and style from the novels Lessing wrote before exploring Sufism as to suggest a completely new train of thought.[13] Aside from a few direct quotes from and allusions to Sufi sources, they have more in common with the earlier *Children of Violence* series in terms of characters, plot, and style than they do with the *Canopus in Argos: Archives* series. The *Canopus* series, written in what

Lessing has termed the *space-fiction* genre, demonstrate a definite break from Lessing's earlier work and raise questions regarding her revised purpose.

The urgency that readers sense in *The Four-Gated City* can be attributed to the emergent impact of Sufi worldview on Lessing's degree of patience with her readers.[14] Prior to the 1960s Lessing was perhaps anxious to rescue Martha Quest out of her marriage trap and she may have been impatient with apartheid, but it was not until after she was immersed in Sufi thought that she dared bring about an apocalypse—as a warning, if not a threat, to us all. Yet, despite such intentional insertions or perhaps subconscious borrowings from Sufi material, Lessing denied in a letter to Mona Knapp that *The Four-Gated City* "owed anything to Sufism" (102). It is possible to read most of Lessing's post-*Golden Notebook* novels in light of Sufi mysticism, although this does not necessarily exclude other readings. At the same time, a Sufi reading sheds light on some aspects of these novels that otherwise remain hidden. When we receive Martha Quest of *The Four-Gated City* on ordinary grounds of reality, as a person who belongs to *this* world alone, her transformation appears to be out of character. But when Lessing's mystical side is acknowledged, it not only becomes easy to grasp Martha's exceptional wisdom but also becomes necessary to expect even greater changes in her being.

In *The Four-Gated City* Lessing includes direct quotations from various Sufi sources: a dervish teaching story from Shah's collection in the dedication; a quotation from Rûmî in the opening to part 4; and another quotation from Shah also before part 4. The dervish story in the dedication sets the tone for the whole work and explicitly asks that characters in the novel be regarded as kindred spirits to the fool in the story:[15]

> Once upon a time there was a fool who was sent to buy flour and salt. He took a dish to carry his purchases.
> "Make sure," said the man who sent him, "not to mix the two things—I want them separate."

111

CONSEQUENCES

When the shopkeeper had filled the dish with flour and was measuring out the salt, the fool said: "Do not mix it with the flour; here, I will show you where to put it." And he inverted the dish, to provide, from its upturned bottom, a surface upon which the salt could be laid. The flour, of course, fell onto the floor. But the salt was safe. When the fool got back to the man who had sent him, he said: "Here is the salt."

"Very well," said the other man, "but where is the flour?"

"It should be here," said the fool, turning the dish over.

As soon as he did that, the salt fell to the ground, and the flour, of course, was seen to be gone. (Shah, *Way* 212–13)

Lessing makes direct use of this tale to demonstrate the equally futile and senseless human endeavors described in the first three parts of *The Four-Gated City*, endeavors that fail from a lack of integration similar to that of the flour and the salt. Characters suffer from the separation of their knowledge from their experiences, and of their thoughts from their feelings, so that each is affected by the various results and side-effects of that segregation.[16] Shah explains: "Doing one thing which they think to be right, they may undo another which is equally right. When this happens with thoughts instead of actions, man himself is lost, no matter how, upon reflection, he regards his thinking to have been logical" (*Way* 212–13).

In the novel most of the characters have done away with their feelings by turning solely to their reason, and all of them, save for the few who have gone "insane," have lost the ability to bridge the gap between their knowledge and their daily experiences. Jimmy Wood, an associate of Mark Coldridge, remains a fool despite the books he owns on Rosicrucianism, Buddhism, Yoga, Zoroastrianism, the *I Ching*, Zen, and Sufism. He has read them but never internalized them to make them his own. Consequently, he is unable to exercise any of the wisdom in these books when his prudence and discretion are called for: when Mark's Communist brother flees to Soviet Russia— whereupon his wife commits suicide and their young son is left behind to be raised by Mark and Martha—Jimmy is asked to keep quiet, not expose the family to the press, and not give the family's new unlisted phone number to anyone; however, he gives it anyway and explains that the news reporter sounded "as if he really wanted it" (159). When the number is changed again, he again gives it out, because, he explains, he thought "that the man asking for it was an electronics expert" (159). Despite all pleas to him to use discretion with news-hungry journalists, he tells them everything he knows when-ever he is asked, his actions being as separate from what he has learned intellectually in his readings as the salt is from the spilled flour in the story.

Dorothy, one of the lodgers in the Coldridge household in London, demonstrates her own lack of integration and whole-ness when she ineptly tries to hire help to repair a leaking faucet: "I rang five plumbers. Three didn't answer . . . The fourth said he would come at nine. He never came at all. The fifth said he would come on Saturday morning at ten. Satur-day morning . . . I went out shopping. Lynda went to sleep. The man came while I was out. I telephoned him. His wife answered" (191). Dorothy's story continues until she has to turn off the water at the main valve because the leak has got-ten worse, and she is in a state of frenzy and has to go to bed to hide from the world. She and Lynda live on tranquilizers to ward off the helpless irritation they too frequently feel. Lynda reasons, "I'm no use to anyone, so I might as well be asleep" (123). Indeed, she spends most of her days in sleep; it is not until Lessing destroys the old order with an apocalyptic dis-aster that Lynda awakens to find her "madness" of use in the new world order.[17] In a 1969 interview with Studs Terkel, Lessing said:

> One of the ideas that helped create Lynda was a woman I knew in London who was fifteen before she realized that everybody didn't know who was at the other end of the telephone and did-n't hear what other people were thinking . . . Through a series

of circumstances [Lynda] comes under pressure, cracks up emotionally . . . has a lot of treatment such as shock treatment, insulin treatment, the whole gamut, and is so damaged that she spends the rest of her life in and out of mental hospitals. At the same time, she has these *powers*, increasingly, the capacity to *hear* what people are thinking and to *see*. (26)

Sufi quotations in the opening to part 4 of *The Four-Gated City* are placed at precisely the point in the novel when the old order as it had been established in the first three parts begins to disintegrate, and the necessity of a new order becomes apparent. Lessing's quotation from Rûmî declares the pressing need for a revolution of minds:

From realm to realm man went, reaching his present reasoning, knowledgeable, robust state—forgetting earlier forms of intelligence. So, too, shall he pass beyond the current forms of perception . . . There are a thousand other forms of Mind . . .

But he has fallen asleep. He will say: "I had forgotten my fulfillment, ignorant that sleep and fancy were the cause of my sufferings."

He says: "My sleeping experiences do not matter."

Come, leave such asses to their meadow.

Because of a necessity, man acquires organs. So, necessitous one, increase your need . . . (448)

The events in part 4 that unfold following this opening demonstrate a profound change in the environment, a consequence of the fact that the fools who make up the novel and their contemporaries have been asleep all their lives: the atmosphere is polluted by toxic fumes with disastrous effects; yet this catastrophe is accompanied by the birth of a new breed of human beings who have indeed acquired new organs of perception with which they can see, hear, and intuit better than their ancestors of the old order. These beings are born knowing the past of the human race as though they contained all of history within themselves. Even as young children, they command authority by the mere fact that they are wise and knowledgeable beyond their years. Lessing also quotes from Shah, whose words reinforce the idea of new organs coming into being as a result of need—and signal the change that is about to take place in the protagonist's world and in the people around her:[18]

> Sufis believe that, expressed in one way, humanity is evolving towards a certain destiny. We are all taking part in that evolution. Organs come into being as a result of a need for specific organs. The human being's organism is producing a new complex of organs in response to such a need. In this age of the transcending of time and space, the complex of organs is concerned with the transcending of time and space. What ordinary people regard as sporadic and occasional bursts of telepathic and prophetic power are seen by the Sufi as nothing less than the first stirrings of these same organs. The difference between all evolution up to date and the present need for evolution is that for the past ten thousand years or so we have been given the possibility of a conscious evolution. So essential is this more rarefied evolution that our future depends on it. (448)

Clearly, Lessing asks us to read the development of new powers in the children born on the uncontaminated island in light of this quotation from Shah and the previous one from Rûmî, and to recognize the birth of the special children as a sign of that "rarefied evolution" upon which "our future depends." She knows that ordinary individuals in their physically defective and spiritually sterile states live in Rûmî's "dungeon" and cannot inhabit the same world with conscious beings. Therefore in the end of the novel she guides her readers out of the special island back to the "dungeon." One of the miracle children described earlier is sent from Rûmî's "rose garden" to this "dungeon" to give advice in various fields of activity. The official, a man with ordinary faculties who is to receive this emissary, asks in a letter: "I take it that your statement that he is ten years old is a misprint?" (654). Lessing ends her novel here with this question. Of course, in the eyes of ordinary "people," this miracle child is only misprinted information—he cannot be real. Lessing urges her readers to see that unless ordinary beings heighten their sensitivity so that they are able to recognize the light when it begins to flicker, they will remain in the dungeon no matter how many Christ figures or Sufi masters may appear on earth to rescue them.[19]

A number of passages in *The Four-Gated City*, in addition to the direct quotations from Sufi literature, explicitly echo Sufi truths. For instance the idea of developing new organs is first introduced in part 2: "One hadn't heard before, because one had nothing to 'hear' with. Living was simply a process of developing different 'ears,' senses, with which one 'heard,' experienced, what one couldn't before" (236). When this idea is repeated two hundred pages later in the form of passages quoted from Rûmî and Shah in part 4, a Sufi reading of this and other similar passages becomes necessary. Yet another fifty pages into part 4, the desperate need for new organs is demonstrated as Martha observes the defective human beings around her: "their eyes were half useless—many wore bits of corrective glass over these spoiled or ill-grown organs; their ears were defective—many wore machines to help them hear even as much as the sounds made by their fellows; and their mouths were full of metal" (506). This description of eyeglasses, hearing aids, and amalgam filling in teeth points to the human decay and the need for new organs of perception, such as the third eye or inner ear, which would make sensory aids unnecessary.

Lessing uses one of her characters in *The Four-Gated City*, Mark Coldridge, to describe a dream city with an inner and an outer layer.[20] In a novel that Mark writes, he elaborates on this city: the inner layer has harmony, order, joy. Outside are power-hungry people fighting for money and recognition. Naturally, the inhabitants of the outer city wish to buy the secret wisdom of the inner city that makes one happy. And when told that they cannot buy but must earn the secret, they overrun and destroy the inner city only to find that knowledge is nothing material that can be carried away: it is to be acquired with experience (141). In Sufi terms, this story can be read as the destruction of the inner circle of humanity by the outer circle who cannot understand or tolerate it.

Some Sufis in the Muslim world today would claim that their own particular brotherhood was similarly attacked and forced to go underground at some point in history, as indeed many Sufis were, as a result of the wave of nationalism and secularism at the end of the nineteenth century. The classical Sufi poet Omar Khayyam (d. 1132) expresses the necessity for discretion and secrecy in the following lines:

> The secret must be kept from all non-people:
> The mystery must be hidden from all idiots.
> See what you do to people—
> The Eye has to be hidden from all men.
> (Shah, *Way* 59)

Coexistent with this secrecy is the Sufi aim that always remains the same: to transmit knowledge to people in the outer circle, that is, to philosophers, scientists, sociologists, historians, economists, and politicians, who practice solely in the domains of fact and value, not in the domains of the unknown and the unpredictable, the timeless. Lessing's inclusion of Mark's novel about the inner city within her novel strengthens the claim that, like Sufis who continue to teach those in the outer circle of humanity, Lessing teaches us Sufi truths whenever and wherever she can.

Paralleling the concept of secrecy and discretion with regard to real knowledge, Lynda tells Martha to "be careful, Martha, careful, you mustn't say what you know, they'll lock you up, they want machines, they don't want people" (503). Martha's response to her own awakening is horror; for now, in

Rûmî's "dungeon," she sees all of the deformities and defects in those around her. She thinks, "The price you paid for being awake, for being received into that grace, was this, that when you walked among your kind you had to see them, and yourself, as they, we are. She did not want it again, not so soon—" (509).[21]

A parallel set up to the "dream city" in Mark's novel exists in his own household but remains undetected by him. Just as the inner city in Mark's book contains a hidden octagonal white room under the library, the basement in his own home serves as the inaccessible recesses of the mind. His mad/wise wife Lynda lives in the basement with her friend Dorothy from the psychiatric ward; Mark, Martha, and the two boys live upstairs, or in the outer layer, from whence each pays visits downstairs to Lynda's inner domain for friendship and advice. Whenever Martha feels close to a breakdown, she feels that there is no one else who can understand her but Lynda. The visits are also occasionally reversed; yet whenever Lynda and Dorothy come up for dinner, the results are disastrous. This disjunction between what happens above and what happens below is best explained by the parallel with the underground Sufi communities that find themselves uncomfortably surrounded by secular societies. Lynda and Dorothy's friends from the psychiatric ward congregate in the Coldridge basement to share their perceptions that are more acute and almost dangerously too honest to be uttered in the outer city.

At times, Lynda's character is cast in a similar role to that of the renowned fool and teacher, Mulla Nasrudin, as illustrated in the interaction between Lynda and Martha:

> "Lynda, do you know who you are?"
> "Me," said Lynda.
> "Do you see that when you look in the mirror?"
> "No. Not often. Sometimes."
> "When?"
> "Oh, I don't know. There are times, you know." (226)

The explicit parallel between this passage and the following Sufi anecdote, which Lessing quotes in *Landlocked*, is impossible to overlook not only in content but also in its cryptic style:

> The Mulla walked into a shop one day.
> The owner came forward to serve him.
> "First things first," said Nasrudin; "did you see me walk into your shop?"
> "Of course."
> "Have you ever seen me before?"
> "Never in my life."
> "Then how do you know it is *me*?" (Shah, *Sufis* 79)

A similar anecdote involves Nasrudin on a journey. When he tires and finds a place to sleep on the street, he becomes concerned that he will not find himself upon waking. When he confides in his neighbor, he is told to tie a marker on his leg, which he does, and falls to sleep. To play a prank, his neighbor removes the marker and ties it to his own leg. When the bewildered Nasrudin awakens to discover his marker on his neighbor's leg, he is forced to ask, "I can tell by this tag around your leg that *you* are *me*. But if *you* are *me*—who, for the love of goodness, AM I?" (Shah, *Exploits* 152).

Lynda develops telepathic powers at the end of the novel and becomes a wise one who survives the apocalypse. This is also true for Watkins's experience in *Briefing*. Through Lynda's or Watkins's experiences, Lessing blurs the fine line between madness and extrasensory perception.[22] For her, "madness" is not a disease but a natural state. Schizophrenia and multiple personality disorders, she believes, must not be treated as illnesses but respected as signs of a person's high sensitivity or as an incomplete state, and of one's need to evolve. She commented on this subject in a 1969 interview with Studs Terkel: "These people [schizophrenics], I maintain, are probably not mad at all . . . a lot of perfectly normal people, with certain capacities, are being classed as 'ill'" (19–20). Rubenstein discusses Lessing's indebtedness to R. D. Laing, who regards schizophrenia as "a natural process of mind-healing"; that is, madness or loss of one's self is regarded as a positive affliction that eventually can help one achieve self knowledge and true identity.[23] According to Laing, the mad person is "prophet of a possible new world, a world governed by forces of unity rather than separation" (Vlastos 246). Likewise, when a seeker on the Sufi Path appears—or is pronounced—"mad," he or she may be in a state of heightened perception and sensitivity, or a state of ecstasy at finally having gotten a glimpse of the Beloved and tasted his or her love. When and if that is the case, a Sufi would say, would that we could *all* become that mad. In *The Memoirs*, for instance, the narrator who claims to walk through walls and to hear voices would be considered quite mad by ordinary standards, whereas in a Laingian reading she may be healing a painful childhood, or in the Sufi context she may be involved not only in a harmonious cure of her psyche but also in a more Hallâj-like ecstatic union with "The One." Sufis believe the mad are mad because they can *see* more and yet are not developed enough to comprehend and sustain their hallucinations, which come and go at random. The enlightened are those who survive their madness, who have learned how to understand and control their visions, and can achieve those visions at will.[24] In her 1969 interview with Studs Terkel Lessing said,

> I think [scientists] have an unconscious, or perhaps not so unconscious, bias to prove that these things don't exist. This is their problem. I met a girl in New York who said she read this book [*The Four-Gated City*] and she had a great burden taken off her because she was like Lynda. She suddenly realized she'd never been ill. Now this made me so happy. (28)

The Diary of a Good Neighbour

Lessing overtly emulates Mulla Nasrudin's character and behavior in the character of Maudie Fowler in *The Diary of a*

Good Neighbour (1983). She relates anecdotes resembling Sufi tales and attributes them to Maudie as though Maudie experienced and performed them. These anecdotes are unmistakably of the spirit of Nasreddin Hodja. Like Nasreddin, Maudie, too, is both helpless and powerful, both foolish and wise, and always utterly and rightfully honest when she speaks. This resemblance cannot be coincidental, for Lessing not only has acknowledged having read Shah's collections of Sufi tales, but also has promoted them in various lectures, reviews, and essays. Lessing seems to want at least to introduce Sufi ideas at a surface level as jokes, without regard to whether the average Western reader is familiar with Nasreddin Hodja or Sufism. Given her commitment to the work of Shah and given her acknowledgment of Sufi thought as valid and relevant, Lessing clearly uses her novels as tools to familiarize the Western public with Sufism in any way she can. Sufism is meant to be contemporary and fresh, not to be treated as an ancient wisdom only to be studied by antiquarians. Therefore Lessing's way of introducing the *spirit* of Sufi doctrine through her tales while relegating the *letter* of Sufi law to a secondary position becomes the appropriate thing to do.

In *The Diary* traces of Sufism occur mostly near the end of the novel. Here, the progression is not directed toward teaching Sufism; rather, Sufism underlies the conception and creation of at least one character, Maudie Fowler, thematically and mimetically. In looking into Maudie's character and the stories about her, Phelan's definition of the term *character* and the distinctions that he makes among the mimetic, synthetic, and thematic dimensions of character will be helpful. As Phelan elaborates, these three dimensions are in turn sometimes converted into three distinctive functions that characters may perform to varying degrees in the narrative. In Phelan's terms, the diary is kept by Janna (Jane) Somers in her mimetic dimension and function as a single, successful middle-aged career woman with various strengths and weaknesses, friends, family, and memories, who lives and records her life in her diary. She befriends Maudie Fowler, mimetically a poor, lonely, sick woman past ninety who refuses to go to a home and who opts to fend for herself. The novel also depicts Janna in her synthetic dimension and function as the narrator.

While Janna narrates the majority of the novel, the novel is also narrated directly by Maudie herself whenever the stories are about Maudie's past rather than about shared events in the present. At these instances the mimetic dimension of Maudie's character is foregrounded: she is portrayed as an old crone who has nothing left but her reminiscences and who enjoys indulging in nostalgia. At the same time she also functions synthetically as a narrator of old people's stories. When, rather than allowing Maudie to speak directly, Lessing uses the character of Janna in her synthetic role as narrator to retell Maudie's memories, it is because Maudie is too sick to speak for herself, or she is dead. At these points in the novel Lessing casts an aura of mystery around the character of Maudie who becomes a greater-than-life heroine embodying ideas such as suffering and survival: she is suffering from, and at the same time surviving, old age and stomach cancer with their accompanying discomforts that rob her dignity. Then, having become a "theme with legs" (Phelan 9), Maudie functions as a Sufi master who teaches through demonstration and through direct contact with her medium. In this thematic role, as in her mimetic role, she behaves in a cuttingly truthful manner, always telling it like it is. In her honesty and curtness she is reminiscent of Mulla Nasrudin.

The progression of *The Diary* moves by Janna's visits to Maudie that are sometimes pleasant and sometimes trying for Janna. The progression also moves by numerous flashbacks to Maudie's past that detail the kind of person Maudie used to be and, to a great extent, still is. From the beginning of the novel, Lessing establishes an instability within Janna regarding her undertaking Maudie's welfare when she herself is already too busy with her work at *Lilith*, the women's magazine she publishes, and her own daily life in general. She rightly wonders, "What is the *use* of Maudie Fowler?" to which her answer is, "By the yardsticks and measurements I've been taught, none" (25). Given this conclusion only twenty-five pages into the narrative, Janna's return visits to Maudie's house to look after her are a surprise to the audience that sympathizes with her inner struggle and with her disgust at the pungent odor of the urine and excrement in which she always finds Maudie soaked at each of her visits. At the same time, the audience also knows full well that this is a novel about Janna's being a Good Neighbour to Maudie and expects Janna to continue returning to Maudie's despite her aversion. In this sense the novel is about the breakdown of Janna's resistance to and disgust for "old people" and, in her eyes, their stale and useless lives. This is a personal triumph for Janna, given her guilt surrounding her inability to have provided emotional support and practical assistance for her own mother years ago when she was sick and dying.[25] Throughout the novel Janna moves by degrees to a place within herself where she does not give in to her disgust but develops sincere love for Maudie. With compassion, she overcomes her instinctive repulsion by the decay of old age and reverses her earlier automatic judgement of Maudie's uselessness.

The narrative also progresses as a result of a second instability that is established in the opening pages between Janna and Maudie. Upon every visit by Janna, Maudie reproaches her with remarks about not having come the day before, or for having come late, conveying her fear that Janna may be coming only out of pity and a sense of obligation. Thus we read to discover the degree of Janna's willingness to visit Maudie, and to learn the result of the arguments that ensue between the two women as a prelude to many visits. The outcome of these two instabilities is already apparent early in the narrative, as the two women always settle down to an exchange of stories about their lives, Maudie's past and Janna's current life. But we read further to discover the ultimate extent of Janna's transformation through her sacrifices as a Good Neighbour.

CONSEQUENCES

A third point of interest for the audience is the unfathomable chasm created by the contrast between the stench and depravity of Maudie's existence and the sensual luxury of Janna's life, which includes hot bubble baths, scented dressing gowns, and leisure to do her nails. Janna is fully aware of and somewhat disconcerted by this contrast, and she frequently brings it up in her diary for us to view and to judge. Although the instability within Janna and that between her and Maudie carry the action forward mimetically, the narrative also progresses synthetically by the mere changes of scene between Maudie's dreadful poverty and sickness, on the one hand, and Janna's glamorous life, on the other. These blatant switches back and forth between Maudie's wretched quarters and Janna's immaculate flat are impossible to overlook, and they serve as shocks that propel the narrative forward to its obvious conclusion: Maudie's eventual death and Janna's inevitable transformation.

Phelan argues that thematic reading of a novel alone results in our selection of one theme over another without regard to the development of character or to the progression of events in the narrative, which amounts to a partial reading. For instance, in *Pride and Prejudice* it is not enough to isolate Elizabeth Bennet as "prejudice," just as it is not correct to regard Winston Smith in 1984 only as "the last man in Europe." Their mimetic functions are also significant, though they are subordinated to their thematic functions. However, in Lessing's novels written after the mid-1960s, the mystical and didactic elements are so strong and Sufi material is so liberally integrated in the narratives that thematizing in the Sufi Way is not only naturally suggested but self-consciously imposed in passages such as when Maudie is in the hospital with stomach cancer, and Janna tells us:[26]

> The family have already been, the tribe, admitted to her presence in twos and threes.
> "Are you coming to see if there's anything for you when I'm dead?" [Maudie] inquires. "You should know better than that, you've had everything off me years ago."

124

"Oh Auntie!" say nieces, nephews, and, "What sort of talk is that, Maudie?" inquires the matriarch [her sister].

"You know what kind of talk," says Maudie, and turns her face to stare away from them; and she does not reply to their Goodbye, Auntie, Goodbye, Maudie. (215)

Not only is Maudie being honest about how she feels about the relatives, but she is also right about their motives. Nasreddin Hodja is caught in the grips of a similar bout with honesty when a neighbor asks to borrow his clothesline: "I am sorry, but I have spread flour on it," says Nasrudin. When his neighbor asks, "How can you spread flour on a clothesline?" he retorts, "I *can*, if I don't want to lend my line!" (my rendering from the Turkish oral tradition). This joke, in Turkey, is used among friends who aren't afraid to "tell it like it is" to each other.

On a rare occasion, Lessing also makes use of a minor character in the novel to comment on Maudie's uniqueness: Vera Rogers fulfills the mimetic role of a social worker who looks after the needs of the old who choose to live on their own. She takes care of their Home Help, Meals on Wheels, Good Neighbours, and medical needs. When Janna calls Vera to tell her that Maudie has died, Vera bursts into tears and says, "Oh, I don't know why [I'm crying], there was something about her, what was it?" (249). This "something about her" sees Maudie through her life and her death. At the funeral, the son of Maudie's nephew, another minor character in the novel, comments that "Auntie Maudie had her sense of humour all right, oh she liked her little joke" (251). Such comments serve to add further credence both to Maudie's mimetic dimension as a lovable old witch and her thematic dimension as a spirited survivor of life's miseries—a potential Sufi, as illustrated in the following examples.

In her synthetic role as record keeper and in her mimetic role as Maudie's only friend, Janna retells a story about Maudie that she hears from the son of Maudie's nephew:

CONSEQUENCES

People [for whom Maudie] cleaned house . . . had a fruit and vegetable shop, and the woman said to her, "Would you like to taste this season's new strawberries?" And set in front of the expectant Maudie a single strawberry on a good plate, with the sugar bowl and the cream.

Maudie ate the strawberry, and then said to the woman, "Perhaps you'd like to sample the cherries on the tree in my back garden?" Brought the woman a single luscious cherry in a large brown-paper bag, and gave her notice there and then. (251)

This anecdote is not about Maudie getting even but about justice being served. Countless collections about Nasrudin abound with jokes that are variants of the same model in which the antagonist deserves what he or she gets, and the protagonist is avenged. It is impossible to resist two of the variants here, as they not only demonstrate that the above story emulates Sufi anecdotes but also are so witty and entertaining. In a popular case retold frequently in Turkey, Nasreddin Hodja arrives at a dinner party wearing his street clothes. He is told to go to the back door and wait in the kitchen. After a while, since no one has paid any attention to him, Hodja leaves. He returns wearing his fur coat and knocks on the front door once more. This time he is treated like royalty, and is seated at the head of the table. They promptly bring him a plate. As soon as the food comes, Hodja grabs a spoon and begins to dish out the food onto his fur coat saying, "Eat my fur, eat!" (my rendering from the Turkish oral tradition). This punch line is in fact famous by itself as a Turkish saying (*Ye kürküm, ye!*) and everyone knows the message it conveys, without needing to repeat the whole story. Another time, the Hodja is at a Turkish bath, where the attendants treat him poorly because he looks shabby. As he leaves, he pays with a gold coin. On his next visit to the bath, he is of course treated royally. This time as he leaves, he hands the attendants a copper coin and explains that this is for his last visit, as the last time's payment was for *this* visit (my rendering from the Turkish oral tradition). The justice of Nasrudin's payments at the bath equals the justness of Maudie's act in bringing a single cherry for sampling.

Nasrudin and Maudie both are thematic figures who are victimized and laughed at, but who rise above their circumstances simply by their strength of spirit. Janna tells Maudie's relatives another story, which once again demonstrates Maudie's utter sense of justice and fairness and her unwavering faith in God who can work miracles, even if, in Maudie's case, they are rather small miracles:

> [Maudie] was out of work, because she had flu and had lost her cleaning job. She was walking home with no money at all in her purse and she was praying, God help me, God please help me . . . And she looked down and saw a half-crown on the pavement. And she said, Thank you, God.
>
> She went into the first shop and bought a currant bun, and ate it standing there, she was so hungry. Then she bought bread, butter, jam, and some milk. There was sixpence over. On her way home she went into the church and put the sixpence in the box, and said to God,
>
> "You've helped me, and now I'll help You." (252)

Nasrudin behaves in similar ways in an infinite number of situations, and in his case he is even more of a knave than Maudie, as when he is out in his garden, praying for a hundred gold pieces, shouting at the top of his lungs. A miser who lives next door hears this, and to play a trick on Hodja, throws down a bag full of gold. "Thank you," says Nasrudin to God. When the miser appears at the door to expose his trick and to reclaim his money Hodja tells him, "You may have been the *instrument*, but the gold did not come as a result of my asking *you* for it!" (Shah, *Sufis* 106). In this story the miser's presence complicates Nasreddin's experience. He must deal with not only Allah but the miser. Nasreddin turns the miser's mockery against him before he proceeds to praise Allah. In Maudie's case the exchange with God is much simpler and more direct.

CONSEQUENCES

This faith in Allah's help above that of humans is demonstrated again and again in anecdotes in which Nasreddin Hodja is rewarded by a twist of fate that blurs the distinction between divine and human intervention. Another time, Nasreddin is again convinced that Allah will provide when a man complains to him that he has been robbed. To prove Allah's power, Nasreddin takes the man to the mosque, where he rolls on the ground and calls loudly upon Allah to restore the man's silver coins. Annoyed by the commotion, the congregation takes a collection and hands the sum to the surprised loser. "You may not understand the means which operate in this world," [says Hodja,] "but I trust that you understand the end when it is handed to you in such a concrete form" (Shah, *Pleasantries* 132).

The Diary remains one of Lessing's less self-consciously didactic and less overtly Sufi works when contrasted to her space fiction. Still, it makes a definite point about self-work, self-sacrifice, service, and the inevitability of old age. It especially focuses thematically on Maudie's spirit, which is her saving grace, and Janna's altruism. These two characteristics bring these predominantly mimetic figures together in a bond of friendship that occasions the writing of *The Diary*.

The Marriages between Zones Three, Four, and Five

In the *Canopus* series Lessing's style is more radically different and seems to be much more intentionally altered to accommodate her didactic purposes. Rightfully labeled "Archives," each novel is written deliberately as a historical account of a civilization whose existence and reality must be preserved for posterity. The narrator of *The Marriages between Zones Three, Four, and Five* (1980) calls this, "maintaining Memory" (99). In *The Making of the Representative for Planet 8* Doeg, one of the narrators, is referred to as a "Memory Maker" and "Keeper of Records" (22).[27] The narrators of every novel (each novel has more than one narrator) in the series call themselves "chroniclers" and they diligently tell the story of their particular planet as though the events being conveyed really took place. The chroniclers in *The Marriages* comment on how particular events turned into folk stories and legend in the retelling. Often, following the depiction of an event, they remark, "This scene is known as 'Jarnti's Walk,' and gives much opportunity for humour to our artists and tellers" (19). Or they write, "This scene, too, is one much depicted" (16), stressing the fact that these episodes really did happen once and that they now have become legend.

The Marriages* and *The Representative* also recall Sufi teaching stories.[28] Sprague and Tiger explain, "The fable form seems to have provided Lessing with a way to subvert the conventional novel without going the way of modernism" (16). In their estimation, *The Representative* "becomes a fable about learning to die." They acknowledge, in fact, that "Sufi teachings about suffering and transcendence all too plainly motivate the ethos of the novel" (17). And at the same time, they point out Lessing's impulse to ground her fable in factual events such as the Scott expedition to Antarctica. The chroniclers of *The Representative* call the novel a "tale": "You ask us how the Canopean Agents seemed to us in the days of The Ice. This tale is our answer" (121). In turn, recognizing this as a Sufi tale could be *our* answer.

In *The Marriages*, Lessing combines history and art—real life and fiction. The resulting tale is thus enriched not only by music and poetry but also by a sense of the human past that adds credibility and depth. This layer strengthens the qualifications of the *Canopus* series to act as Sufi teaching stories. In the Sufi tradition, it is customary to spin a fantastic tale and then to attribute it to Genghis Khan, Tamerlane, Solomon, or any number of other rulers or saints and their friends who might have lived centuries apart. Casting the tale in an actual historical period and in a real place increases its impact and staying power. Similarly, Lessing invites us to suspend judgement and to entertain the possibility of the mimetic

129

dimension of her characters because this helps her to communicate her Sufi message.

For instance, many Nasreddin Hodja anecdotes take place in the land of the terrifying Mongol conqueror Tamerlane, even though the two lived centuries apart. There are many anecdotes about Nasreddin that ground him in history. The following depicts him in a town where the fierce Tamerlane decides to set up camp. When Tamerlane asks the townspeople to feed and care for his elephant, they are distraught by the burden, for they are too poor to feed themselves. The Hodja is selected to confront their feared guest, to tell him the town cannot care for his elephant. He agrees on one condition: that the whole town follow and stand by him when he approaches the ferocious king. They set out on the road to Tamerlane's camp. When Tamerlane roars "What do you want?" the terrified Hodja turns for support to his townspeople, only to find that they have fallen back and snuck away in fear. Upon this discovery the Hodja blurts out to Tamerlane, "We are so pleased to be looking after your elephant that we were wondering whether you might have a *second* elephant for us to keep!" (my rendering from the Turkish oral tradition).

Like this Hodja tale, which blends history with fiction for added credibility, Lessing's *The Representative* is presented as though it were an objective historical account of what happened to Planet 8 during the time of "The Ice." At the same time, Lessing wants us to learn from *The Representative* as though it were a teaching tale. This combination of history and story is poignantly demonstrated in the novel when Doeg, the chronicler and representative of Planet 8, says, "It was then I first noticed that always when one is telling of something done or seen or experienced, it becomes a story, a tale . . . at any rate, our people listened as if to some tale or legend" (54). Lessing (like Doeg) in turn suggests to her readers to listen as if *her* novel were a tale or a legend but to assume that it is also fact. Combining history and story, Doeg tells us how "We *listened*—the eyes of every one of us had in them always a look of waiting to hear or receive some news, or message or information" (33).

The novels in the *Canopus* series also share the qualities of space fiction. When this is combined with the objectivity of a chronicle, Lessing is equipped with the ideal tools with which to illustrate her perception of the reality of foreign regions beyond the earth, regions that ultimately correspond to the inner worlds in which we live in our minds, fantasies, and dreams. In *The Marriages* these worlds are clearly "Zoned" off to correspond to the various levels of consciousness in Sufism.[29] By using the genre of space fiction, Lessing is able to escape the limitations of the known world and to explore spheres and Zones never encountered in ordinary life. In addition, her claim to be writing a historical text adds further legitimacy to the reality of these otherwise unrecognizable Zones or levels of consciousness only known to other Sufis.

Sufis accept the simultaneous existence of several levels of consciousness in the world as we know it. Therefore the same event might be experienced and perceived to differing degrees by different individuals. This inequality is apparent in the marriage of Al·Ith to Ben Ata: Al·Ith is capable of experiencing, feeling, and perceiving more deeply than Ben Ata because she belongs to Zone Three. The chroniclers of Zone Three tell us, "Her ways seemed too difficult for him, or at least unfamiliar, or out of his reach just then. And his were striking him as crude" (46). Because of the unique circumstances defining this marriage, Rowe aptly describes *The Marriages* as "romantic fiction put through a space transformer" (194).

As suggested earlier, our acknowledgment of the mimetic dimension of Lessing's characters is essential to our understanding of Lessing's Sufi-inclined ideas, because they are more than mere literary devices that she uses to convey messages from an alien world. Their real-life experiences as model Sufi masters or disciples are crucial to our acceptance of some of Lessing's teachings. Bazin regards Al·Ith as Lessing's most committed and authentic mystic, because "she abandons all

131

the rewards of the material world, lives simply, and devotes herself to her quest" ("Evolution" 164). While I propose that we accept Al·Ith's mimetic reality, I am aware at the same time that when Al·Ith and Lessing's other science-fiction characters are closely analyzed, their thematic and synthetic dimensions seem to overshadow their mimetic dimensions.[30] In doing this, Lessing encourages an allegorical reading while never fully letting go of the mimetic plausibility of her story line.[31]

For example, in *The Marriages* Al·Ith's synthetic dimension is qualified by the requirement that she act as a person with certain traits would act in order to further the plot and to illustrate and advance Sufi teachings in the novel. Attention to the plausibility of her mimetic dimension is necessary for our full acceptance of her as a Sufi. For instance, Rowe comments on the limits of mimesis in *The Marriages* and observes that except for Al·Ith and Ben Ata, the characters are rather like "cardboard." Even in the cases of Al·Ith and Ben Ata, we get few details. In *The Marriages* Al·Ith is hardly a mimetic character, despite the chroniclers' claim to the historical verity of her experiences. She functions more as a set of characteristics embodying the nature of Zone Three than she does as a woman with a mind and a body of her own, making her own decisions, feeling pain or joy.

Like Al·Ith, Ben Ata is, more often than not, a two-dimensional figure: he is a king, embodying barbarism and crudity, while Al·Ith is a princess and later queen, embodying independence, sensitivity, and lightheartedness. Both function more often as fixed devices fulfilling "the Order" of "the Providers" and acting out the traits assigned to them by the master scriptwriter, Lessing. The clash between the traits that they embody is evident in their first lovemaking: "as he held her still so that he could enter her, she shrank from him and tightened as if everything in her repudiated him" (46). About them Rowe asks, "Do they have moles? Big or small feet?" (199). We are given only those characteristics that are relevant to their thematic roles. As they grow and change as a result of the marriage, their characteristics also change. In other words, as their thematic roles change, their mimetic characteristics adapt to their new roles.[32]

Throughout the novel Al·Ith always behaves according to what would bring about a balance between the Zones, simply fulfilling her thematic role as the sacrificial bride, there to offer herself for the sake of equilibrium in the cosmos. Likewise, the character of Ben Ata is there to act out the theme of brute force and violence. His plot functions include taking Al·Ith at his will and by force, yet also becoming somewhat hewn and changed by Al·Ith's grace. Meanwhile, the words the couple exchange always stress their irreconcilable differences. Al·Ith tells Ben Ata, "If you were set down in the middle of our land you would not understand anything that was going on. Do you know that as soon as I cross into your land I cease to be my real self? Everything I say comes out distorted and different" (99). Al·Ith's sentiment against integrating the Zones is supported by the counting game that the children play in Zone Three. They recite, "Great to Small / High to Low / Four into Three / Cannot go" (3). The Sufi Way, too, goes against the grain, against learned habits and childhood rhymes. Breaking habits is the first and most difficult step toward breaking free. In ordinary life, "working" on oneself to rise in one's level of being is next to impossible to achieve.

When Al·Ith goes to Zone Four it is with the understanding that she is there to cultivate the properties of Zone Three in those she meets, starting with her husband, Ben Ata. Even this she neither chooses nor wants to do. From the very beginning of the narrative the chroniclers make it clear that what happens to Al·Ith is decided by "the Providers," and it is always "they" that direct her. We are told early in the novel that Al·Ith was "taken" to Zone Four. She did not go of her own volition, but submitted to a higher will as a Sufi would. In fact, *islam* means "surrender." While Al·Ith as a synthetic character submits to Lessing-the-author's will, Al·Ith in her mimetic and thematic dimension submits to the will from "Above." The chroniclers note that the inhabitants of Zone Three see "what was in store for her—and they were about to raise their voices in lament, keening, but she lifted her hand and stopped them. 'There is no help for it' she said in a low voice, her lips trembling. 'We have our orders'" (16).

Lessing accomplishes her purpose to demonstrate different levels of being not only by narrating the unequal and incompatible experiences of Al·Ith and Ben Ata, but also by translating these invisible layers into geographical space. In the novel, the Zones have actual frontiers where one ends and the other begins, denoting a change in the quality of the atmosphere when a person moves from one Zone to another: "The inhabitants of Zone Three, straying near the frontier, found themselves afflicted with repugnance, or at the least by an antipathy to foreign airs and atmospheres that showed itself in a cold lethargy, like boredom" (4). While Zone Three is marked by a purity, innocence, and lighthearted friendliness, Zone Four is the space allotted for war, violence, and barbarism, and Zone Two "is as if you looked at blue mists—or waters or—but it is blue, blue, you've never seen such a blue" (74). Al·Ith's goal is to grow into Zone Two, even purer than Zone Three. She describes Zone Two to Ben Ata: "All I can say is that you stand and gaze and look, and never have enough of it" (74). When we accept Lessing's characters as mimetic individuals (even when they are only slightly so), we have to allow them room to grow and evolve and to exhibit their depth of spirit.

Other critics have also identified the Zones as stages of enlightenment on the "Sufi Way."[33] Not only are these Zones or levels of consciousness (*maqam*) a central concept in Sufism but they are even expressed in similar forms in Sufi literature, as the Sufi tale in the following pages illustrates. Stated most concisely, *maqam* is the level that one achieves in one's personal growth and training, such as patience, faith, or certainty. These levels are "commonly ordered in a set sequence, one achievement laying the groundwork for the next" (Hodgson 1:

406). Lessing emulates these sequential achievements on the Sufi Path when she enables Al·Ith to travel through the Zones or *maqams* of the human soul.

Lessing's demonstration of many levels of being, the boundaries of which some of her characters penetrate in *The Marriages*, also bring to mind C. S. Lewis's cosmology in *The Great Divorce*. Lewis presents an image of the hereafter: a group of people depart on a bus from a smog-polluted city, arguing and fighting about everything, and arrive in another world where the light is so strong it hurts their eyes and the blades of grass are so substantial they pierce their feet. The higher beings who come to meet them here explain how this is only an intermediary world and that it is as low as they themselves could possibly come in order to meet the newcomers. They explain that this for them is darkness; to them, everything here appears ghostlike. In this manner Lewis contrasts the levels of consciousness: what is darkness and a mere blade of grass to a higher being with refined senses appears to a lower being, with coarser organs of perception, to be as brilliant as white light and as sharp as steel.

These levels of being also recall the Sufi story from the sixteenth-century manuscript entitled *Hu-Nama* (Book of Hu), written by Nawab of Sardhana and translated by Idries Shah. In this story, which is considerably longer than the Nasreddin tales we encountered earlier, unknown and invisible worlds are demonstrated in terms of what is accepted to be the "known" by ordinary organs of perception. The synchronicity of events, thought patterns, and levels of being are illustrated by the use of an elaborate frame structure within the narrative, tales within tales.[34] While *The Marriages* is not written in the style of a frame structure, it shares with the following Sufi story the same message regarding the reality of many worlds existing simultaneously at any given moment. Different people exhibit different levels of consciousness that correspond to literally different worlds; therefore, different people occupy different psychic spaces although they may be in the same room.

CONSEQUENCES

The question of the possibility of being aware of different levels of consciousness and living in more than one world at the same time was debated in the seventh century when Islam was first introduced to the Arabian peninsula. Controversy arose among the first Muslims in reference to that occasion, when the prophet Muhammad was said to have been taken from his bed directly up to heaven where he saw Abraham, Moses, Jesus, many angels, hell, and the beautiful gardens of paradise, all of which he could describe in detail upon his return to earth. He was able to give accurate descriptions of the people he saw on his way who could verify his account—and yet while all of this had taken place, his bed was still warm when he returned, and a pot of water which he had overturned and spilled was still not empty. Naturally, this account led to debates over the issue of whether Muhammad ascended to heaven corporeally or only spiritually and, in turn, whether there exist more worlds than the world that we know.

In the eighth century, four different viewpoints on the reality of the prophet Muhammad's ascent were reported by the Muslim historian Ibn Ishaq in his *sirat*, or account of Muhammad's career as a messenger of God. In these four accounts, the following conclusions were reached: according to several narrators, the ascent was the way God chose to reveal himself to Muhammad; according to al-Hasan, Muhammad really went to heaven (Jerusalem), because he said so upon his return; according to Muhammad's young wife, Aisha, only Muhammad's spirit was transported, while his body remained in Mecca; and according to Mu'âwiyah b. Abu Sufyan, it is immaterial whether the experience is real or visionary, because it came from God! A saying of Muhammad's supports this argument: "My eyes sleep while my heart is awake" (Ishaq 181).

These versions provided the fertile environment for a teaching story, *The Sultan who Became an Exile*, that calls to mind Lessing's Al·Ith, the queen who became an exile. Recorded in the sixteenth century, this story is about a Sufi

136

shaikh who tries to show a skeptical king that different time-
and space-frames must be used to understand what really happened to Muhammad the night that he ascended to heaven.
The story stresses the dictum of Muhammad to "Speak to
everyone in accordance with the degree of his understanding"
and aims to "demonstrate the unknown in terms of what is
called 'known' by the audience" (Shah, *Tales* 38). When analyzed in terms of coexistent spaces, the outermost space (or
rhetorical frame in this story) would describe the sultan of
Egypt holding a conference of learned men. In the conference,
a controversy arises over Muhammad's night journey. Some
say it is possible that Muhammad really ascended to heaven,
but the sultan is skeptical. Hence a Sufi *shaikh* attempts to
demonstrate to the sultan how Muhammad's ascent to heaven
could have taken place.

In a frame parallel to the first, a quick reference to the
night journey is made, following which the Sufi *shaikh* moves
to a third frame, hoping to "show" his wisdom to the sultan
instead of using words to explain. To do this, the narrator uses
the framing device, not only synthetically in the discourse but
also mimetically within the narrative, by allowing the *shaikh*
to open each of the four windows in the court chamber and
bid the sultan to look out. As the sultan looks, so do we.

Out of the first window (or yet a fourth frame), the sultan
and we see an invading army. After the window is shut and
opened again, there is not a soul in sight. Opening another of
the windows (or a fifth frame, which parallels the fourth), we
look out to see the city in flames. Upon shutting and opening
that window, we see no more fire. Similarly, the third window
(a sixth frame paralleling four and five) reveals a flood, then
no flood; and the fourth window (a seventh frame, which parallels four, five, and six), reveals a garden of paradise, then it,
too, vanishes.

In the third frame, the Sufi *shaikh* orders a vessel of
water to be brought and asks the sultan to immerse his head
in it for a moment. Here, yet an eighth frame is introduced: the

sultan, upon putting his head in the water, finds himself alone on a seashore. When asked who he is, he says he has been shipwrecked, and after a series of inconceivable experiences, he marries a woman of significant wealth. After seven years, this wealth is squandered, and he has to work as a porter to provide for his wife and seven sons. One day when taking ablutions before prayer at the same spot where he had arrived at this land, he is suddenly transported back to the palace in the third frame.

The *shaikh* tells the sultan that it has been only a moment since he immersed his head in the water. Indeed, the basin of water is still standing there. However, the still disbelieving and now furious sultan returns to the court where the dispute had originally started (the first frame) and orders the *shaikh* to be beheaded, upon which the wise *shaikh* escapes to the second frame, or the rhetorical digression to Muhammad's ascent to heaven, where he transports himself corporeally to Damascus and to safety. From there he writes a letter to the sultan, who is in the first frame. Here the moral of the story is given: it is not important whether something has happened; what is important is the *significance* of an event. "In your case," writes the *shaikh*, "there was no significance. In the case of the Prophet, [however,] there was significance in the happening" (Shah, *Tales* 38). At the end of the discourse the first two frames are left unresolved. These must exist simultaneously, and they must be left to individuals who hear the story to resolve in accordance with their own level of comprehension of the events that took place in frames three through eight. Interpretations from one extreme (that of the skeptical sultan) to the other (that of the faithful *shaikh*) are thus offered to the audience within the same tale. Likewise, Lessing offers us Al·Ith's travels that transcend the borders between worlds that represent similar extremes.

While *The Marriages* is much longer than even the longest Sufi tale, it can be read as a teaching story with layers of meaning for readers to extract for themselves.[35] Knapp

138

points out that ironically, although Lessing rejects Christianity, she "has been credited with writing a Christ-parable, Al·Ith being the female savior who descends to a baser realm, sows the seeds of redemption and is then agonizingly reunited with her true spiritual home" (163). Here we have a Sufi parable with a female protagonist who, much like Christ, sows her love and compassion.

The progression of *The Marriages* depends on the major instability and friction created by Al·Ith and Ben Ata's incompatible Zones. The reader knows that the more refined Al·Ith must arrive ultimately at Zone Two but also that first she and Ben Ata must work out their differences. While the outcome of the narrative is not hard to guess, we read to discover just how the characters will evolve to the higher frames (i.e., those with lower numbers) and exactly what effect their personal evolutions will have on the frames that they represent.

We also saw this type of movement between worlds in *The Memoirs*, in which Emily's growth, like Al·Ith's, depended on a similar regression to a lower level of being. She first had to return and take a look at her miserable childhood in order to be able to move forward in her adult life. Likewise, Al·Ith seems to move backwards from a finer to a cruder Zone in order to make real progress. Greene, too, sees this need to reach back in time before further growth, which she describes as "the way forward [being] the way back" (*Poetics* 26). If we were to draw a perfect parallel between *The Marriages* and *The Memoirs*, we could surmise that Zone Four represents Al·Ith's past, as the space behind the wall represents Emily's past. As the guardian/Emily in *The Memoirs* first had to purge her past, Al·Ith may be investigating a Zone she occupied at some earlier point in her life, before the beginning of the novel, in order to come to terms with herself and to earn the privilege to move up to Zone Two. When one approaches Sufism, one undergoes a similar form of regression before being able to move forward and "work" toward attaining higher states of being. This is why Rûmî speaks of awakening in the dungeons

139

before achieving the rose gardens. Greene explains, "[Al·Ith's] story is pitiable, wrenching, and, like other of Lessing's works, it demonstrates that freedom can only be earned the hard way" (*Poetics* 180). Indeed, Al·Ith's freedom comes at a high price.

While Zone Four is at war with Zone Five, the chroniclers explain that the war is the reason Zone Four has become so barbaric: "A realm at war did not need the courtesies" (5). Naturally, it goes against the grain for inhabitants of Zone Three to mingle with those of Zone Four. When Ben Ata sends a curt message to Zone Three, the chroniclers note, "Here was proof of the rightness of our reluctance to be brought low by Zone Four" (5). This is also the reason why Al·Ith, in her thematic role as peacemaker, must go to Zone Four and marry Ben Ata. On the Sufi ladder to enlightenment, those above must pull up while those below push them up. The teacher needs the student as much as the student needs the teacher. Therefore, only after Al·Ith has pulled Ben Ata up toward Zone Three can she herself gather the necessary strength to proceed to Zone Two, and in turn, only then can there be more free movement between the Zones. Al·Ith believes "that this great lump of a man so newly introduced in her life must balance in some way those far blue heights of Zone Two" (61). The chroniclers know that "Zone Three [is] only one of the realms administered generally from Above," and they are aware of the necessity of integration among the Zones. They explain, "We did think, when we thought in these lines [about integration] at all, of ourselves in interaction with these other realms, but it was in an abstract way. We had perhaps grown insular? Self-sufficing?" (6). And it is precisely because "the Zones [can]not mingle, [are] inimical by nature" (4) that "the Order" comes from "Above" for Al·Ith to sacrifice herself to a higher cause and accept Ben Ata in marriage. She explains to Ben Ata, "We are here for a purpose—to heal our two countries and to discover where it is we have gone wrong, and what it is that we should be doing, really doing" (76).

In this novel as in others, Lessing demonstrates the break-down of barriers whenever beings at different levels strive for a way to connect and communicate with one another.[36] In its depiction of segregation among Zones and the difficulty of integration, *The Marriages* also recalls *The Four-Gated City*, in which the same necessity for integration is illustrated by the opening Sufi teaching story about the fool who is sent to buy flour and salt, both of which he loses while trying so hard to keep them separate. The progression of *The Marriages* depends on this instability among the Zones, or levels of consciousness. Furthermore, the thematic dimensions of both Al·Ith and Ben Ata are essential for our grasp of the progression. For instance, insofar as Al·Ith, in her function as a theme, represents the whole of Zone Three, her actions and her suffering in her function as a mimetic figure reflect on and directly affect Zone Three. This direct correlation between Al·Ith and Zone Three mimetically affects the people, plants, and animals who live on Zone Three: when Al·Ith suffers, they suffer, and some even die. Al·Ith's marriage to a lower being is such a step backwards for her that its initially destructive effects are felt in all of Zone Three, the Zone she abandons to marry Ben Ata.

This tight bond between Al·Ith and Zone Three is best understood when the novel is read as an allegory in which Al·Ith functions as the embodiment of all of Zone Three, there to fulfill her thematic role of scapegoat. When she suffers the crudity of Zone Four through Ben Ata's embrace, the whole of Zone Three experiences the same suffering: animals ail and lose their fertility; people lose their cheer and vitality. Since Al·Ith left, all are "sad enough to die." It is reported that "They have lost the zest for living" (17)—a state that Al·Ith hopes to ameliorate by conceiving Ben Ata's child, thereby uniting the Zones. Meanwhile, Al·Ith and Ben Ata's "differences [are] so great that they [are] both always being overtaken by feelings of astonishment that they [can] be there together at all" (75). In the end when Al·Ith does evolve as expected, Zone Three rejoices and evolves with her. Thematically, the change in her reflects a profound change in her level of being as a result of her suffering and of her efforts at overcoming that suffering.

The episodes in *The Marriages* not only suggest Islamic influence by Al·Ith's act of surrender, which defines the word *islam*, but also suggest non-Western influence by the names Lessing chooses for her characters, such as *Kunzor, Jarnti, Ben Ata, Al·Ith, Murti,* and *Vahshi*, names that are foreign to the Western ear.[37] Some names in *The Marriages* reveal the characters' makeup as well as Lessing's thoughts. Names with possible resonances from the world of Islam include *Murti*, which is slang for "wife" in Arabic. *Arusi* means "my bride" in Arabic, and *Dabeeb* describes a kind of a "walk." *Vahshi* is a word in Turkish, Persian, and Arabic meaning "wild, ferocious, savage, bestial, and brutish," which fully describes the warrior queen from Zone Five, whom Ben Ata marries and tames, as Al·Ith once tamed him. The word *vahshi* also describes Zone Five itself, perfectly. Ben Ata and Vahshi's union, like his earlier experience with Al·Ith, is contracted in hope of bringing about an equilibrium between two Zones, this time, Zones Five and Four. When the savage and wild queen unites with the more-evolved Ben Ata, her people can hope to evolve also into Zones Four, Three, Two . . . in time.[38]

While not all names in Lessing's cosmology correspond to an Islamicate language, the few that do suggest that there is more to Lessing's cosmology than meets the Western eye. Arguing along similar lines, Sprague thinks names in *The Marriages* "vaguely suggest semitic and Indian origins, not Euro-American origins" ("Naming" 13). For instance, *Al·Ith* suggests *alif*, the first letter in the Arabic alphabet . . . *Al* is also the Arabic definite article, "the" (13). *Alif* is the letter with which God's name, *Allah*, begins. Classical Sufi poets have made much of the letter *alif* primarily because of this. Poems are written to beautiful girls named *Alif*, who happen to personify *all* of the beauties of God, the Beloved. For instance, the Turkish love poet (*aşık*) Karacaoğlan has composed a song to the accompaniment of *saz*, a long-necked stringed instrument, in which he praises *Alif.*

In Turkish *ata* means "forefather" and *ben* means "I." Thus by definition, Ben Ata embodies all of his heritage and ancestry in Zone Four. When Zone Three wishes to unite with Zone Four, Al·Ith is chosen to be sacrificed to the cause by marrying a man who can sire children to bridge the gap between the past, or Zone Four, and the future, or Zone Two. Considering the earlier resistance to such a fusion of Zones, Al·Ith and Ben Ata's sexual union can be interpreted in terms of Sufi symbolism. The idea of this union as a thematic function is simulated in Al·Ith and Ben Ata's lovemaking at the mimetic level: "She held him as if she were drowning and could only be saved by his driving body. She felt as if he did not do this, extinguish her, knock her out, sink her deep, drive out of her all the tensions and the electricity, that she would go crazy, explode. Why? she had no idea. This was Zone Four! This was how it was" (181).

It is impossible to separate time and space in *The Marriages* because the characters function more as two-legged themes than mimetic people, and these themes are easily spirited past the frontiers of Zones and beyond the limitations of time. Al·Ith has only to ride her horse some distance for her character to enter another Zone. Given the restrictions that would have to be placed on a well-rounded character with mimetic traits, the idea of the synchronicity and simultaneity of events in *The Marriages* seems best expressed by Lessing's use of the two techniques demonstrated in the previous pages. The first is the way she enables characters to transcend barriers between Zones. To do this, Lessing uses allegory that affords characters in their thematic functions the freedom to behave in ways unlike primarily mimetic characters could. The second technique is her depiction of different levels of consciousness on the Sufi ladder to enlightenment by means of geographical time/space Zones that exist simultaneously.

A reading of *The Marriages* as a Sufi teaching tale need not be in conflict with rhetorical, scientific, or psychoanalytical readings. The subtlety with which a Sufi tale teaches is inherent in its structure: what appears "on the surface as tales or jokes . . . are in fact *structures*—formulated to bring into cognition patterns which the mind finds difficult or impossible to render and receive in any other way" (Courtland 88). Sufi stories teach on different levels and demonstrate the interconnectedness and synchronicity of events. Likewise, *The Marriages* teaches through the use of the space-fiction genre that breaks down our ordinary barriers of perception and allows Lessing to convey the synchronous experiences of people in different Zones as well as the simultaneity of Zones or levels of being in a single individual. In Al·Ith's nature, for instance, we see traits of primarily Zone Three behavior, but also traces of Zones Two and Four. Too, she and Ben Ata coexist while Al·Ith manifests primarily Zone Three traits, and Ben Ata expresses the crudity of Zones Four and Five.

A Sufi tale is said to stimulate the right half of the brain, which is often ignored by formal education. Modern scientific research has shown that the brain is divided into two hemispheres: the left half is the source of logical, rational thought; and the right half deals with nonverbal, nonsequential, nonlogical information. It is where creativity originates, and it has an "all-at-once" approach to data that it encounters. The didactic Sufi tale requires exactly this type of all-at-once approach in order to be grasped properly (Courtland 88). Likewise, Lessing's *The Marriages* invites readers to abandon traditional expectations about a novel and to make themselves receptive to new ideas as demonstrated through allegorical Zones or depths of consciousness. Hence, one may speculate that the left half of the brain that reasons is inevitably required to suspend disbelief as Lessing's characters are swiftly spirited between levels of being that are Zoned into geographical regions.

Sufi teaching stories aim to break up rational thinking and to block the interference of logical thought patterns. By forcing the audience to depart from analytical reasoning, the Sufi story addresses a less inhibited audience, in an altered state, who listens not for the logical but for the *intuitive* sense of the story. Similarly, Lessing wants to teach something fresh by breaking away from empirical analysis. At the conclusion of *The Marriages* her characters acquire the ability to allow themselves to be transported to a higher Zone than that in which they found themselves in the opening of the novel: "There was a continuous movement now, from Zone Five to Zone Four. And from Zone Four to Zone Three—and from us up the pass [to Zone Two]" (245). In a traditional novel with mimetic characters there never could have been such free movement in time and space; neither would Al·Ith have endured the abuses of her barbaric husband so patiently and for so long, without the plot developing radically differently. However, since Al·Ith serves primarily a thematic function in the allegorical realm of the narrative, the audience is not as inclined to question the suffering she endures. For the same reason, it also does not trouble us when she simply disappears one day: "One day when Al·Ith climbed the road to visit the other Zone, she did not come back. Others of her friends disappeared in the same way—[past the frontiers and into Zone Two]" (244).

At the end of the novel Al·Ith's mimetic sacrifice is rewarded by a thematic commingling of Zones: "There was a lightness, a freshness, and an enquiry and a remaking and an inspiration where there had been only stagnation. And closed frontiers" (245). Once she fulfills her thematic role, Al·Ith is no longer needed and can recede into the watery blueness of Zone Two, presumably a Sufi plane. Having submitted to the higher will of the "Providers" and having endured the consequent suffering, she earns the right to reside in heavenly Zone Two forever. But understandably, Mona Knapp notes that to the rational thinker this is "small comfort" compared to what Al·Ith had to endure (160).

Lessing is successful in offering us a Sufi teaching story through *The Marriages*, the second novel in the *Canopus* series. She communicates something new about spiritual levels of being or psychological levels of consciousness in Sufism to the layperson who might not otherwise take an interest in Sufism. Lessing's is a consciousness interested in a revolution and an awakening of minds and hearts that may be induced through exemplary fiction.

The Making of the Representative for Planet 8

In *The Representative* (1982), the fourth novel in the *Canopus* series, Lessing subordinates the mimetic characteristics of Doeg, Johor, and others to their synthetic and thematic functions even more than she does in *The Marriages*. The mimetic function is restricted to such a degree in *The Representative* that even the characters' names periodically change. The narrative foregrounds the synthetic component of several such characters, whose synthetic dimension recedes into the background whenever his thematic dimension requires attention. Alternating between their synthetic and thematic dimensions, characters seem even more puppet-like than Al·Ith or Ben Ata of *The Marriages*. They do not act out a plot but rather recite and perform a lesson much like in a medieval morality play.

In his synthetic dimension, Doeg, who is properly labeled "Memory Maker" (22), serves as Lessing's agent.[39] He tells Lessing's tale for her and teaches many morals through his experiences in his limited mimetic capacity as one of the victims of The Ice. He is also a thematic character who embodies the idea of selflessness or of having no identity: "Here I am!" he says, "and add to it the thought: But the 'I' of me is not my own, cannot be, must be a general and shared consciousness" (65). As Lessing's message bearer, he reassures his compatriots on Planet 8 that their "qualities will be reborn somewhere" (80). These words recall the message in the Sufi teaching story "The Tale of the Sands," in which a stream is challenged to give itself up to the wind in order to cross the desert. When it does so, it is not annihilated but rewarded by rain on the other side of the desert which forms into a new river, in essence containing the same water.

A stream, from its source in far-off mountains, passing through every kind and description of countryside, at last reached the sands of the desert. Just as it had crossed every other barrier, the stream tried to cross this one, but it found that as fast as it ran into the sand, its waters disappeared.

It was convinced, however, that its destiny was to cross this desert, and yet there was no way. Now a hidden voice, coming from the desert itself, whispered: "The Wind crosses the desert, and so can the stream."

The stream objected that it was dashing itself against the sand, and only getting absorbed: that the wind could fly, and this was why it could cross a desert.

"By hurtling in your own accustomed way you cannot get across. You will either disappear or become a marsh. You must allow the wind to carry you over, to your destination" . . .

[Giving itself up to the wind was not acceptable to the stream, as it feared losing its individuality, but . . .]

. . . Dimly, he remembered a state in which he—or some part of him, was it?—had been held in the arms of a wind. He also remembered—or did he?—that this was the real thing, not necessarily the obvious thing, to do.

And the stream raised his vapour into the welcoming arms of the wind, which gently and easily bore it upwards and along, letting it fall softly as soon as they reached the roof of a mountain, many, many miles away.

The stream was learning. But the sands whispered: "We know, because we see it happen day after day . . ."

And that is why it is said that the way in which the Stream of Life is to continue on its journey is written in the Sands. (Shah, *Tales* 23–24)

As the stream in the tale is made to act out the role of egolessness, so too are Lessing's characters required to display only those specific traits that are relevant to the teaching. In both "The Tale of the Sands" and *The Representative*, the necessary behavior to be learned and evaluated by the audience is a sacrificing of self and identity in order to gain a higher, more evolved self or true identity. Doeg's description of himself is reminiscent of the egoless stream that allows itself to be absorbed by the wind: "I imagined as I stood there looking at my face, my body, how stretching behind me, to each side of me, in every direction away from me, stood slight modifications of me, some very similar indeed, some hardly at all. I filled a town with these variations of myself, then a city, in my mind, whole landscapes. Doeg, Doeg, Doeg again" (81). As the desert teaches the stream in the Sufi version of this lesson, so does Johor, the agent from mainland Canopus teach Doeg in Lessing's version of the same lesson. In both versions one can identify the Sufi teacher (the wind/Johor), his disciple (the stream/Doeg), and the external strife that the disciple must face (the desert/The Ice). In both cases the necessary friction inevitably becomes an internal struggle to hold onto one's identity for fear of losing one's self in death. Both allegories teach that selflessness is rewarded in the end, that, in fact, ego is not one's anchor in life, but the primary obstacle. Both cases require surrender (*islam*) on the part of the disciple or would-be Sufi with no promise of any personal gain.

Lessing depicts Doeg as hardly any more mimetic than the stream in the Sufi tale. Doeg is given no real traits to make him more human than a stream or rain, and he has no feelings except a curiosity, which serves the author's purpose to tell her tale. The more questions Doeg's curious mind can throw at Johor, the further the narrative can progress in the form of questions and answers that allow both Doeg and Johor to fulfill their synthetic functions as mouthpieces for Lessing's version of the Sufi doctrine. At fleeting moments Doeg protests this lack of identity and asks, "What is Doeg but an attempt, and even a desperate and perhaps a tragic attempt, to make the faint coloured shadow, memory, stronger?" (90). Johor's answer is even more shocking: "I am not sure what your name is, when you ask these questions, but it is not Doeg!" (90). This is so, because being Doeg involves surrendering to his

148

synthetic role as a Representative and a Memory Maker, and to his thematic role as someone with no ego. This parallels the necessary subordination of his character to the allegorist's design. In order to serve the higher aim of the planet as dictated by Canopus and the greater aim of the author, both the thematic Doeg (the egoless representative) and the synthetic Doeg (the puppet/player) must remain a humble servant to the end. By serving Canopus he can survive The Ice; by serving Lessing he can demonstrate for the readers how to survive physical death.

Conclusion: Lessing's Teachings

Sufi ideas clearly afford Lessing-the-seeker the opportunity to investigate the possibilities of tapping other spheres of consciousness that in turn force Lessing-the-novelist to experiment with new fictive techniques in order to convey her messages better. Among Lessing's messages is the fact that not all beings live on the same level of consciousness, but that all beings are given equal opportunity to rise above the level at which they were born, as suggested in *The Marriages* and *The Representative*. In *The Four-Gated City* the opening teaching story encapsulates Lessing's message in a nutshell: beings who think they can survive compartmentalizing their lives or isolating parts of themselves in neatly divided quarters are fools. Lessing also emphasizes that people like Maudie in *The Diary* are not useless to society; on the contrary, it is often the seemingly helpless Maudies of the world who, like Nasreddin Hodja, are the stronger and the more powerful in the inner realm.

Contrasted to Martha Quest's and Janna Somers's lives, the lives of the protagonists in Lessing's space fiction require a change in fictive technique. Characters such as Al·Ith or Johor seem to have made demands on Lessing's choices of genre, mode, and style that can enable them to exercise the fullest

149

freedom within their fictional worlds. As a limited mimetic figure, Al·Ith cannot function in the traditional world of *The Diary* any more than Doeg or Johor, who are even less mimetic than Al·Ith, can ever belong to the postwar London of *The Four-Gated City*. Consequently, they require Lessing to provide for them a revised vision, and a new cosmology to match that vision, for them to inhabit.

In Lessing's galaxy, the unnamed masses who suffer Shikasta's fate, or Al·Ith who suffers the alienation of the wise, or both the Representatives and the represented who have to be annihilated, are most important in the roles they play as envoys and models for us, and less so as whole individuals with completely mimetic lives.[40] It therefore seems irrelevant whether Alice in *The Good Terrorist* and Janna Somers in *The Diaries* are successful in their daily struggles, so long as we witness them striving to become who they were meant to be. Ultimately, what matters, Lessing impresses upon us, is their contribution to the greater plan. Saul Green, Anna Wulf's "other" self, describes his contribution to this common cause: "There are a few of us in the world, we rely on each other even though we don't know each other all the time. We're a team, we're the ones who haven't given in, who'll go on fighting. I tell you, Anna, sometimes I pick up a book and I say: Well so you've written it first, have you? Good for you. OK then I won't have to write it" (642).

In keeping with Sufi teachings, Lessing stresses the importance of commitment to self-remembering[41] so that one may live by the guidance of one's mind, body, and heart, and make discoveries about the self who perpetually approaches that elusive shadow of the Other one is to know. Like a Sufi master, Lessing impresses upon us our responsibility for the small part we are privileged to play in the greater evolution of humanity and the universe, by fulfilling our individual destinies.

Part III

Implications

Four

Lessing between Spirituality and Science

One of the major implications of the influence of Sufism on Lessing is that Sufism enabled her to offer more faith and hope in her novels than she was able to before. Today, to the extent that she imports the Sufi faith, Lessing is in the minority in the West. She has departed radically from the secularized worldview of the twentieth-century West. This distinguishes her novels from those of most of her Western contemporaries and places her somewhere between the Eastern and Western traditions.

153

IMPLICATIONS

A second major implication of the influence of Sufism on Lessing is the fact that the fresh subject matter she found in Sufism precipitated a new perspective that instigated her choice of a new genre and a new style of narrative. It is Lessing's Sufi message in her post-1960s novels that positions her uniquely between East and West and between spirituality and science. The quotations that head this chapter indicate the two worlds and eras that Lessing negotiates in her difficult balancing act between East and West: she is more of an "educated, thoughtful" person, which aligns her with the twentieth-century British novelist Forster's protagonist, Mr. Fielding, than she is "the candle . . . consuming [herself]," like the "true lover" in the lines of the twelfth-century Persian Sufi poet, 'Attâr.

My analysis of Lessing's novels in this book has demonstrated the extent to which Sufism added a new layer of thought, a new set of stories, images, and new blood, to her work. This transfusion enabled her to write about metaphysical subjects with authority. At the same time, this is not to say that Lessing writes Sufi literature. The only conclusion we can make with any certainty about Lessing is that there is not a single tradition out of which she writes. She is neither British nor Rhodesian nor Persian, neither Christian nor Muslim, neither a fully pessimistic Western novelist nor a fully Sufi writer, but she is a seeker who is not afraid to question the status quo and to try out new ways of communicating to her readers.

Greene aligns Lessing with Eliot, Yeats, Pound, Lawrence, and Joyce for turning to myth as "a place beyond determinism, a place beyond culture" described by Eagleton as "a flight from contemporary history" (qtd. in *Poetics* 71). Bazin has compared Lessing to James Joyce and D. H. Lawrence in her use of epiphanies and in her compulsion to warn her readers ("Moment"). Kaplan and Rose sum up the 1978 MLA special session on Lessing; during it, speakers compared her to George Orwell, Ursula Le Guin, and Aldous Huxley and concluded that like these writers, Lessing is "mystical," "religious," and a "visionary" (27). Drabble holds similar views when she writes, "Doris Lessing is a prophet who prophesies the end of the world. She is much read but not perhaps much heeded, for there is very little that can be done, in her view, to avert catastrophe" (50). Yet, Drabble adds, despite the helplessness on which Lessing insists, "[s]he is the kind of writer who changes people's lives" (50). Drabble characterizes Lessing as one of the few novelists who insists on deciphering our world. She also asserts that "for a writer who consistently foresees and confronts the worst, [Lessing] is neither depressing nor apparently depressed" (50). Given her Sufi outlook, Lessing is not depressed because she is not writing in the dark, nor from out of darkness. Due to the Sufi influence, she writes with self-assurance and is able to reassure her readers even as she prophesies doom. She is, if not prophet, definitely mentor to those who will listen.

In order to evaluate Lessing's complex role as message bearer to the West, we need to recognize the filter through which she received the Sufi message. This filter includes the Western literary traditions that Lessing shares with her contemporaries and the twentieth-century Western intellectual approach to God, that is, the cessation of even questioning the idea of God and accepting his nonexistence. Only then can we appreciate the balance between the Sufi-like faith in a higher power on the one hand, and trust in the material world and in art on the other that characterizes Lessing's novels. Lessing writes of Sufi truths and teaches *islam* or active surrender to the higher will of Canopus or God, while she also demands of her characters uncompromising independence and twentieth-century style rationalism and skepticism.

Spirituality in Literature

In the history of English literature, there have been many and diverse relationships between spirituality and literature.

155

IMPLICATIONS

Of the numerous modern Western writers who have represented a (usually) *re*contextualized aspect of one of the many religions of the world, some have been orthodox, some mystics, others atheists, and still others uncommitted. Through drawing parallels, comparisons, and contrasts, the following pages will point out shared tendencies between Lessing and other canonical writers in the Western literary tradition who have been engaged in spirituality as a direct or peripheral subject of their writing.

In the absence of a strong religious impetus, twentieth-century writers bemoaned the emptiness and alienation in the contemporary world and wrote to explain and to redefine their godless universe. At the turn of the century, novelists wrote of the death of God, and poets offered themselves as prophets of the secular age; many writers preached liberation and self exploration; a few writers turned to Eastern traditions for their inspiration; E. M. Forster explored Hinduism and Islam as he found them in India; Herman Hesse explored the occult; C. S. Lewis looked deeply into Christian faith; and Lessing turned to Sufi truths as she encountered them in the West. Her prophetic side drew into prose what is usually done in poetry as prophecy. In a 1986 interview with Stephen Gray, Lessing commented:

> with *Canopus* I didn't plan a new series, I planned one book. I wanted to write the Bible as science fiction because somebody had said to me that nobody had ever done this very simple thing, which was to read the Old Testament and the New and the Apocrypha and the [Qur'ân] right through; it's a continuing story, it's the same play, with the same cast of characters . . . what they have in common is "messengers" or prophets who come and say to human beings, "You stinking lot of no-good-nicks, pull your socks up and do better, or else." (116–17)

The writers and thinkers used here for comparisons with Lessing include Carl Jung, William Blake, John Steinbeck,

Albert Camus, William Faulkner, D. M. Thomas, Virginia
Woolf, Margaret Atwood, Flannery O'Connor, Samuel Beckett,
Harold Pinter, E. M. Forster, Ursula Le Guin, Arthur C.
Clarke, Stanislav Lem, David Brin, Mary Shelley, and others.[1] Such a brief list naturally is not representative of all religious, pseudo-religious, or anti-religious themes and fragments
in Western thought and literature. Only a few writers are
cited out of a vast array of thinkers, poets, novelists, and play-
wrights whose uses of and references to spirituality or whose
anti-religious inclinations provide characteristic examples for
comparison and contrast with Lessing's uses of and references
to Sufism. For example, Camus, Beckett, and Pinter offer perfect points of contrast to Lessing, while C. S. Lewis, Jung, or
Blake might be exceptional allies and fellow seekers, and
Forster and Hesse remind us that Lessing is not alone in
drawing on an Eastern spiritual path.

Lessing acknowledges the absence of God in her present
audience when she characterizes the twentieth-century reader
of literature in the person of Martha Quest. In *A Proper
Marriage* she writes of Martha Quest, "She was of that generation who, having found nothing in religion, had formed themselves by literature" (61).[2] Her subsequent novels illustrate
this assumption. She writes metaphors and allegories of Sufi
truths from Eastern lands for a predominantly secular Western
audience that has evolved out of the Age of Reason and its
incessant probings into the nature of God. She is familiar with
the shortcomings of believing in the divine when that belief is
interrogated by the moderns. Given her position between a
world of religiosity and one of disbelief, she writes didactic novels that proselytize. She is like Nasreddin Hodja, who knows
that to make yoghurt one must stir a spoonful of yoghurt into
warm milk, yet kneels by a large lake and stirs a spoonful of
yoghurt into it. When a passerby tells Nasreddin that that is
not the way to make yoghurt he retorts, "I know, I know, but
what if it takes?" (my rendering from the Turkish oral tradition). The punch line, "What if it takes?" is an expression in

IMPLICATIONS

Turkish (*Ya tutarsa?*) used when one wants to communicate that something is worth trying, that one *must* have faith.

Perhaps in her urgency to make yoghurt, Lessing does not always allow the yoghurt culture time to multiply on its own, but stirs all the more vigorously. It is this tendency that has earned Lessing the reputation of being a didactic writer who likes the soapbox. Given the existential and individualistic Western readership that resents being told what to do, this reputation has been difficult for Lessing to live down.

To continue the yoghurt metaphor, Lessing's yoghurt includes survivors of the Enlightenment and its suppressed spirituality. During the Restoration and the eighteenth century most essayists and poets[3] conceded that men and women must think, sense, reason, intuit, and seek for themselves, rather than blindly believe in Christianity. Even as they wrote, they were aware that humanity's collective knowledge was neither final knowledge nor the limit of knowledge. As a result, many lost their faith and turned to empirical reasoning for comfort.

When we scan the last few centuries in terms of scientific breakthroughs, it becomes apparent why the foundations of faith were so irreversibly shaken by the findings of researchers to the degree of discrediting and even completely discarding the religious side of the Western tradition: studies in geology expanded the beginning of time back millions of years; studies in astronomy expanded space beyond the earth-centered universe of the Bible; studies in biology and Darwin's discoveries gave a more modest place to humans as one of many mutable species in the animal kingdom; studies in archeology extended the Europeans' awareness to include civilizations beyond the West; anthropologists and geologists uncovered ancient civilizations that made it more difficult to overlook the reality of non-Western paradigms; textual critics found the Bible to be just another text that had evolved in time and that included human errors and gaps. Such findings eroded the absolute quality of Christian faith and demystified Jesus. The Bible was obviously *not* an absolute and holy source of knowledge handed down from Mount Sinai. Contextual critics argued that it was one more myth among many mythologies and that the story of the life of Jesus—a dying God being reborn—was *not* unique to Christianity. There were many sides to every question, something westerners had been reluctant to acknowledge. An active imagination refused to settle on absolute truths any more. By the time of the Victorian age, increasing knowledge of the world and intense questioning of existing truths had undermined Western men and women's ability to believe as the past had believed. No new sustaining values were offered in place of the old traditions, except painful doubt and agnostic science. These characteristics left their indelible imprint on the psyche of the modern Western seeker.

In addition to the emphasis on reason which was passed down to Western twentieth-century writers from the thinkers of the Enlightenment and the emphasis on imagination bequeathed by the Romantics of the early nineteenth century, Lessing and her contemporaries received from the Victorians (who lived in a fragmented industrial society) the despair, sense of loneliness, isolation, and the longing for serenity and joy—a rather stark contrast to the steadfast faith that is characteristic of classical Sufi poetry. In the modern age the times not only changed for the worse, becoming more unstable, but also allowed for no pacifying prayers, reassurances, or morals to which one could cling. In a 1981 interview with Christopher Bigsby Lessing commented, "we now live with our heads in the middle of exploding galaxies and thinking about quasars and quarks and black holes and alternative universes and so on, so that you cannot any more get comfort from old moral certainties because something new is happening. All our standards of values have been turned upside down, I think" (72).

Need usually precedes a search; it was the need for new values to fit the times that led Lessing to her search. Lessing wrote in "Learning How to Learn" in 1982,

IMPLICATIONS

I could no longer accept the contemporary "package." This consists of materialism, socialism or an association with one of the
many churches of Marxism and atheism—belief in material
progress and that the betterment of society can come only
through political action. Now I see this package as pitifully
meager and empty, but it was hard to jettison because I did
not know how to look elsewhere. I read and read: the various
kinds of Buddhism, the yogas, Christian mysticism, Hinduism,
Islam. (12)

And in the early 1960s, she read *The Sufis* by Idries Shah.
Lessing recognizes thinkers in Islam for having done much to
further psychological philosophy in the Islamic world, including study of dream states, inspiration through dreaming, and
complicated notions about cognition and consciousness. She
includes even Carl Jung, one of the few mystically oriented
thinkers in the West, among those who left her dissatisfied
with what the Western tradition had to offer. She writes, "I
think Jung's views are good as far as they go, but he took them
from Eastern philosophers who go much further. [Ibn al-'Arabî
and al-Ghazzâlî] in the middle ages [twelfth century] had more
developed ideas about the unconscious, collective or otherwise,
than Jung, among others. He was limited. But useful as far as
he went" (qtd. in Rubenstein, *Novelistic* 230–31).

In fact, Jung would have agreed completely with Lessing's
reasons for looking outside the European tradition for religious truths, since he regarded Europe to be the "mother of all
demons" (*Wisdom* 2) and looked elsewhere, himself. At the
conclusion of his autobiography he writes, "When people say I
am wise, or a sage, I cannot accept it. A man once dipped a hat-
ful of water from a stream. What did that amount to? I am not
that stream. I am at the stream, but I do nothing . . . The difference between most people and myself is that for me the
'dividing walls' are transparent. That is my peculiarity . . . To
some extent I perceive the processes going on in the background, and that gives me an inner certainty. People who see

nothing have no certainties and can draw no conclusions" (*Memories* 355–56). Jung was conscious of the stream of knowledge that is greater than any human achievement. Therefore for him, perhaps Ibn al-'Arabî or al-Ghazzâlî, too, were mere mortals who dipped their hats in the stream of knowledge but who did not become that stream.

Jung himself expresses his own discontent in a letter to his friend Mountainlake, the Pueblo chief in Taos, New Mexico: "My Dear Friend, Mountainlake—All you tell me about religion is good news to me. There are no interesting religious things over here, only remnants of old things" (*Wisdom*). Indeed, Jung was very much impressed with his Native American friend's belief that it was he and his tribe's daily morning rituals and meditation that assured the sun's rising every morning: Mountainlake, like all of the Pueblo, believed that if they stopped their daily prayers, within a few years the sun would stop rising and the world would come to an end—a faith that Jung deeply respected and admired.

Jung stands out in the West for stating the kinds of things that Sufis or members of Native American or African tribes would have considered obvious. In contrast to the purity of faith that Jung encountered among the Native Americans and among the people he met in Africa, he saw that the Western culture had departed from the instinctual life and from God. For him, all things were richly spiritual, all things on earth—including places—had a soul and a psyche. He "intuited an imbalance in Western culture in favor of one whole style of analysis, logic, external achievement, social hierarchicalism, and he asked [like Lessing,] 'What happened to the other side?'" (*Wisdom* 2). In his attempt to answer this question, Jung went to Africa "to seek that part of himself that had become invisible in the European tradition" (*Wisdom* 2) and brought dreams and the unconscious to the foreground in the West.

Lessing studied Jung for a time. Jung's assertion that the twentieth-century West has no soul appeased her in the knowledge that she was not alone. One of Jung's earliest childhood visions, when he was a schoolboy, sums up the source of the void and alienation that Lessing and her Western contemporaries were feeling: "I saw before me the cathedral, the blue sky. God sits on His Golden throne, high above the world—and from under the throne an enormous turd falls upon the sparkling new roof, shatters it, and breaks the walls of the cathedral asunder" (*Memories* 39). Allowing himself to recognize this vision freed Jung from his entrapment in Christianity. He continues, "So that was it! I felt an enormous, an indescribable relief. Instead of the expected damnation, grace had come upon me, and with it an unutterable bliss such as I had never known. I wept for happiness and gratitude" (*Memories* 40). Jung recognized that Christian myth was deficient and no longer satisfactory because it did not include the feminine; it excluded matter, treating it as the devil, and ignored and denied evil (*Matter*). By acknowledging the imperfection of Christianity, Jung won half the battle; by seeking to compensate for that shortcoming, he fought the other half, as did Lessing, by looking for answers in non-Christian traditions.

The mystical poet William Blake was another striking exception to Western thinkers and writers. His poetry of vision put him more in line with the Sufi masters of the East than with the inheritors of the Enlightenment in the West. Lessing's novels cannot be compared to Blake's mystical poetry, but Blake becomes important to our understanding of Western Sufism, for his poetry provides a touchstone that is mystical in outlook within Western literature. With the questioning "I" and "eye" that he inherited, Blake looked closely at life—a leaf, a grain of sand, a small child—and saw in them both the objective, empirical information that they yield to a scientifically oriented, careful observer, and also the whole of infinity that they disclose to a spiritually inclined ardent seeker. With his poetry full of mystical insights, Blake combined the Puritans' assertion to live up to one's inner light and Francis Bacon's invitation to study nature, since studying nature was really studying the works of God.

In "There is No Natural Religion" Blake warned his readers to be alert to the entire process of life, because our finite senses alone cannot acquire a knowledge of God and of the natural world. Without dismissing the conclusions of his predecessors, which included natural religion and empirical reasoning, Blake insisted on man's godlike capacity for imagination and for vision to enable him to grasp reality and infinity directly (1493). In this insistence on direct communion with God, Blake was among the few Western thinkers who came the closest to the classical Sufi Way. His poetry is testament to the Christian and Sufi ideal of being totally in the world, but not of it. Like the Sufi Way, Blake's way bypassed, transformed, and replaced reason with visionary powers which grasped the mysteries that had so intrigued the thinkers of the Enlightenment.

Blake was in the minority, however. Rather than pose questions about God, his contemporaries—the Romantics—asked the question, What are we to make of *human* life? They found their answers in a combination of the sublime in nature, the ordinariness of everyday life, and the wealth of the human imagination. Poets such as Wordsworth, Shelley, and Coleridge found meaning in the natural world made all the more glorious in their own imagination, while Blake went even further and both conceived and interpreted his own visions. That Blake was in the minority among the Romantics means the chances of Lessing's finding satisfactory answers to similar probings were slim in the West. The war among upholders of Christian faith, miracles, and skepticism had resulted in the coexistence of two worldviews in the West, with a heavier, this-worldly emphasis on rational, secular thought.

Lessing appears to have sought compensation for the repressed spirituality of the European tradition in Sufi thought and literature that, in contrast to the predominant thought and literature in the West, emphasized faith and the reality of the ineffable. For instance, in one of many Sufi orders in the East, in the order of the Whirling Dervishes (the Mawlawiyyah) that has its origins in thirteenth-century Central Anatolia, members to this day learn to reach heightened states of perception by way of turning with the right arm and palm reaching upwards to God, and the left arm and hand curving downwards to the earth. With their right hand they harness the truth and receive God's grace, which they pass with their left hand down to the earth presumably while levitating in the frenzy and passion of the act. Many of Lessing's later characters, such as Johor, Al·Ith, or Maudie, are closer in spirit and experience to these and other Sufis than they are to their more limited counterparts in Western literature, such as Jay Gatsby, Nora Helmer, or Stephen Dedalus. Sufism helps Lessing to bring out an element of her own tradition that was subordinated, enabling her to solve problems in the European tradition. Sufi thought helps her to stretch the boundaries of human capacity and to mitigate the West's insistence on the rational mind to the exclusion of other pathways to understanding. Yet even as Lessing's characters and stories demonstrate an affinity to Sufism, her novels appear to be imbued with competing ideologies.

In John Steinbeck's *The Grapes of Wrath*, Casy the ex-preacher sums up the West's waning faith in God in the decade that led up to the bomb, when he tells Tom Joad, "There ain't no sin and there ain't no virtue. There's just stuff people do. It's all part of the same thing. And some of the things folks do is nice, and some ain't nice, but that's as far as any man got a right to say" (24). Like Karl Marx, the prophet of the industrial age, Casy believes that one does not have a soul of his own, but "[m]aybe all men got one big soul everybody's a part of" (24). "I figgered about the Holy Sperit and the Jesus road," he continues, "I figgered, Why do we got to hang it on God or Jesus? I figgered, maybe it's all men an' all women we love; maybe that's the Holy Sperit—the human sperit—the whole shebang" (24). This approach may have comforted Casy, Steinbeck, and some readers. Insofar as Marxism offered an ardent love of the people as a solution, and to the extent that it recognized art as political, it provided a new ideology—but only for a time.

Unlike Sufism, Marxism did not comfort those who sought a universal reality. It faltered under the scrutiny of someone like Lessing, who is concerned with establishing finer distinctions between true salvation and existential rationalization.

If "religion" were defined in worldly terms as a discipline and practice that helps humans to perceive the universe as a meaningful whole, to place themselves within that whole, and to restore confidence, and if "God" were defined as the sense of rightness that humans experience when they have found their place in the universe, so that they may withstand life's challenges and obstacles, then literature *is* a new "religion" for the twentieth-century reader. Lessing partly implies this definition when she writes in *The Four-Gated City* of a generation forming itself by literature after having found nothing in religion.

However, more dominant in Lessing's mind seems to be the other definition of religion as a system of beliefs in higher powers that guides humans to develop and transform themselves and transcend death by overcoming imperfections and by fighting the limitations of human capacity. In this case, twentieth-century Western poetry, fiction, and drama naturally fall short of serving as guidebooks to transformation, or as literary models to emulate, propelling Lessing to look elsewhere for answers. When Lessing turned to Sufism, it must have been clear to her that the contemporary West had failed to replace sacred texts with literature, since it celebrated strictly an earthly paradise and had nothing to do with God. The absence of a believable and trustworthy God had left the moderns with a profound sense of being totally alone and condemned to free will, to the absurd, and to death, all of which, according to the existentialists, one had to accept with heroism in order to lead a committed life. Men and women were burdened with the responsibility to be totally accountable to themselves, and not to any gods. Meursault in Albert Camus's *The Stranger* expresses this well. He tells the priest who offers to absolve him of his sins before he is to be executed, "I'd very little time left and I wasn't going to waste it on God" (150).

IMPLICATIONS

The spiritual sterility and the impending doom felt in the twentieth-century West are expressed in countless instances of modern fiction, which include Benjy's wailing in William Faulkner's *The Sound and The Fury* or Nadia's howl and Kolya's scream in D. M. Thomas's *The White Hotel*. Dilsey, one of the few sincerely spiritual characters in modern fiction, recognizes Benjy's bellowing as something greater than the wailing of an idiot. In her opinion it symbolizes the cry of all humanity for its lost past, lost tradition, lost faith, and lost compassion. Faulkner's narrator in the "Dilsey" section of *The Sound and The Fury* says, "It might have been all time and injustice and sorrow become vocal for an instant by a conjunction of planets . . . he bellowed slowly, abjectly, without tears; the grave hopeless sound of all voiceless misery under the sun" (172). Similarly, D. M. Thomas writes in *The White Hotel* that during the massacre of a quarter million Jews, Ukrainians, gypsies, and Russians at Babi Yar, "The mouth of the three-year-old [Nadia] was open wide in a soundless howl" (286) and the eleven-year-old Kolya's scream "was only one strand in a universal scream, mixed with the happy shouts of the soldiers and the barking of dogs, but it was the one that stood out" (283).

European and North American writers have offered only a broken and useless savior or mundane solutions in response to the collective cries of humanity. In *The Waves*, Virginia Woolf symbolizes faith by the "sad figure of Christ" (179), which recalls Margaret Atwood's "alien god," or "dead man in the sky watching everything [we] do" (84). Woolf's solution to the absence of God, who could have offered a cohesiveness to the multiplicity, is to turn to one's friends for spiritual affirmation and guidance. Bernard in *The Waves* feels "so imperfect, so weak, so unspeakably lonely" (267) without his friends that he is lost but for the comforting memories of his dead friends. He says, "Some people go to priests; others to poetry; I to my friends . . . the touch of one person with another is all" (266).

In *Surfacing*, Atwood's solution to the absence of a satisfactory religion is equally this-worldly. Her protagonist converts to an ancient Indian religion inspired by the underwater cave paintings. However, these Indian gods who had "marked the sacred places, the places where you could learn the truth" (171), are as illusory as Christ. The protagonist's newfound gods serve more as an aid in this life on earth, than offering her salvation in any other life after death. Hers is a secular god, as her immersion and rebirth have been psychological, not religious experiences (Rigney 50–51). In the end, she comprehends more of *herself*, rather than of Christ's or God's mysteries.

Flannery O'Connor offers an alternative when she suggests in *Wise Blood* that Christianity is inevitable and that her characters, like us in the West, are Christians (or Jews or Muslims) *in spite of* themselves. Hazel Motes is haunted by Christ no matter how far he flees; his response to the fact that Jesus died for him is to say, "I never ast him"! He ultimately blinds himself with quicklime and fills the bottoms of his shoes with small rocks and glass, on which he walks daily to mark the fact that he has stopped running from Jesus— behavior that provokes readers to question the dark God O'Connor envisions suitable for her characters who suffer modern living in the West. Some Sufis in history have been known for similar asceticism. However, Sufi mystics have never regarded God as a force to escape but a power to embrace.

In general, Lessing's Western contemporaries resort to murder, assassination, suicide, or materialism as resolutions to their plots. Commands in twentieth-century novels and plays come not from a Judeo-Christian or Muslim God, but from earthbound figures, such as Pinter's "dumbwaiter," Faulkner's "player," or Steinbeck's and Marx's "masses." The God of the moderns works at random like Faulkner's "player," who makes Joe Christmas murder, flee, and get caught, and who makes Percy Grimm chase Joe, castrate, and execute him; or he is a landowner like Godot, and has the power to keep Vladimir and Estragon waiting; or he is a ringleader who makes Pinter's assassins carry out the orders that he sends down to them by means of the dumbwaiter. This worldly god

even has servants, such as the messenger boy whom Godot
sends to Vladimir and Estragon; and he knows how to operate
modern machinery as in Pinter's "Dumbwaiter." In most cases,
he is an unreasonable and inconsiderate absentee slumlord
and gangster, not a savior. *This* is the god that Lessing rejects
by turning to Sufi mysticism. In Lessing's space fiction, commands come from Planet Canopus, while those living on subordinate planets surrender (*islam*) to the will of Canopus.

Before she turned to Sufism, Lessing's vision was pessimistic, as we can see in the choices made by her protagonists: suicide in "To Room 19," divorce and abandonment of
one's baby for the sake of one's sanity in *A Proper Marriage*, or
mental breakdown in various forms in different novels. Later,
she sought and found a new faith, new perspective, and new
vocabulary in the wealth of Sufi literature and ideology, creating a rift between her work and the works of her contemporaries. Through the mitigation of Sufism, Lessing seems to
have embraced more positive endings such as Emily's salvation at the end of *The Memoirs*, Doeg's transformation and
rebirth after the freezing of Planet 8, or Al·Ith's evolution to a
higher plane in *The Marriages*.

It may be useful to analyze E. M. Forster's representations of religion for a point of reference to Lessing. Unlike the
kind of perverse religiosity suggested by O'Connor, religion as
it used to be before the age of disbelief is reintroduced in
Forster's *A Passage to India*, one of a few works in modern
fiction that directly addresses the failure, as well as the ongoing practice of, religion today. The novel is divided into three
sections, entitled "Mosque," "Caves," and "Temple," perhaps
representing Islam, Christianity, and Hinduism. In the "Mosque"
section we meet Dr. Aziz, a Muslim Indian who defends the
sanctity of the mosque when he sees Mrs. Moore, a foreigner,
enter the mosque, since, as a Muslim, he considers all non-
Muslims "infidels." In the "Caves" section we learn of the
British Mrs. Moore's Christian faith, contrasted to the
Brahmin professor Godbole's Hinduism. And in the "Temple"

section we witness the Hindu festival. Mrs. Moore necessarily dies in the end of the novel because she is one of the last true believers in Christianity. In the opening of the novel when she is reproached by Dr. Aziz for not taking off her shoes in the mosque, she replies that she indeed removed her shoes, even though there was no one else to see, because "God is here" (20). It is this faith that endears her to Dr. Aziz and professor Godbole.

Mrs. Moore believes that "God has put us on earth to love our neighbors, and to show it" (51), but, she wonders, "like an elderly woman" (150), that perhaps we are all "merely passing figures in a Godless universe." She is disappointed that in spite of "[c]entury after century of carnal embracement, . . . we are still no nearer understanding one another" (135). When she encounters the strange echo in the dark, featureless, and empty Marabar caves that reduce all sounds to "boum," she wonders "with the cynicism of a withered priestess," whether all of the divine words of "poor little talkative Christianity," from "Let there be Light" to "It is finished," also do not only amount to "boum" (150). Characters in Lessing's novels do not come close to the sincere religiosity of Mrs. Moore, Dr. Aziz, or Godbole. After her departure from India and her death on the boat bound for home, Mrs. Moore is even travestied into a Hindu goddess. Forster writes, "At one period, two distinct tombs containing Esmiss Esmoor's remains were reported: signs of the beginning of a cult—earthenware saucers and so on" (256–57).

On the other hand, Mrs. Moore's son Ronny, whose religion is commonplace, is representative of Lessing's generation. Forster's narrator tells us, "Ronny's religion was of the sterilized Public School brand, which never goes bad, even in the tropics. Wherever he entered, mosque, cave, or temple, he retained the spiritual outlook of the Fifth Form, and condemned as 'weakening' any attempt to understand them" (257). Ronny approves of religion only when it endorses the national anthem and objects when it threatens to touch his life. He is a believer in Christianity to the degree that God saves the king and supports the British police. He believes religion is "a symptom of bad health" (52), much like the empirical British philosopher Thomas Hobbes for whom the word *God* was "little but a philosopher's fatigue" (Willey). The "religious strain," Ronny believes, appears only when one is aging and approaching death. For him, conversation becomes unreal whenever Christianity enters it, and he breaks it off by retorting, "I don't think it does to talk about these things, every fellow has to work out his own religion" (52)—a typical Western individualist sentiment.

Godbole's spirituality is perhaps the most positive of the religions we encounter in all of twentieth-century Western literature. The Brahmins reenact the birth of a new "Lord of the Universe" every year during the Hindu festival, and with the symbolic birth of the child god Shri Krishna, manifested as a silk baby, they bear witness to the Lord's salvation, which strengthens their faith. To the degree that this is about a real event and that real people partake in the celebration, Forster's depiction of Hinduism far surpasses all testaments of faith expressed in Lessing's novels under the influence of Sufism. Yet it is essential to note that Forster's models of religiosity are not westerners, nor do they look to the West. Forster looks on from an Orientalist's distance and perhaps with nostalgia at the religious faiths of Godbole and Aziz.

In contrast to the lost traditional and religious values of the westerners, the Muslim Indian doctor Aziz feels himself deeply "rooted in society and Islam" (121). Whether he genuinely believes in Islam or not, he feels that "[h]e belong[s] to a tradition which [binds] him, and he [has] brought children into the world, the society of the future" (121). His identification with Islam allows him to feel "placed," unlike the various Western protagonists we have looked at, who dangle, like Adela Quested, "at the end of [their] spiritual tether[s]" (263). The basic conclusion Dr. Aziz derives from the difference between East and West is, "So this was why Mr. Fielding and

170

a few others were so fearless! They had nothing to lose" (121). In contrast, Islam for Dr. Aziz is "an attitude towards life both exquisite and durable, where his body and his thoughts [find] their home" (19). Muslim poets offer him "[t]he secret understanding of the heart" (20) and his greatest desire during the excursion to the Marabar caves is, "We shall be all Moslems together now" (131). Dr. Aziz also writes poems "about the decay of Islam and the brevity of love" (268); but still, he is not disillusioned with his God in the same manner as are his Western counterparts. He knows that Islam offers its adherents *more* than a body of thought. It supplies them with a way of life and a body of knowledge that accompanies those who are willing to practice Islam and to "seek wisdom from the cradle to the grave," as the prophet Muhammad commands.[4]

For our purposes here, these considerations of Forster are important for two reasons: first, the similarity of Forster to Lessing since both have imported the spiritual content of their work from the East; second, the disparity between their critical reception because of the style in which each presents that spirituality. Within the configuration of *A Passage to India*, Forster privileges the Indian characters Dr. Aziz and Godbole over the British characters Ronny, Adela, Mr. Fielding, or even Mrs. Moore. Like Lessing, Forster imports an Eastern tradition into the Western novel and shows the inspiring qualities of Dr. Aziz's Muslim tradition and Godbole's Hindu tradition. He presents his readers with the notion that there is something valuable to be learned from the East. Contrasted to the other Western writers discussed in this chapter, excepting Jung and Blake, Forster is like Lessing in his portrayal of spirituality. For him, as for Lessing, spirituality is transformative, not this-worldly in its scope. Forster's and Lessing's depictions of spirituality in literature are serious, and not only a symbolic substitute for what's missing, nor a playful exercise in artistic freedom.

Forster's representations of spirituality are more realistic than comparable passages in Lessing. His characters are not in outer space, but in British-ruled India. Yet his protagonists observe the mystically oriented Hindu festivities from a foreigner's distance—unlike Lessing's characters, who are in the eye of the storm at all times. Even Mrs. Moore does not partake in Godbole's Hindu practice beyond exchanging a few friendly conversations with him, while Lessing's characters are always participants in, not observers of, the mystical events. For instance, Doeg does not watch the struggle against The Ice, he is *in* it. Emily does not watch others undergo time and space travel, she is at the *center* of it. In an even greater contrast to Lessing, Forster is less overtly didactic and much less focused on guiding his readers out of the echoing void of the Marabar caves. He is satisfied simply to present the differences between the British and the Indians and their religious traditions as he sees them. Forster's readers are less likely to resent him for his spirituality, because he has not adopted the mode of confrontation or the role of prophet, even as he takes a strong stand against British colonialism in India.

Science in Literature

Robert Reilly explains that at least works written before 1945 were able to look up to science as "the key to all truth [that] would enable man to understand, manipulate, and thus transcend the painful reality of his ordinary existence" (4). But after the holocaust and Hiroshima, even those who believed in science were left with uncomfortable questions. Reilly places the blame for twentieth-century pessimism directly on the atom bomb, and he notes that it was immediately after Hiroshima, a "scientific" tragedy which irreversibly altered late-twentieth-century Western thought, that holocaust novels became abundant.

Since the West never totally recovered its faith in Christianity after the challenges posed to it by the various scientific explorations, science became the new authority in the West, the "New Religion." It is fascinating that until Francis Bacon's "New Science" in the seventeenth century, the word *science* used to refer to *all* learning, *all* knowledge, *all* truths, with no distinctions made between the "spiritual" and "material" components. However, starting with Bacon's arguments in *Advancement of Learning*, published in 1605, an unprecedented distinction emerged between divinity, which Bacon called "inspired theology," and science or philosophy, which he called "natural theology." He stressed the excellence of the latter, which produces "profane and human" knowledge (which is practical and useful for everyday life), such as knowledge of "artillery, sailing, printing, and the like." When Bacon promoted science, he explained that God has revealed himself to man by means of two scriptures: the written work (Bible) and creation (nature); therefore studying nature was really studying (the works of) God. While Bacon stressed the scientific study of nature for the goal of making knowledge useful and practical, he never intended to take God out of the formula altogether or to discard "God's other revelation," the Bible. Bacon promoted secular learning because he mistrusted deductive reasoning from given "truths," disapproved of equating knowledge with virtue, recognized the impossibility of making theology rational, and saw the need for a pragmatic approach which could improve the standards of daily life in seventeenth-century England.

Today, after four hundred years of studying the second causes, or nature, and abandoning the search for first causes, or God's hand, we are finding that the separation between the study of God and nature that was so necessary for Bacon's time has gradually produced an irreparable schism between spirituality and science, including a dismissal of the reason Bacon had proposed for studying nature: "God worketh nothing in Nature but by second causes." While for Bacon undertaking scientific study did *not* exclude God, we in the modern age have turned completely to science for reasons that are not always connected with discovering God's mysteries. We find

173

ourselves placing complete faith in science and making *it* our present myth (except perhaps for some astronomers, physicists, and cosmologists). Our complete investment in science is reflected even in our language as when, for example, we speak of getting something "down to a science."

In the seventeenth century, religion was the towering power over people's lives and it was in no danger of being overshadowed. Then, the idea of studying nature was a novelty and was called "The New Science." Today, the reverse is true: as science and technology tower over the twentieth-century West, various spiritual paths, including Sufism in the West, are dismissed as "new age religions"; and what was once the New Science now has become our New Religion. We continue to give our tacit consent to discarding spirituality and to placing our faith in science. For instance, in writing about science fiction, Reilly seeks reasons for why authors of science fiction use spirituality in their works and concludes that "[t]he scientists themselves are a sort of priesthood. Science fails to conform [to a definition of religion] only with respect to the postulate of 'a power' to explain the order" (3).

As a direct result of the shift in focus from religion to science, science fiction has become the modern mythology in art and literature. Jung calls science our latest religion in the West. He draws parallels between science fiction and mythology in order to emphasize that "myth is not only something people dance to naked or tell around the camp fire" (*Wisdom* 3). In his writings, Jung was interested in exposing the "narrow-mindedness of rationalism" (*Wisdom* 3) and the imbalance of favoring science at the expense of spirituality. Lessing has said in a 1980 interview with Nissa Torrents, "Science, which is the religion for today, looks for the metaphysical, as with Catholics of old. Hence the boom in science fiction, which reflects this preoccupation and which moves in the world of the non-rational" (66).

As we grow accustomed to this, we are not surprised by the science-fiction and magical-realism plots in our films and literature, nor by psychics, visionaries, or products of genetic engineering and mutation. Extraterrestrials and spaceships invade the big screen and our consciousness with ease, while we glory in our intelligence matched against that of the aliens; nor do we have a problem with learning that our poets sometimes consult the Ouija board, as James Merrill did in composing many of his poems. We are not disconcerted by the uses of spiritual divination for secular purposes, nor by the emergence of scientific archetypes that define our reality. We have placed our split faith in science as our new religion while assigning science fiction the ambiguous role between science/technology and the supernatural/metaphysical.[5] The box office hit *Independence Day* (1996) is a testament to this.

Suvin defines science fiction as follows: "Science Fiction, then, is a literary genre whose necessary and sufficient conditions are the presence and interaction of estrangement and cognition, and whose main formal device is an imaginative framework alternative to the author's empirical environment" (7–8).[6] In the *Canopus* series there are estrangement and cognition, and definite alternative frameworks to Lessing's empirical environment. But there is also spirituality. Lessing is interested in the "and, and, and" frame of mind, not "either, or." Her fiction is inclusive, comprehensive, spiritual, and didactic beyond the definition that Suvin allows for science fiction. When Lessing writes *space fiction*, her themes tend to follow a pattern that is *other* than what we witness in science fiction within the limits of Suvin's definition. Given her immersion in Sufi teachings, Lessing's "archetypes" are not accidentally or loosely woven but are more consciously calculated to exemplify a Sufi truth. This renders Lessing's novels *Sufi fiction*, so to speak, and not *science fiction*, although this is not to say she is writing spiritual tracts. It is important to remember that Lessing herself carefully refers to the *Canopus* series as *space fiction* and not *science fiction*. In reference to the *Canopus* series Lessing commented to Margarete von Schwarzkopf in a 1981 interview:

IMPLICATIONS

I wouldn't classify these books as science fiction. They don't have much to do with "science," that is, scientific knowledge and technology. I leave that to my colleagues who really know something about technology . . . No, my novels are fantasies, or utopias in the truest, most precise sense of the term, to be sure, rather less related to Orwell and Huxley than to Thomas More and Plato. (107)

Draine recognizes a split in some critics' definitions of science fiction. She writes that according to Kingsley Amis, Darko Suvin, Donald A. Wollheim, Sam Moskowitz, and David Ketterer, "[s]cience fiction is at pains to be natural, not supernatural; secular, not sacred; rational, not irrational; empirical, not philosophical, religious, or mystical; turned outward to the tangible realities of the cosmos, not turned inward toward the personal psyche or 'upward' toward God or any other spiritual reality." If we use this definition of science fiction as our measuring stick for Lessing's space fiction, Draine concludes, "[Lessing] claims for science fiction a scope much wider than many of its own practitioners and theoreticians would grant" (*Substance* 146). This is true for some of the other science-fiction writers, as well.

Draine notes the tension between the strands of science fiction and spirituality in *Shikasta* and looks at the degree to which *Shikasta* fits into the science-fiction genre and the degree to which it qualifies as sacred literature. Some of what Lessing does, Draine argues, are "cardinal sin[s] against the integrity of science fiction" (144). For instance, while Johor is comparable to the emissaries in Ursula LeGuin's *The Left Hand of Darkness*, Arthur C. Clarke's *Childhood's End*, and Olaf Stapledon's *Last and First Men*, he has distinguishing "messianic overtones" that make him a Christ figure unlike other emissaries (151). Draine does not necessarily credit Sufism with the difference that she finds between Lessing and LeGuin, Clarke, or Stapledon, but in her discussion of the Zones in *The Marriages*, she does credit Sufism and its stages

176

of enlightenment for Lessing's concept of the levels of consciousness.[7] In her discussion of *The Marriages*, Draine recognizes Lessing's point of departure from the codes of science fiction, when she describes the Zones that have stars and that are like "concentric shells around the planet" (5). She explains that Lessing feels no need to address the realistic problem of how every Zone can possibly see the stars. Instead (as in the Sufi tradition), Lessing asks us to suspend our disbelief and not demand scientific explanations and proof (157).[8]

Like Draine, Bazin, too, argues that "Lessing's space fiction is basically religious and moral in its intent; it is scientific only to the extent that scientific theory (concerning, for example, evolution or psychic phenomena) can enhance her moral vision. Throughout her works, the 'lodestone,' against which all is tested, is the polarized experience of painful self-annihilation and ecstatic oneness that occurs in the mystical moment" ("Evolution" 165). Bazin explains this by quoting from Lessing's "Testimony to Mysticism": "the best scientists, those on the highest levels, always come closer and closer to the mystical . . . Much of what Einstein said could have been said by a Christian mystic, St. Augustine, for example" (160). Bazin concludes that in Lessing's novels, and "for our survival, the mystical is just as essential as the scientific" (160).

My view of Lessing's space fiction in *Between East and West* acknowledges the dual faiths, worlds, directions, and genres that Lessing straddles. I align Lessing with those science-fiction writers who deal more seriously with spirituality. Many critics have connected science fiction to spirituality, such as in James Blish's "Cathedrals in Space"; Disch Thomas's "Science Fiction as a Church"; John Platzner's "The Mystification of Outer Space: Pseudo-Mysticism and Science Fiction"; or Robert Reilly's *The Transcendent Adventure: Studies of Religion in Science Fiction/Fantasy*, a collection of essays that includes a bibliography of further readings in spirituality in science fiction. C. S. Lewis, most overtly with his very Christian orientation, places God at the top of his sytem.

IMPLICATIONS

The trilogy *The Memory of Earth*, for which Orson Scott Card used the Old Testament as his model, explores spiritual themes. Other science-fiction writers also negotiate splits between spirituality, the social sciences, and science. David Brin's ecological concerns are expressed through a pantheistic perspective that is reminiscent of Native American practices. Arthur C. Clarke's novel *Childhood's End* has a mystical quality about it and deals with the idea that humans will evolve into a new form of consciousness. In the works of the Polish writer Stanislav Lem, themes of politics and social issues are woven together. Ursula Le Guin's fiction is influenced by anthropology as well as by science. Some use the futuristic disguise to avoid censorship in their country and to make a social and political commentary as is the case in *Slaughterhouse Five* by Kurt Vonnegut or *Left Hand of Darkness* by Le Guin. While some science-fiction writers draw on religious models for solutions to the problems they pose, others propose solutions that are politically and socially responsible, with a focus on the mundane. They are more concerned with saving humans or warning humans *on earth*. In this sense, Lessing's fiction seems to be most consistently aligned with C. S. Lewis's work in its degree of commitment to spiritual salvation.

When Mary Shelley wrote perhaps the original science-fiction novel, *Frankenstein*, she did so to combine her art with empirical learning and the new scientific discoveries of the times. The monster, as if warning future scientists about the atom bomb, gets out of hand to the horror of his creator and of Shelley's readers. In Lessing's fiction, on the other hand, there are no scientists, no laboratories nor Frankensteins, but only seekers. Fantastic events and creatures are brought about not by advanced scientists but by a higher power that is closer to a spiritual force than to technological gadgetry. Lessing is more concerned with educating the human heart than with stretching the capacity of the human brain to perform superhuman feats.

According to Jung, most science-fiction plots have a basic theme of extraterrestrial intelligence (*Wisdom* 3). A Jungian analysis of *Star Wars*, for instance, discloses loose Jungian archetypes such as "lady in distress," "young hero," "superhuman powers," and "a battle of good and evil," confirming Jung's assertion that myths are repeated throughout time and new ones are created all the time. (*Star Wars* is also of course quintessentially Freudian: an oedipal battle between father and son.) As a popular film, it represents a stereotypical form of science fiction, with all of the technological hardware—unlike some of the more serious science-fiction novels with social concerns or scientific plots. Still, this film helps us to consider some of the *shared* characteristics of science fiction, perhaps the lowest common denominator. Battles such as that between Luke Skywalker and Darth Vader in *Star Wars* recall the battle that Ahura Mazda, the Wise Lord of Zoroastrianism, fought with Ahriman, the force of evil. However, in science fiction, unlike Zoroastrianism, the pearls of wisdom are dropped here and there *at random*, with *no* expectations or demands placed upon the participants or observers. The battle of good and evil was the central image around which Zoroaster (Zarathustra) founded his teachings, with the promise that in the end, good would command evil, or God would triumph over Satan.[9] In *Star Wars*, Ahura Mazda's "sea of light" becomes Luke Skywalker's "Force," and the battle that took place in ancient Iran or ancient Greece of the Zoroastrians is transported to outer space.[10]

In *The Empire Strikes Back*, the sequel to *Star Wars*, the characters have telepathic powers. Whenever "the good guys" part from one another they say, "May the Force be with you," just as a Christian or a Muslim says, "May God be with you." Only in the former, "the Force" is rather impersonal and aspiritual, unlike the Christians' God-the-Father or the Muslims' Allah. Some of the *Star Wars* characters are even as wise as Confucius himself: "You must unlearn what you have learned," they tell our hero Luke, so that "the Force" can enter him.

They are well versed in a kind of pop-wisdom shared by most religions, and they don't hesitate to throw it around: "Energy surrounds us and binds us," they believe; and "you must feel the Force around you, everywhere, even in a rock"—precisely what Jung was insisting upon, that even the soil we walk on has a spirit and a mood because it literally contains the blood and sweat of those who died on it (*Wisdom* 2).

However, there is a major difference between Jung's (or the Sufis') spiritual outlook and the utterings of Luke, Princess Leia, and the others. In the latter, the wisdom is not grounded in a cohesive body of teachings such as the Navaho faith, Zoroastrianism, Christianity, or Sufism. Rather, it is a grab bag of religions and philosophies. Granted, *Star Wars* can*not* represent all forms, styles, and subject matter of science fiction; but it *does* represent what typically can be found in science fiction that reaches audiences beyond fans of the genre. *Star Wars* gestures toward spiritual teaching but never asks its viewers to change their beliefs or to behave differently. The film does *not* offer a spiritual teaching behind the fiction. Although the implication in the fictional world of *Star Wars* is that the Jedi master does in fact have a specific body of thought and practice to transmit, this remains in the fictional realm. Readers will doubtless recognize the following examples, which simultaneously recall a variety of religious traditions. "I don't believe it," Luke says, when he is told that the Force will help his fight; "That is why you fail," he is told. He is ordered, "No, don't [just] try; do, or do not." When he asks "How do I tell good from evil," he is told, "First you must be calm and quiet." So he stands on his hands for several hours, upside down, as though practicing yoga, in order to receive "the Force." Yet, unlike Lessing's characters who guide and are guided according to the Sufi body of knowledge, Luke, R2-D2, or Leia are obligated to no particular system of thought, and they have no perceptible spiritual goals beyond gaining *physical* command over the galaxy.

Lessing's characters are in outer space because they have exhausted their possibilities on earth, which, Lessing warns us, can become our fate, if we do not take heed. In Lessing's space fiction, extraterrestrial characters are spiritually superior to their counterparts in most other science-fiction plots, by the mere fact that they serve as mimetic models as well as serving their synthetic and thematic functions. Lessing implies that they are masters or seekers on the Sufi Path. Any commentary Lessing's narrators make is not concerned with the identifiable politics of a particular nation. Rather, she offers a developed theology. There is a method to her madness. While much science fiction is overtly anti-religious, and more specifically anti-Christian or sometimes pagan in orientation, Lessing promotes Sufism, a sophisticated and complex tradition that competes with Christianity.

Much serious science fiction has a much greater sense of the contingencies of history than does Lessing's space fiction. Science fiction offers an investigation of technological developments, the real possibilities of connections between time and motion, and the human ability to control the future—all, potentially, by means that are accessible to the human mind and that fall within the limits of human potential and the laws of physics. Outer space, science, and technology provide writers of science fiction with fresh artistic possibilities and a brand new stage on which to stretch the human potential. This is also telling in the professions of some science-fiction writers, such as the Polish writer Stanislav Lem, the best-known representative of European science fiction, who is a medical doctor, or Ursula Le Guin, who is an anthropologist, like her parents. Science fiction offers them a way to combine all that they have learned, as it was so clearly the case with Mary Shelley in the previous century. Comparing her own work to Stanislav Lem's, Lessing has commented, "Of course I don't really write science fiction. I've just read a book by the *Solaris* bloke, Stanislav Lem. Now that's real classic science fiction . . . full of scientific ideas" (Frick 159).

When Lessing turned to outer space, she appears to have done so in order to increase the spiritual and psychological possibilities of her characters. Some science-fiction writers do resemble Lessing in their spiritual slant; but more writers seem to have turned to science fiction to solve social, political, and psychological problems posed by human limitations on earth. Many seem to have turned to science fiction because they were looking for creative ways to "fix" the disintegration they felt around them by plunging into cosmic distances. When the earth that had satisfied Shakespeare for a stage became crowded and restricted, science-fiction writers seem to have turned to outer space as their new stage—or as their brand new laboratory where the artist/scientist could carry out experiments yet untried. These offered potential solutions to problems that were created by humans in the first place, such as environmental issues, political dilemmas, and the consequences of scientific breakthroughs; they did not imagine new human beings created in *God's image*, but new scenarios under predictable circumstances, given the *laws of nature*. While this certainly is not to be dismissed as insignificant, it did not free humans from their fate: characters still loved, suffered, fought, and died, "bound by the same laws of pain, love, and death, no matter what space suits [they wore] or what utopias [they built]" (Baranczak 155).

Lessing's use of outer space appears not only to be for aesthetic and stylistic reasons. She can also envision psychological levels of being or Sufi states of consciousness, and she gives these levels and states actual geographical and spatial locations. For example Al·Ith must live in outer space so that Lessing can expand her spiritual possibilities beyond the limits of ordinary human existence.[11] Lessing's characters may have limited mimetic characteristics, but they serve as believable Sufi models in addition to their thematic and synthetic functions. Although the famous Luke Skywalker of *Star Wars* may be oblivious of planet Earth, he is still prone to human failures, his lot is still cast with that of the human race, he is still a mere earthling. His earthly life is inevitable. He walks the skies and flies in his spaceship only because it is so much fun to do so, fun for us to fantasize about, and fun to watch. "The Force" may be with him, but his travels are not aimed at Nirvana nor a union with Allah, while Al·Ith, Johor, or Emily's goals can be read as the Sufi Path to enlightenment.

In a 1987 interview Lessing told Thomas Frick that she was invited to be the guest of honor at the World Science-Fiction Convention in Brighton, England (158–59). She interpreted this gesture to signal a breaking down of the strictly defined boundaries between science and religion that guard the genre. At the same time, she was impressed by the number of people at the convention who came up to her to ask what she was doing there, when surely she was not a science-fiction writer. While this boundary maintenance is clearly intact in all disciplines and trades, one of the many reasons for which we admire Lessing has to do precisely with the boldness with which she oversteps boundaries, tries new forms, and crosses over to places where she is not completely welcome—at first. She can do this because she refuses labels—she wants to be no more a science-fiction writer than she had once accepted being a feminist writer.

When Lessing writes of a new human species that rises out of the ashes of the apocalypse at the end of *The Four-Gated City*, she does not create fantastic plots, but seems to envision the Sufi ideal. For instance, she names the wise black child who is born with the collective knowledge of mankind and with higher powers of perception, "Joseph," reminding us of the biblical and Qur'ânic Joseph who overcomes the evil jealousy of his brothers to become a king (according to all of the three Abrahamic traditions) and also a prophet (in the Islamic tradition). In Lessing's version, too, Joseph is a Prophet. Like the Joseph of Judaism who is a descendant of Adam through the line of Jacob, Isaiah, and Abraham, and heir to the Jews' covenant with God, Lessing's Joseph is a carrier of the genealogical line of the "chosen" human race at the end of *The Four-Gated City*. Just as the biblical and Qur'ânic Joseph could tap into God's thoughts through dreaming and through his ability to interpret dreams, Lessing's Joseph is born with the knowledge and consciousness of all of humanity already in him, as though he had read God's mind. He is the new Adam who will work as a gardener to cultivate the postapocalyptic earth. There are other children like Joseph who are born after the world cataclysm, who can both "see" and "hear," and, as Lessing's narrator tells us, these children "don't have to be shielded from the knowledge of what the human race is in this century—they know it . . . they are beings who include that history in themselves and who have transcended it" (647)—a theme also used in Arthur C. Clarke's science-fiction novel *Childhood's End*. In a 1969 interview with Studs Terkel, Lessing commented that "it's possible that we're changing into people with greater capacities for imagination, and that we are going to be regarded as the 'missing link,' the transition people, and we'll have much better people" (30).

If Joseph in the Qur'ân represented the active surrender (*islam*) of Muslims to God's plan, Lessing's Joseph represents the moderns' last resort in him to facilitate a new beginning on earth. Martha Quest writes to Francis Coldridge at the conclusion of *The Four-Gated City*, "Joseph, the black child, will come to your settlement near Nairobi, and you will look after him. So he says. He says more like them are being born now in hidden places in the world and one day all the human race will be like them. People like you and me are a sort of experimental model and Nature has had enough of us" (648). That this Joseph has more in common with the Joseph in the scriptures than with the usual science-fiction super heroes supports the argument in this chapter that Lessing is more spiritually (than scientifically) driven.

Conclusion

This book's aim has been to clarify the reasons why the spiritual strand of Lessing's arguments must not be overlooked, because what we have here deserves interfaith (Muslim and Judeo-Christian), interdisciplinary (psychological, anthropological, philosophical, theological, literary), and cross-cultural (Eastern and Western) interpretations. Lessing wears many hats and negotiates many angles at the same time: at least two faiths (Eastern mysticism and Western humanism/materialism), two worlds (East and West), multiple directions on the compass, many continents, and several genres (novel, novella, fairy tale, teaching story, space fiction, fantasy). Rûmî's quatrain may help us appreciate the degree of the significance of Sufism in Lessing's work. It points out the worlds of difference that something or someone can make in one's state of being.

> When I am with you, we stay up all night.
> When you're not here, I can't go to sleep.
> Praise God for these two insomnias!
> And the difference between them. (*Open Secret* 6)

In the Sufi poet's case, the difference between these two insomnias is his Beloved Allah. Whether he has his Beloved with him makes a difference in *how* he doesn't sleep all night. In Lessing's case, the difference is Sufism.

The above distinction of Joseph's identity is crucial to locating Lessing's novels between the literature of the Sufis from the East and modern literature in the West, as well as between spirituality and science in literature. For centuries, Sufi literature and tradition have been in existence in the Muslim world, preferred by scholars and historians of Islam as the "classical" version of Sufism and referred to more accurately as *tasawwuf*. Classical Sufi poetry consists of predominantly autobiographical love poems that bemoan the mystical poets' anguish in the absence of their Beloved and express their exhiliration at the moment of enlightenment and union with the Beloved. The version of Sufism encountered in Lessing has a *different* flavor to it. If not devotional, it is modern, relevant,

185

and applicable to contemporary life. If not real-life testimonies such as those about Rûmî's love for Allah, it is *fictionalized autobiography* that is based on a combination of *all* that Lessing has learned—from Communism to Eastern religions, of which Sufi thought constitutes a recent layer.

A reasonable compromise, therefore, would be to read Lessing wearing metaphorical bifocals, for she insists on straddling East and West, tradition and modernism, spirituality and science, intuition and logic, and fantasy and realism. With her characteristic didactic urge, she demonstrates that it is *imperative* to seek understanding both rationally, in the external world of statistical truths, and intuitively, in the dreams and myths of one's own mind and heart, the latter being the only place where anyone—from the East *or* West—has ever found the Beloved.

Part IV

Appendixes

Appendix A

Tasawwuf in Islam

Many are now willing to accept the Islamic origin of Sufism and the unbreakable link connecting Sufism to Islam, rather than following the older practice of explaining Sufism away as some kind of alien influence within Islam.

—Seyyed Hossein Nasr,
Sufi Essays

Nasrudin found a weary falcon sitting one day on his window-sill. He had never seen a bird of this kind before.

"You poor thing," he said, "how ever were you allowed to get into this state?"

He clipped the falcon's talons and cut its beak straight, and trimmed its feathers.

"Now you look more like a bird," said Nasrudin.

—Idries Shah, The Exploits
of the Incomparable
Mulla Nasrudin

According to scholars of Islam, *tasawwuf,** or the classical Sufi Way, has undergone a trimming process similar to that inflicted

---

*All foreign terms that appear here are Arabic unless otherwise indicated.

by Nasrudin on the falcon in the above story, a trimming inflicted both intentionally and unintentionally in an effort to make it accessible to the moderns. They argue that, in spite of what the moderns have done with *tasawwuf* in both the East and the West, it has a long history, integrity, and power competitive with what the moderns have labeled "Sufism." This discussion elaborates on that history.[1]

Marilyn Waldman likens the history of *tasawwuf* to the footpaths on college campuses that students form through the dirt and grass.[2] After years of being trodden by students who choose the best way to travel between classes, paths emerge through grass lawns until eventually the administration notices the rows of trampled grass and packed-down dirt and acknowledges their use by laying asphalt or concrete. Walkways are thus established where footpaths used to be. This is how the various Sufi orders were established and assigned to a master who was long dead; it is also how the history of *tasawwuf* was traced: in retrospect. Furthermore, whereas it may take colleges and universities a year or two to lay down a walkway, it took Sufis centuries to concretize a "Way." For this reason, among others, talking about the Sufi tradition as if it were a single or tangible phenomenon is impossible. Hodgson writes, the Sufi tradition dominated the whole inner life of Islam (1: 394). Therefore, the following historical background of Islam is offered here to contextualize *tasawwuf* within the Muslim framework.

The faith of Islam, or surrender of one's will to the will of God, was revealed to the prophet Muhammad in Mecca in the Arabian peninsula from 610 C.E. until Muhammad's death in Medina in 632 C.E. Because of the direct manner in which the Qur'ân (lit., "revelations") was revealed to Muhammad, Sufi mystics, who are known for their aspirations for direct communion with Allah, upheld the Qur'ân as the supreme authority to guide them. Allah's speaking to man *directly* was proof enough for them that direct access to him is possible (Arberry, *Sufism* 13). So long as the prophet Muhammad was alive, the first Muslims who composed the Muslim community (*Ummah*) were able to rely upon his connection with God through the Qur'ân. However, upon Muhammad's death, the Muslim community encountered questions that had not been an issue before: What is a good Muslim? What is a good caliph or *khalîfah* (deputy or successor)? What constitutes a true community? What is piety? What is sin? In trying to find answers, several factions developed within Islam, and these questions were fought out for a century and a half. Sufis offered one of the many answers to these questions.

Four caliphs ruled after Muhammad: Abû-Bakr (ruled 632–34), 'Umar (ruled 634–44), 'Uthmân (ruled 644–56), and 'Alî (ruled 656–61). The latter two were assassinated as a direct result of disagreements over answers to the above questions. Their successors, the Umayyads (ruled 661–92) and the Marwanids (ruled 692–750), were accused of being too worldly and of practicing *bid'ah* or "innovation" instead of striving to follow the Qur'ân and Muhammad's example to the last detail, and were overthrown in 750 by the 'Abbâsids who claimed *nass*, or "authority," from Abû-Hâshim of the Hâshimite line who left his authority, at his death, to Muhammad b. 'Alî of the 'Abbâsid line. The 'Abbâsids claimed direct descent from the prophet Muhammad's uncle 'Abbâs and called themselves the Ahl al-Bayt, or "people of the house [of the Prophet]." They were accepted by "a majority," or Jamâ'î-Sunnî, as absolute heirs to the caliphate, since like Muhammad in the first century of Islam, they were successful in uniting the *Ummah*, or "the community of Muslims."

However, the original questions that had divided the community at Muhammad's death still were not successfully answered, and unrest persisted. A minority of Muslims, the Shî'ah (party [of 'Alî]), believed that only 'Alî (Muhammad's nephew and the fourth caliph) and his line of descendants (*imams*) could carry the divine light of God, and therefore, that the "right" ruler could only be chosen from among 'Alî's family.

As a result of the Muslims' search for a precise knowledge of right and wrong in the eyes of God, it became necessary to develop an independent body of sacred law (Sharî'ah) and several schools of thought (*madhhab*s) came into being. The basic intention of all *madhhab*s was to arrive at God's will and, from that, at correct behavior: if Muslims were to surrender (*islam*), they needed an exact law to which to surrender. In order to arrive at such a law, a variety of *fiqh*s, or "proper legal understanding," were devised to understand God's commandments for correct behavior. For instance, since the Qur'ân said to "fear God and look to Muhammad," reports of what Muhammad had said or done during his lifetime (*hadîth*) were collected and recorded, together with a careful recording of *isnâd*s, or "the chain of names of all the transmitters of each *hadîth* report." For Sufis, as for all Muslims, the recorded *hadîth* served as their second source of guidance after the Qur'ân.

Muslims also turned to *ijmâ'*, or "consensus," of how the Muslim community in Pristine Medina during the first century of Islam behaved, since in the *hadîth*, Muhammad was quoted to have said that "Muslims will never agree on a mistake." Finally, *ijtihâd*, or "personal reasoning," was added onto these three sources, in order to allow the *faqîh*, or "legal scholars," room to make analogies (*qiyâs*) between a circumstance and one of the three sources for guidance. Within a short time the Sharî'ah and religious scholars ('*ulamâ*'; sing. '*âlim*) became very authoritative, having a say on every aspect of life from personal hygiene to worship.

The ninth century saw a new development: *Falsafah*, or "philosophy," was devised by an elite group of philosophers (*Faylasûf*) who asserted that God was pure reason, that humans could achieve that same pure reason through using their rational capacity, and that the philosophic search was the truest way of honoring and worshipping God.

Out of the challenge of the *Faylasûf*s and in reaction to the zealous followers of the Sharî'ah, there developed a countermovement, the Mu'tazilî disputation called *kalâm*, or "systematic theological discourse." The rationalistic Mu'tazilites argued that the Qur'ân was not co-eternal with God, and therefore the Sharî'ah was not divine; the Qur'ân, created in time—that is, created in *this* world—was open to interpretation. Naturally, this position gave the 'Abbâsid caliphs free rein to interpret "God's commands" as best suited their personal interests. However, although the Mu'tazilî movement became the official position endorsed by a series of 'Abbâsid caliphs, beginning with al-Ma'mûn (ruled 813–33), it lost its popularity after a short time.

The last resort of Muslims wishing to reconcile the nature of God, the nature of the Qur'ân, and their relationship to each other was to exercise *bila kayfah*. Meaning "without regard to the how," this term was coined by al-Ash'arî (d. 935). By it Ash'arî expressed his conclusion that some things cannot be explained by human reason, and divine intention is one of them. God's will was to be *accepted*, not disputed—which, after all, was the meaning of the act of *islam*: surrender to a higher will. And it was widely agreed that while it was true that God has superior intelligence, it was equally true that humans do not have access to that intelligence. Hence, as in all monotheistic religions, a gap still remained between God and humans. It is this gap that Sufis claimed to overcome. They sought intimacy with Allah directly.

The mystical movement in Islam sprang out of asceticism. During the late seventh and early eighth centuries, ascetics such as Hasan al-Basrî (d. 728) emerged in Islamdom. He was a pious Muslim who, influenced by Christian asceticism, practiced *zuhd*, or rejection of the world, and preached that the life of an ascetic is the only way to achieve God's intimacy while living on earth—an abhorrent and a hateful place in God's eyes. And when, a century later, Muslims began to refer to themselves as "Sufis," Hasan al-Basrî was dubbed "the first Sufi" in Islam.

Equally important to Sufis in hindsight was Râbi'ah al-'Adawiyyah of Basrah (d. 801), who formulated the Sufi ideal of ecstatic love for God. Also a pious Muslim and an ascetic like al-Basrî, she was a strict vegetarian, trusted and loved by animals. Her ideal of an ecstatic and disinterested love of God soon developed into a major Way of the Sufis, the Drunken Way, which welcomed those who were intoxicated in their love for God, and who had forsaken their earthly senses for this love. Râbi'ah also became a significant figure in the history of Islam as the first female mystic to be recognized. An anecdote about her describes her running through the streets with a jug of water in one hand, a fiery torch in the other. She is said to have exclaimed that she intended to put out the flames of Hell and to burn up the gardens of Paradise so that "people should no longer worship God from fear of Hell or desire for Paradise, but only from love of God Himself" (Hodgson 1: 402).

Sufi practice allowed a place for Muslimas (Muslim women) and offered them the only religious sphere within Islam where they could find a voice. Although Sufi associations (*tarîqah*[s], lit. "the Way") were by definition male-clubs, women could enroll as associates and could be appointed as leaders to organize women's circles, even though female circles never developed into independent *tarîqah*s or orders. On Fridays in many locales, the contrast between male and female religious practices became apparent: while the men went to pray at the mosque, the women visited the local saint's tomb and made offerings and petitions to the spirit of the saint.

The fluidity of the early Muslim population must be kept in mind when considering the lives of the various Sufis during the eighth century. The mobility of Sufis and the degree to which they traveled necessitated retreats or hospices to accommodate wanderers seeking a master. By the eleventh and twelfth centuries, these gatherings at rest-houses focused around a particular master (*shaikh*) and looked to the master in a new way, which resulted in a shift in orientation: now mystics were not simply gathering at rest-houses, but were gathering around a master. The hostel (and later school) building consisted of a central courtyard with cloisters along two sides, within which were situated cells where Sufis slept. On one side was the main hall, where devotional exercises took place and where the *shaikh* usually sat on a sheepskin, observing the exercises. A separate mosque contained the kitchens and offices, and sometimes a bath-house. These retreats have been called *zâwiyah* in Arabic, *khâniqâh* in Persian, and *dergâh* or *tekke* in Turkish. Their evolution into spiritual schools from the eighth century on has been a major step in the institutionalization of *tasawwuf* in Islam.

As the nature of the retreats changed, they became *tarîqah*s or "schools" which were handed down from one master through *silsilah*, or "a spiritual pedigree," to another. In this manner, the spiritual heirs and successors (*khalîfah*s) who claimed to have inherited the *barakah* (blessedness) of the great *shaikh* could theoretically keep a mystical school (*tarîqah*) alive for centuries after the original master had died. The step toward congregating at retreats also required a change in the nature of the adherents of *tasawwuf*. Whereas earlier Sufis might have been hermits, isolating themselves from the world, now Sufis constituted a large body of visible people in Islamdom. Later Sufis lived quite ordinary lives and became active members of society, even occupying positions in politics.

Two strains of Sufi practice were identifiable during the late eighth and early ninth centuries. One was that of Abû-Yazîd al-Bistâmî (d. 874), an important figure whose Way, like Râbi'ah's, was rapture, ecstasy, and intoxication. He pursued unity with God through being "drunk" with love. The other was that of Abû'l Qasim al-Junayd (d. 910), who, during approximately the same time period, taught sobriety, self-possession, and control. The Sober Way, since it was more in accordance with the Sharî'ah, was more widely adopted by Sufi *shaikh*s. Even those orders which were heterodox in their Ways claimed Junayd as their ancestor. The Malâmatiyyah movement (Blameworthy Ones) represented a variation of

Bistâmî's Way. Its members not only rejected the "self" but also deliberately worked to attract humiliation. For example, Bistâmî himself is known to have eaten bread in public during Ramadan, the month of fasting. While this was legal for him because he was on a trip, the crowd only saw the fast-breaking and abandoned him (Hodgson 1: 398). Although these distinguishing factors appeared to establish a variety of "Ways," according to Hodgson, the Sufis still were reasonably homogenous and they even kept in mutual contact despite the fact that they were dispersed throughout Islamdom (1: 393).

Sufis varied somewhat in terms of the *degree* to which they adhered to the Sharî'ah. While some of them followed it closely, others ignored it, and still others carried out its commands to an excess: for instance, if required to pray five times a day, they did it ten times, the result being as antinomian as not praying at all. They differed considerably in type of worship and direction: sobriety, dream world, ecstatic intoxication, asceticism, retreat, austerity, worldliness, use of drugs, dance, fasting, self-mutilation, prayer, and various breathing exercises. These were tried and practiced in order to induce perfect union with God. A common trait of the Sufis was their ability to believe in and to perform supernatural feats. These included eating live snakes, extinguishing flames in their mouths, entering blazing ovens, walking barefoot on hot coals, or mutilating themselves with knives without suffering physical harm. These acts were intended to demonstrate their victory of spiritual command over their flesh.

This kind of innovation seemed to call for orthodox behavior, and the tenth and eleventh centuries saw a growth in the number of Sufi theorists. As Arberry puts it, "the need produced the men and the men produced the books eminently suitable for the purpose" (*Sufism* 66). The earliest manuals on Sufi theory were treatises and guides on manners and practice for the *shaikh* and his pupils. They showed how the Sufi ritual was "now a traced-out Way, a rule of life, by following which the novice [could] attain union with God, founded upon a series of observances additional to the common ritual and duties of Islam" (Trimmingham 29). While they were instructive, however, these manuals were very tedious to read. Nonetheless, during less liberal times in the history of Islam, Sufis could survive, provided they curbed their zeal for an individual expression of Allah's presence in their lives and behaved according to the laws governing Islam as interpreted by the theorists.

At the end of the eleventh century, Muhammad al-Ghazzâlî (d. 1111) somewhat reconciled the differences between orthodox Muslims and Sufis by carefully and skeptically studying *fiqh* (discipline of elucidating the Sharî'ah), *kalâm* (theological discourse), *Falsafah* (philosophy), Ismâ'îlî Shî'î thought (believing in an absent imam or leader), natural sciences, and *tasawwuf*. The conclusion which al-Ghazzâlî reached in his great compendium, *Ihyâ' 'Ulûm al-Dîn* (The revival of the religious sciences), was that the Sufis' intimacy and deep love for God had to be combined with Sharî'ah. Reflection and meditation could become a part of the religious life of Muslims without threatening their practices. This conclusion helped to legitimate the Sufi Path, so that, by the twelfth century, mysticism was fully recognized by the *'ulamâ'*, the legal and religious scholars.

When the Sufi Way was thus legitimized, there evolved an important division of labor in Islam: the Sharî'ah and the *'ulamâ'* who enforced it directed the outward activities of Muslims, while the Sufis assumed responsibility for the inner life. Although both groups looked to Muhammad, the former stressed Muhammad's role as revealer, concerning outward law, while the latter stressed his role as friend and intimate (*walî*) of God, concerning inner grace. Furthermore, while the *'ulamâ'* taught *islam*, or surrender to God, Sufis taught *'ishq*, or love of God.

The earliest formally organized *tarîqah* that is known to us is the Qâdiriyyah order, which gathered around the figure of Muhyi al-Din 'Abd al-Qâdir b. 'Abd Allah al-Gilani (d. 1166),

who was from Gilan, Persia. The Qâdiriyyah became especially powerful in India. While the earlier groups were loose
organizations held together by enthusiasm and a common
devotion, the *silsilah-tarîqah*s were more formally organized
and united by a structured *shaikh-murîd* (elder-disciple) relationship. In this relationship, all members clearly consented to
following the Way, or *tarîqah*, of the founder and his spiritual
ancestry as listed in the *silsilah* (pedigree, or chain of transmission of knowledge). It was not uncommon for a Sufi order to
trace its origins back to the prophet Muhammad.

During the time of the Seljuks in Anatolia (12th cent.),
Sufis began to practice the Shî'ite custom of *bai'a*, or initiation
with an oath of allegiance to the *shaikh*. A simple *bai'a* used in
the Shâdhilî *tarîqah* (order of the Shâdhilîs), for instance,
would run thus: "O God, I have repented before Thee, and
accept as my teacher *Shaikh* X as my *shaikh* in this world and
in the next, as guide and leader to Thy Presence, and as director (*murshid*) in Thy Path. I will disobey him neither in word
nor in deed, neither overtly nor covertly. Confirm me, O God, in
obedience to him and his *tarîqah* in this world and the next,
and in the *tarîqah* of the *shaikh* of *shaikh*s and *imm* of *imm*s,
the *Qutb* [pole or axis] of the community, my Lord Abû'l-Hasan
ash-Shâdhilî, God be pleased with him!" (Trimmingham
186–87).

Also during the twelfth century, an association between
the Sufis and the *futuwwah* orders became apparent. The
futuwwah were groups of chivalrous young men who modeled
themselves after the figure of 'Alî. 'Alî was Muhammad's
nephew who later also became Muhammad's son-in-law and
the fourth caliph. Especially in the eyes of his partisans, the
Shî'ah, 'Alî was believed to embody the characteristics of
courage, generosity, endurance of suffering, love of truth, hos-
pitality, and aiding the weak. The young men who looked to
'Alî as their ideal gathered in groups, or *futuwwah*, that sub-
stituted for lack of official institutions of protection in
Islamdom. They resembled certain men's voluntary organiza-

tions. Sufi orders were also connected with occupational guild organizations which were involved with craftsmanship or trade, somewhat similar to the Masons. They in fact styled themselves after the hierarchical structure of the guilds which had a grand-master, master-craftsmen, and apprentices. Similarly, the religious orders established a hierarchy of masters, initiates, and novices. The members of a particular *tarîqah* often were also members of a certain futuwwah and/or a guild. Hence, with the more formal arrangement of the orders, *tasawwuf* became not only a legitimate spiritual activity, but also a vocation.

The second formally organized order after the Qâdiriyyah was the Suhrawardiyyah, which claimed its beginnings with Shihâb al-Din 'Umar b. 'Abd Allah al-Suhrawardî (d. 1234). Some say the movement really began with the uncle Diya' addin Abû Najib as-Suhrawardî (d. 1168), who taught his nephew the *Hadîth*. This is a typical example of the way in which many Sufi orders were formed generations later, in retrospect, requiring some guessing with regard to the origins of a teaching. The founders of many Sufi orders were recognized retroactively when a group of men had gathered around a *shaikh* and had devised a *silsilah* (pedigree) of their spiritual ancestry going back to the designated founder. Furthermore, any *silsilah* was also always connected back to either al-Bistâmî or al-Junayd of the tenth century, who were credited with establishing the two main Ways among the Sufis: (1) the Drunken and (2) the Sober Way, respectively.

Other Sufi orders which emerged were the Shâdhiliyyah, the Mawlawiyyah (known in the West as the Whirling Dervishes), the Rifa'iyyah, the Yasaviyyah, the Kubrawiyyah, the Chishtiyyah, and the Naqshbandiyyah. Once these Ways or *tarîqah*s had been formed, all subsequent *tarîqah*s claimed to be derivatives of one or more of them. The forming of the derivatives depended on disciples who returned to their own countries after their training and founded daughter institutions. Once established, they usually developed in their own Ways and broke ties with the mother institution. Thus by the fifteenth and sixteenth centuries, a traveler would be certain to come upon one or another *tarîqah* anywhere he went.

The experiences of a newcomer at a *tarîqah* would basically require his complete faith in the *shaikh*'s knowledge and guidance. The master's task was to open the eyes of the adept (*murîd*) and to act as a physician of the soul. Although different Sufi orders had their own distinctive Ways for initiating and training a newcomer, they basically followed a similar succession of events. First, the master tested the adept to determine his willingness to undergo the hardships that awaited him. There were numerous methods for testing the future Sufi: usually, this took the form of three years of service—"one year in the service of the people, one in the service of God, and one year in watching over his own heart" (Schimmel 101), at the end of which it was decided whether one could be accepted for tutelage. These years were spent doing such tasks as begging, cleaning latrines, carrying water, and so forth; the aim of this was to develop humility and discipline.

After these three years, the adept could receive the patched robe (*khirqa*) as a badge of admission into the particular Sufi order. This was a dark blue robe formerly worn or touched by the blessed master or *shaikh*. After receiving this robe, the novice was called an aspirant or an initiate. By being in contact with an object belonging to his master, he was said to acquire some of the master's mystical blessed power (*baraka*). At this point the initiate was required to go into a forty-day seclusion in a dark room which simulated a tomb, and his robe, a shroud, the experience aiming to help the initiate to change his consciousness deeply.

There were also special cases of Sufis who were said not to be initiated by a human guide or *shaikh*, but to be touched spiritually by the prophet Muhammad or rescued from the wilderness by the immortal prophet Khidr, a servant of God and companion of Moses, said to have drunk from the water of eternal life. Khidr is the patron saint of travelers, always cloaked in green, the color being symbolic of the life force in him. He was adopted by Muslims from the Zoroastrian tradition and is associated with the coming of summer. In some Middle Eastern countries, May 6 is celebrated by building bonfires at night and jumping over the fires all night long in memory of the prophet Khidr.

After being initiated either through a *shaikh* or through more mystical means, the student followed three basic steps which led him to God: the first was Islamic law (Sharî'ah). Since "no path [could] exist without a main road from which it branche[d] out, no mystical experience [could] be realized if the binding injunctions of the Sharî'ah [were] not followed faithfully first" (Schimmel 98). Sufi thought did not abolish the external laws, but rather followed an inner consciousness which was an internalization of external rites and commands. Hence Sufis performed the ritual prayer, fasting, recitation of the Qur'ân, giving of alms to the poor, and pilgrimage to Mecca which the Islamic law or Sharî'ah commanded, and they often added more laws to the Sharî'ah, making even more exacting demands on themselves. According to Hodgson, "the Sufis' starting point was ever the Qur'ân, whose inward meanings they explored, attempting to get behind the surface of the words" (1: 394). Ultimately, they hoped to experience what Muhammad must have experienced when he received the words of God, and "to relive the spiritual states out of which the words [of the Qur'ân] had been formed" (1: 395).

The second step the initiate took to reach God was the Path (*tarîqah*), less concretely defined, more difficult to follow: one wandered through different levels of being or stations (*maqâm*), and experienced various states of consciousness (*hâl*), which are gifts of God (or insights) that come unbidden after much work and suffering on the path (Schimmel 98). After this, the third step was taken, which was the ability to see the truth or reality (*haqîqa*) that God is One. It was at this stage that many Sufis were accused of committing heresy by declaring that they were one with God, which was misinterpreted to mean they were God. For example Mansur al-Hallâj (d. 922), one of the most visible and powerful exponents of *tasawwuf* during the tenth century, was perceived to be a threat to the authority of the 'Abbâsid caliphate and to orthodoxy for preaching his faith publicly and for exclaiming, "I am God." He was arrested and brutally put to death, his martyrdom thus becoming a symbol of the conflict between orthodox Muslims who chose to follow the Sharî'ah, and Sufis who chose to subordinate the Sharî'ah to a more individualistic inner light.

By the thirteenth century the Sufi schools were forming not only around a master or a rest house, but around the *barakah*, or blessedness of a place, person, or tomb, so that blessedness itself began to be institutionalized. A result of this transition was that when a great *shaikh* died, and sometimes even while he was alive, he was venerated as a saint or *walî*, and members began building shrines around saints' tombs, starting a new trend of pilgrimage. This activity further incorporated the belief that the material of which the tomb was built must be holy too, and people began chipping away at the concrete gravestones, or picking at the cloth coverings over a tomb in order to carry away some *barakah* (blessedness) with them.

It was in connection with the institutionalization of *barakah* and the belief in Sufi saints that the Sufis declared the prophet Muhammad to have been the "first Sufi." They reasoned that a true *walî* or saint does not necessarily know that he is one. Therefore, just as they were assigning sainthood to their dead *shaikh*s, so they also nurtured a reverence for Muhammad's sainthood and made sure that their *silsilah*s (or spiritual pedigrees) were traced back to the prophet Muhammad. Some in fact claimed to have been commanded in a dream by Muhammad to found a new *tarîqah*. This added further legitimacy to *tasawwuf* within Islam.

During the fifteenth century, along with the growth of the Ottoman Empire, the Sufi *tarîqah*s had become very influential in the arts. They were the inspiration for a vast and rich tradition of poetry and music, written in Arabic, Persian, Turkish, and Urdu, both in the educated and sophisticated circles and in simpler spheres. When the ruling classes of the Ottoman Empire divided into the men of the sword and men of learning in the sixteenth century, the Sufis were the only reconciling factor between these two contrasting groups of citizens. During this time it was they, and not the *'ulamâ'* (religious and legal scholars), who were the significant representatives of religion; and it was the shrine, not the mosque, that was the symbol of Islam (Trimmingham 67).

Scholars of classical Sufism in general regard such popularization of the brotherhoods as the beginning of the decline in the *authenticity* of mystical feeling. According to Trimmingham, by the eighteenth century, every Muslim male may have been a member of at least one brotherhood whose intent was to spread the Sufi message, recruit more members, and to engage in social service. That they were more involved in the practical rather than the spiritual activities of a brotherhood is viewed by Islamicists as their having been interested in attaining ecstasy for its own sake only, and not as the means to achieving God's intimacy. Trimmingham writes, members even seemed to blame the *tarîqah*s for fettering their creative freedom, binding them to a series of mystical terminology, disciplines, and exercises (103). There emerged many writings of hagiographies and collections of saints which may have taken away from inner practice, and it seemed to have become too easy to establish an order and to claim the rights to its leadership.

To continue the history of *tasawwuf* according to Islamicists, that is, to give the classical model, the nineteenth century saw several revival movements among the Sufi brotherhoods in an attempt to rekindle the extinguishing frenzy of mysticism within Islam. At the same time, the secularization and modernization of Muslim nations was forcing the immediate disappearance of Sufi orders from the popular scene. In

203

İstanbul, for instance, the declaration of the Turkish Republic in 1920 was accompanied by the disappearance from the public eye of seventeen *tarîqah*s which were housed in 258 *tekke*s or hostels and many more smaller groups which used to meet in private homes (Trimmingham 253). By 1925, all Sufi orders in İstanbul either had dispersed or had gone underground. Likewise in Iran, the predominantly Westward-looking public ridiculed and rejected Sufi practice. Similar changes in attitude took place in the rest of Islamdom as well, especially in orthodox Muslim countries. In Saudi Arabia, where fundamentalist Wahhabi Muslims predominate, Sufism is either unheard of or deeply hidden. Still, there is much serious activity within the surviving Sufi orders in Islamdom. In Pakistan, Sufi masters continue to practice and to have a healthy following. The 1961 Lahore District Census Report states:

> *Pir*s [Sufi saint and healer] are held in great esteem and respect by villagers who pay quarterly, half-yearly or annual visits to their *murîd*s [disciples] and get *nazrana*s [offerings] in the form of cash, or clothes according to the economic status of the follower. Besides the living *Pir*s, the people have great faith in the *Pir*s who died centuries ago and attend their shrines at the time of their annual *Ur*s [death anniversary festival]. The hold of the *Pir*s is gradually dying away. (*Population*, qtd. in Ewing 2)

This passage at once acknowledges and denies the existence of ongoing Sufism, at least in Pakistan. As Katherine Ewing writes, it represents modernist discourse that "sets up a series of dichotomies in what today appears a naive celebration of modernity: tradition vs. modernity, rural vs. urban, and (implicitly) wasted economic resources vs. economic rationality" (3). This is, nonetheless, what has been happening to Sufism within "modernizing" nations.

In studying these changes, it is important to note that the development of Sufi thought and practice has been very much in character with its metaphysical orientation toward time, and its dependence on the inner life of each individual. As a result, what has come to be called "Sufism" today derives from much retroactive labeling and reshaping of past persons and events. This process of revision contributed to the limitless varieties which continue to manifest themselves in an infinite number of Sufi guides and orders. Thus even though *Sufism* as an abstraction implies a degree of coherence, there still persists diversity and individualization of the Ways of Sufis. Therein lies the resistance to definition of a teaching that is alive.

Appendix B

Scholarship on Lessing's Mysticism

Please see the bibliography for the full publication data on the following works.

1970s

Clarence W. Richey's "Professor Watkins' 'Sleep of Necessity'" (1972) is a Gurdjieffian evaluation of *Briefing*. Here Richey likens Professor Watkins's sleep to the "asleep" state discussed in George Ivanovich Gurdjieff's system. Furthermore, he sees a resemblance between Lessing's style in *Briefing* and Gurdjieff's *All and Everything*.

"The Sufi Quest" (1973) by Dee Seligman discusses the development of new organs as a result of the Sufi quest in *Landlocked* and *The Four-Gated City*.

Nancy Shields Hardin facilitates our acceptance of Lessing's Sufism in "Doris Lessing and The Sufi Way" (1973) in which she discusses *The Four-Gated City*, *Briefing*, and the *Jack Orkney* collection and introduces the concept of awakening that is central to Sufism.

In "Conscious Evolution in *The Four-Gated City*" (1974) M. Susan Lewis applies Sufi concepts to *The Four-Gated City*. These include destiny, free will, and surrender, as well as the universality of individual experience and the interconnectedness of all evolution, individual, or cosmic. Lewis explains these concepts through her study of Martha Quest and the Coleridge family.

APPENDIXES

Hardin's "The Sufi Teaching Story and Doris Lessing" (1977) compares Lessing's works to parables and concludes that, like the Sufi teaching stories, Lessing's novels can be used as tools to change our thought processes.

Judith Stitzel's "Reading Doris Lessing" (1979) defends Lessing's mysticism against charges of self-indulgence. Stitzel, like the Sufis, is able to comprehend the real meaning of the rational mind and of reason, when she argues that reason is more than limited and fixed logic. She brings fresh air to the subject of Lessing's mysticism, which some fear to be totally irrational, and she illustrates what Sufis call "Learning How to Learn"—a phrase that Shah used as a title for one of his books.

1980s

"The More Recent Writings: Sufism, Mysticism, and Politics" (1982) by Ann Scott is a formalist reading of Lessing's use of religious language in *The Four-Gated City* and *Memoirs*.

"Sufism in Doris Lessing" (1983) by Sarla Kumar is an insightful study of the states of consciousness of the characters in *The Four-Gated City*, *The Golden Notebook*, and *Briefing*.

"Doris Lessing et le Soufisme (*Shikasta* et *The Marriages between Zones Three, Four, and Five*)" (1983) by Cecile Oumhani offers a synopsis of Sufism in the novels of Doris Lessing, beginning with *Landlocked* and including the *Canopus in Argos* series.

Another article that is partly about Lessing's mysticism is "The Evolution of Doris Lessing's Art from a Mystical Moment to Space Fiction" (1985) by Nancy Topping Bazin. Bazin traces the evolution of Lessing's art as it moves from the realistic to the mystical, and into space fiction. She notes as transitional novels *Briefing for a Descent into Hell* (1971), *The Summer Before the Dark* (1973), and *The Memoirs of a Survivor* (1974).

1990s

"A Sufi Model for the Teacher/Disciple Relationship in *The Sirian Experiments*" (1991) by M. Patricia Mosier studies character development in *The Sirian Experiments*, drawing parallels to the Sufi transmission of knowledge.

Article by Nancy Topping Bazin, entitled "Madness, Mysticism, and Fantasy: Shifting Perspectives in the Novels of Doris Lessing, Bessie Head, and Nadine Gordimer" (1992) makes a connection between madness and mysticism.

Article by Phyllis Sternberg Perrakis, entitled "Sufism, Jung and the Myth of Kore: Revisionist Politics in Lessing's *Marriages*" (1992) is a comparative study that evaluates Lessing's *Marriages* from a psychological and Sufi point of view.

Shadia S. Fahim's *Doris Lessing and Sufi Equilibrium: The Evolving Form of the Novel* (1994) studies the theme of equilibrium and the changes and consistencies in the form of Lessing's novels from *The Grass is Singing* through the space-fiction series, with a special eye on comparisons between Lessing's Sufi-influenced novels and classical Sufi literature.

Works by Lessing on Sufism

Please see the bibliography for publication data.

"An Ancient Way to New Freedom"
"Building a New Cultural Understanding with the People of
    the East"
"The East's New Dawn"
"An Elephant in the Dark"
"If You Knew Sufi . . ."
"In the World, Not of It"
Introduction to Idries Shah's *Learning How to Learn*
"Learning How to Learn"
"The Living Stream"

APPENDIXES

"The Mysterious East"
"Omar Khayyam"
"The Ones Who Know"
Preface to Idries Shah's *Seekers after Truth* (French
    edition)
"A Revolution"
"Some Kind of a Cake"
"Sufic Samples"
"Sufi Philosophy and Poetry"
"Unmasking Burton"
"The Way of Mecca"
"What Looks Like an Egg and Is An Egg?"

Notes

Preface

1. Appendix A offers a detailed historical summary of Sufism (*tasawwuf*) in Islam, of which Western Sufism is an off-shoot. This distinction will be discussed in more detail in the introduction and chapter 1.

2. From conversations with Katherine P. Ewing, professor of anthropology at Duke University.

3. Scholars have remarked the influence of *tasawwuf* on an extensive list of non-Muslims. Some of the better-known names are William Shakespeare (see book by Lings), Robert Graves (see his introduction to Shah's *The Sufis*), Ted Hughes (see book by Bishop), and Robert Bly (he continues to perform translations of Sufi poetry to *saz*, a stringed instrument; see the various collections of Bly's versions of Rûmî and of Kabir in the bibliography).

4. More appropriately, therefore, the term ought to be spelled *Sufi-ism*; but for consistency it will be spelled *Sufism* here, throughout.

5. The term *Islamicate* was introduced by Hodgson to distinguish aspects and products associated with the world of Islam, or even just with Muslims, but not necessarily with the religion of Islam—not *Islamic* (1: 57–60, 95).

NOTES

Introduction

1. Aside from a few articles on Lessing's Sufism, the most serious and extensive effort to date has been Shadia S. Fahim's *Doris Lessing and Sufi Equilibrium: The Evolving Form of the Novel* (1994). For an annotated list of the scholarship on Lessing's mysticism, please see appendix B.

2. This is one of many Mulla Nasrudin (also known as Nasreddin Hodja) anecdotes that circulate by word of mouth in the Muslim world, as well as in parts of the former Soviet Union and Greece, where this figure is popular. The Nasrudin stories will be discussed in greater detail in chapter 3.

3. George Ivanovich Gurdjieff was a Russian-Armenian mystic and teacher who combined Sufi teachings with Buddhism and other ancient ways including Orthodox Christianity. Gurdjieff, like Shah, played an important role in transplanting Sufism to the West.

4. P. D. Ouspensky is credited with propagating and explaining Gurdjieff's "system" through his books *In Search of the Miraculous and The Psychology of Man's Possible Evolution*, among others.

5. From conversations with Katherine P. Ewing, professor of anthropology at Duke University.

6. Among them, Lessing mentions the following: BBC, Sussex University, *The Times Literary Supplement*, the *Educational Supplement*, *The Spectator*, *Time and Tide*, *New Statesman*, *Sunday Times*, *Sunday Telegraph*, the *Observer*, the Travel Book Club, the London Film Festival, the New York Film Festival, Orientalist professor James Kritzeck, Richard Attenborough, Dr. Louis Marin (head of the Paris School of Anthropology), Geoffrey Grigson, Isabel Quigley, Ted Hughes, Pat Williams, and Desmond Morris (Letter 51).

7. There have been other works by other scholars and teachers responsible for introducing Sufism to the Western world as well. This book is concerned in most part with Sufism as Lessing received it from Shah.

212

8. According to Nasr, the "good" ones include the works of L. Massignon, H. Corbin, E. Dermenghem, L. Gardet, C. Rice, F. Meier, P. Filipanni-Ronconi, B. de Sacy, R. A. Nicholson, and A. J. Arberry (15).

9. For this group, Nasr offers no examples.

10. According to Nasr, these are by writers such as R. Guenon, M. Lings, J. L. Michon, L. Schaya, F. Schuon, T. Burckhardt, W. Stoddart, V. Danner, J. Canteins, and M. Chodkiewicz (8–9, 15).

11. These orders include the Shâdhiliyyah, Naqshbandiyyah, Qâdiriyyah, Khalwatiyyah, Jarrâhiyyah, and Ni'matullâhiyyah in Europe and America (Nasr 9).

12. These include the Naqshbandiyyah, Mawlawiyyah, Rifâ'iyyah, Qalandariyyah, Chishtiyyah, Malâmatiyyah, Yeseviyyah, Khalwatiyyah, Qâdiriyyah, and Bektashiyyah, among others. *Tarîqah* means "the Way."

13. From conversations (1990–92) with Marilyn Waldman, professor of the history of Islam at The Ohio State University.

14. From conversations (1996) with Katherine P. Ewing, professor of anthropology at Duke University.

15. See also Hardin's "The Sufi Teaching Story and Doris Lessing" and Lessing's Preface to Shah's *Seekers after Truth*.

16. Ornstein writes, "With a current revival of interest in Sufism, sparked mainly by the writings of Idries Shah, many have extended their interest to the classical, theological versions which are the product of the Middle East. But some of this interest is archeological and anthropological as well as spiritual: these two separate factors must be distinguished at the outset" (356).

17. From conversations (1990–92) with Marilyn Waldman, professor of the history of Islam at The Ohio State University.

18. For more on Sufi history, please refer to appendix A.

19. For more on the concept of the *Ummah*, please see appendix A.

20. Rûmî, too, claimed this in his famous invitation to everyone to come and join, whoever they might be, but his disciples were devout Muslims, and those who weren't, converted to Islam. The invitation reads as follows:

Come again, come.
Whatever you are,
An unbeliever, a fire-worshipper, a pagan, come.
Whether you've repented a hundred times,
or a hundred times broken your vow, come.
This is *not* the door of desperation;
come however you are, come!
(Rûmî *Mathnawî*, my translation)

21. In this catalog they write, "Our idea to start a catalog list of Sufi books came from the problems [we] had in finding certain titles when we were in University together. On a research trip to Turkey we stopped over in England and were amazed at the availability of so many books on Sufism" (1).

22. The Golden Sufi Center was founded in 1992–93 and is currently directed by Jungian psychologist Llewellyn Vaughan-Lee in Inverness, California. Vaughan-Lee carries on the work of Irina Tweedie, author of *Chasm of Fire* and *Daughter of Fire*, who taught the Path of the Naqshbandiyyah in London, England, until she bequeathed her teaching to her trusted pupil and friend of twenty-five years. Their work focuses on dream interpretation in the Sufi Way.

23. In *Changing the Story* Gayle Greene studies the different responses of men and women to *The Golden Notebook*. While most male reviewers and critics dismissed and discounted (106) *The Golden Notebook*, the female reception was more positive. Among the male critics, Greene cites Anthony Burgess, who calls *The Golden Notebook* "a crusader's novel" and suggests Lessing ought to have written a manifesto, not a novel (106). Female critics, on the other hand, varied more in their reactions. Greene observes that while Ellen W. Brooks, Elayne Antler Rapping, and Margaret Drabble praise *The*

Golden Notebook for placing women at the center of the novel; Alice Bradley Markos, Elaine Showalter, Ellen Morgan, Jenny Taylor, and Catharine R. Stimpson are at best unimpressed, but—more importantly—they are offended by Lessing's representation of women as victims.

In "Reading *The Golden Notebook* in 1962" Jean McCrindle praises it for its innovative structure and for its variety of themes from Communism to sexual politics, mental illness to motherhood and children. In *"The Golden Notebook*: 'Female Writing' and 'The Great Tradition,'*"* Elizabeth Abel focuses on *The Golden Notebook* as a "self-consciously female" work (102). She observes that change comes not from the male realm of politics but from the female vision, as demonstrated by Anna's numerous notebooks. Abel's view of Lessing foreshadows Lessing's adoption of Sufi views. Sufism promotes ways of seeing a situation all at once, which, as Abel and French feminist critics argue, is a natural and organic result of the female biology and female experience. Mark Spilka has compared *The Golden Notebook* to D. H. Lawrence's *Women in Love* in its treatment of modern men and women who wish to try something different and who pay dearly for that wish. Spilka argues that readers are attracted to the same thing in Lessing and Lawrence: that is, that both writers refuse to give up on humankind. I would add to this that these writers also share the impulse for prophethood: Lawrence with his thoughts on blood consciousness and Lessing, with her commitment to Sufi awakening. Shadia S. Fahim applies "the working together of opposites" (68) in Sufism to *The Golden Notebook* and shows how Anna benefits from reaching the equilibrium between inner and outer realities and among her intellect, psychological makeup, and her intuition. Fahim notes that with *The Golden Notebook* there is a change in the formal structure that Lessing uses to communicate her ideas.

24. In "The Evolution of Doris Lessing's Art," Bazin gives examples from *The Marriages* to substantiate this observation (164). Lessing, however, does not want to represent only

women but all of humankind. Fishburn writes, "For Doris Lessing, writing has always involved a special kind of commitment to other people, a commitment that allows her to function as their artistic representative, taking their side and speaking out when they cannot" (*Doris* 5). Furthermore, Lessing even intends to represent humans in an afterlife, if possible, and shows glimpses of afterlife through her art. Soos observes that Lessing "abandoned her faith that political activism could effectuate lasting change" (25) and became interested in mystical consciousness as a reaction to her disillusionment with the Communist Party. Still, when Lessing turned to Sufism she did not turn away from her earlier interests that she had already assimilated. Rather, Sufism constituted yet another layer.

25. Ruth Saxton notes that Lessing's attitude is like Virginia Woolf's with regard to sexuality and the female body, in that they both regard the female body as a barrier before a woman's true identity. Saxton notes how both writers believe, women can "either procreate or create, but never simultaneously" (95). In both novelists' works, there is a body/mind split, reflecting a fundamental discomfort with the female body.

26. See Wilson 57–72.

27. See also Fahim's 142, 144, 153, and 258. Fahim focuses on the multiple perspectives that Lessing's space fiction forces us to take: the scientific, religious, Darwinian, mythic, historic, and scriptural. "Lessing uses the rhetoric of science fiction not so much to create a foreign world but to challenge our complacency about the habitual one and to help us modify our definition of reality itself" (144). Fahim analyzes how Lessing's space fiction forces the reader to adopt a multidimensional perspective, thus aiding in an expansion of consciousness (153).

28. In a 1991 interview with Tan Gim Ean, et al., Lessing said, "I'm surprised readers term them 'science fiction.' They're more 'space fiction.' Science fiction should examine some scientific idea, exaggerate . . ." (202).

29. This concept has a special meaning in Sufism that differs from that in Christianity. See also Fahim: "Sufis believe that reality is the interaction between the spiritual and the material world and therefore insist on a start from and a return back to ordinary reality" (215). Fahim sees the counterbalancing between the two worlds of inner and outer reality as the line of continuity in Lessing's canon. She writes, "It is precisely that balance between outward and inner modes of perception which attracts Doris Lessing to Sufism and it is in relation to that balance that her career develops" (236).

30. There is a reason why critics such as Sale have said, "Doris Lessing is not a casual person, and has none of the casual virtues. She has no wit, and only a very serious kind of humor. She works terribly hard, at living and at writing, and at her best she reveals the inner logic of human lives with a pain and a joy unmatched among living writers" (4).

31. See also Rubenstein's "Outer Space, Inner Space," where she discusses Lessing's space fiction as being about inner space: space fiction is "a metaphor through which [Lessing] portrays her imagined—but utterly realistic—extension of the present, to show us the human and emotional contexts through which the future might be met and directed" (187).

32. Likewise, we know a lot more about the Jewish tradition than we do about Islam, even though the Muslim population worldwide today is about eighty times greater than the Jewish population and almost equal to the Catholic population. See *Britannica Book of the Year*, 1995 approximations for mid-1994: 1,058,069,000 Catholics; 1,033,453,000 Muslims; 13,451,000 Jews. That is, approximately one billion Catholics, one billion Muslims, and thirteen million Jews. These figures amount to Catholics comprising 18.7 percent of the world's population; Muslims, 18.3 percent; and Jews, 0.2 percent.

33. However, this is changing. See *Britannica Book of the Year*'s approximations for 1995 in the United States: 55.3 million Catholics; 6.5 million Muslims; and 5.6 million Jews.

Our knowledge of Islam *must* expand, especially since Muslim numbers in the United States today are rising rapidly because of immigration, the birthrate, and, to a lesser degree, conversion. Of the 6.5 million Muslims, 1.4 million are Black Muslim followers of Elijah Muhammad and Louis Farrakhan's Nation of Islam.

34. Hodgson uses the term *Islamdom* to refer to the parts of the world where Muslim peoples predominate (1: 57–60, 95).

35. In her essay "Doris Lessing and The Sufi Way" Hardin quotes from one of Lessing's lecture series at The New School for Social Research given on September 25, 1972, explaining Lessing's reflections on ESP. Lessing says, "It's very hard to be a part of that complicated idea . . . that you are a rationalist and atheist and you don't believe and everything is already cut and dried and you already know everything and suddenly start throwing all that out the window and start thinking again. It was very hard for me to do that . . . You can see someone pick up what you are thinking and start talking about it . . . There is something there to be explored . . . if we don't get upset" (570).

Chapter 1

1. According to William James, an experience must have the following four marks in order to be considered "mystical": (1) ineffability, (2) noetic quality, (3) transiency, and (4) passivity (302). James observed that often, the words *mysticism* and *mystical* are used "as terms of mere reproach, to throw at any opinion which we regard as vague and vast and sentimental, and without a base in either facts or logic" (301). See also *Mysticism* by Underhill.

2. On the Sufi position on the place of the intellect, see also Fahim 205.

3. See also Fahim 117–18, 173, 180–81; and Ornstein 380–81.

4. In her discussion of *The Sentimental Agents* Fishburn recognizes that Lessing "is playing the role of Sufi master to our role of disciple," in that she poses questions which she refuses to answer directly. In the style of the Sufi master, she only answers in paradoxes that require work to be understood (*Unexpected* 144).

5. See also Fishburn, who discusses these concepts in terms of physics.

6. See also Fahim 210 and 222, on "getting into tune with the whole plan."

7. Shams was Rûmî's teacher and guide on the Sufi Path.

8. Dick Davis is a poet, translator, and professor of Persian in the Department of Judaic, Near Eastern, and Hellenic Languages and Literatures at The Ohio State University.

9. In *Mystical Poems of Rûmî* A. J. Arberry notes that "In Persian poetry the abode of Jesus after his ascension is usually said to be in the Fourth Heaven (the sphere of the sun)" (150, 218).

10. This is Dick Davis's previously unpublished translation from the original poem in Persian in *Divan-e Shams-e Tabrîzî*, ed. Foruzanfar, vol. 54, 661. Dick Davis has kindly given me permission to publish his translation here.

11. The term "Unreal City" is from T. S. Eliot's *The Waste Land* 465.

12. In *Doris Lessing: The Poetics of Change*, Gayle Greene, too, compares Lessing's novels to T. S. Eliot's *The Waste Land* and points out that Thomas Stern in *Landlocked* is likely to have been named after Thomas Stearns Eliot. Greene cites many references to ruins and to some of the ruined cities of Europe, among them London and Cologne; and she acknowledges Lessing's positive outlook under grim circumstances.

13. Among those who offer grim images and no workable solutions are William Butler Yeats, D. H. Lawrence, T. S. Eliot,

Joseph Conrad, George Orwell, Eugene O'Neill, Arthur Miller, Sylvia Plath, D. M. Thomas, Samuel Beckett, and Harold Pinter.

14. Greene sees a change toward something new in *Landlocked*, which she attributes to a great extent to Sufism. She writes, "The destruction that has so altered the world that we cannot think or talk about it in customary ways is rendered hauntingly, powerfully, by a lyrical mode that strains against the limits of language to express the inexpressible horrors of the century as well as something new emerging from them" (*Poetics* 57).

15. Even critics who doubt Lessing's mystical side acknowledge the seer in her. Jouve writes, "There is no doubting either Lessing's prodigious flair for the topical, her energy, her power. Perhaps one should not doubt either that her vision of a dismal future and her belief in the need for a new humanity to evolve if humanity is going to survive may be right. Time may reveal her to have been a prophetess" ("Of Mud" 123).

16. The true Sufi becomes what is called in German, "ein Gott-getrunken mensch" (a God-intoxicated man).

17. In *The Marriages*, Lessing emulates Rûmî's technique in the form of Zones that correspond to various stages of being, as discussed in chapter 3.

18. In the 1970s, for instance, Lessing, like Herman Hesse, became a cult figure. I knew of people in London in the seventies who began to regard Lessing as their spiritual guide and who heeded her warnings in novels as early on as in *The Memoirs*.

Chapter 2

1. In *The Novelistic Vision* Rubenstein also holds this view: "This orientation of Sufism is easily compatible with the already clear preoccupations and patterns in Doris Lessing's previous fiction: her interest in breaking through the conven-

tional ways of thinking and being, the urge to understand and extend the parameters of consciousness, the mystical intimations expressed in her characters, the desire to overcome the dialectical antitheses of perceived experience in favor of a synthesizing vision of wholeness" (122).

2. In *The Novelistic Vision* Rubenstein observes the process of organic evolution in *Briefing* (181). See also Fishburn's *Unexpected* on the New Physics and Lessing.

3. Draine acknowledges the "enormous scope for [Lessing's] moralizing urge in *Shikasta* and *The Sirian Experiments*," two novels "that provide the context for *Marriages*" (*Substance* 167).

4. In *The Novelistic Vision* Rubenstein, too, raises the point that the quest for the self implicit in Lessing's pre-Sufi novels is not altered but *deepened* in the context of Sufi thought (122–23).

5. For a discussion of the film version of *The Memoirs*, see Jenny Taylor's interview with director David Gladwell. Martin Green identifies the values of *The Memoirs* as "in some sense symbolic and mystical" and says that therefore "it is not a novel at all" (6). Singleton, too, applies Sufism as well as Jungianism to *The Memoirs*, and she has been criticized for ignoring Lessing's rationalism by focusing on the alchemical elements alone. Yet Lessing herself has stressed at various times that accepting the two worlds—inner and outer, or the mind and the body, or spiritual and material—is not a matter of either . . . or, but and . . . and . . . and . . . In "The Feminist Apologues" DuPlessis compares Lessing's *The Memoirs* to Joanna Russ's *The Female Man* (1975) and Marge Piercy's *Woman on the Edge of Time* (1976). She recognizes each work as a teaching story in which "elements like character and plot function mainly as the bearers of philosophical propositions or moral arguments, whose function is to persuade" (1–2). DuPlessis also observes that each of the novels both analyzes the past and projects into the future (2). She believes that in doing so, each writer writes beyond the ending, beyond "closure of historical movement" (2). As a result,

our sense of resolution is altered. Nothing is resolved, nothing is fixed. According to DuPlessis, in "rewriting the beginning and getting beyond the ending," all three writers assert their authority and try to "reconceive the world" (2).

6. When Lessing illustrated Anna Wulf's state of incompletion and spiritual depravity in the 567-page *Golden Notebook*, her initial reviewers were not so impressed by all of Anna's psychological work on herself that left her fragmented. Nordell wrote that "The occasional satisfactions of seeing how bits of the puzzle fit together are not enough" (11). Not enough, that is, unless one is inclined to value a breakdown and reconstruction of the human psyche. Buckler, on the other hand, praised *The Golden Notebook* for the same reason that others found it overbearing: its complexity and fragmentation. Buckler wrote, "However overwrought Anna's sensibility sometimes is, Mrs. Lessing points such powerful significances therefrom that, in comparison, many other highly touted novels dealing with man's acceptance—or defiance—of his fate seem picayune indeed" (18).

7. Fahim analyzes the carpet episode as well as the four-walled garden and the iron egg as mandala symbols that activate "[t]he process of contemplation by inducing certain mental states which encourage the achievement of equilibrium between the levels of perception" (108).

8. In Fahim's reading of *The Memoirs*, rational, psychological, and spiritual modes of consciousness are fully integrated to bring "the different strata of the novel together" (87).

9. Fahim, too, sees a continuation from *The Golden Notebook* to *The Memoirs*. She points out how the narrator of *The Memoirs* breaks through the walls of reality almost in the opening pages of *The Memoirs*, whereas Anna in *The Golden Notebook* and Martha in *The Children of Violence* series spend a lifetime working toward their breakthroughs (85–86). Fahim writes, "As a writer influenced by Sufism, Lessing sees that it is only in the fullest development and balancing of all available faculties that human beings can free themselves from

mere predetermined repetition and so evade catastrophe" (85). Kaplan observes a similar continuity between *The Golden Notebook* and *The Four-Gated City*: "But Martha's evolution of consciousness goes much further. By now, the interpenetration of consciousnesses no longer may be considered a weakness but a precious ability which foresees the future course of human evolution" (125).

10. Jeanne Murray Walker almost concludes that Emily and the narrator are the same person: "otherwise how could the narrator, who is certainly not omniscient, view scenes of Emily's past" (96). In this book I argue that when the narrator and Emily are read as one and the same character, they create a whole, a state of integration to which Sufis aspire.

11. For this reason Melvin Maddocks calls *The Memoirs* "a ghost story of the future" and "a panicked intuition turned into a tentative myth." For Lessing, however, there are more than ghosts in this novel; the imaginary rooms behind the wall are *more* real to Lessing than the realities of everyday life.

12. But Walker is much more interested in the social ramifications of dysfunctional individuals. She recognizes Emily as someone who has failed at "bonding" (102) and failed at "producing" (100); this contributes to the breakdown of society. She therefore concludes that "ultimate salvation comes only to individuals who can achieve wholeness within themselves" (108). Walker is convinced that "reciprocity among individuals is essential if society is to survive" (112), which concern is reminiscent of the concept of "reciprocal maintainance" in some Sufi teachings.

13. Walker argues that "*The Memoirs* is allegorical in the way Spencer's *Faerie Queene* is allegorical; a single image in the novel often signals both social and psychological meaning" (114).

14. In *Under My Skin* Lessing offers revelations on The *Memoirs*'s autobiographical dimension (28ff.).

15. In *Poetics* Greene writes, "To ask what is real in this novel—the realm behind the wall or what goes on in the flat—

is to miss the point . . . Lessing leads us to question not only the evidence of our senses but the paradigm of Western rationalism we've inherited to deal with experience . . . but if we can suspend disbelief, they may teach us to question our perceptual equipment and the spatial-temporal mold of Western empiricism and lead us to something new" (141–42). My reading of *The Memoirs* parts ways from critics who believe in the reality of the world behind the wall only as a narrative experience. I propose that, as a mystic, Lessing means us to take the reality of her narrator's time-travel literally. Fishburn interprets the world behind the wall as no more than a creation of language that Lessing uses to give her readers hope: "in inventing a new world, [Lessing] has taken on the difficult task of inventing a new language to describe it." She acknowledges Lessing's wish "to transform our view of reality" (*Unexpected* 42) but interprets that transformation only as an intellectual exercise in stretching one's perceptions. Fahim argues for the interpenetration of the two realms, the inner and the outer, on either side of the wall (8), and she illustrates how the two worlds nourish each other in the narrator's life (115). She points out Sufi theories of literature to explain the two irreconcilable universes in the world of *The Memoirs*, the realistic and the fantastic. She is interested in Lessing's quest for equilibrium, and she charts that quest by analyzing the transformation in the form and genre of *The Memoirs*.

16. Lott concludes that this difference "may very well reflect the sexual and cultural biases of the authors. Carroll, the nineteenth-century male, finally does return his heroine to the waking world of intellect and reason; whereas Lessing is willing to subsume the rational in a mystical transformation" (178).

17. See also Hardin, "Sufi Way" 571.

18. See also Fahim 109.

19. In "Doubles Talk" Sprague unfolds the layers of doubling in *The Golden Notebook*, such as "joy and spite, male and female, anarchy and order, victim and cannibal, art and

life" (194), and the doubling of characters such as Anna/Molly, Anna/Ella, and Anna/Saul. She focuses on the greater significance of the male doubles in the novel, referring to them as "the madman in the attic" (184). Sprague defines the second self as one who "exhibits displaced characteristics that the public . . . cannot acknowledge" (184). She borrows the term *second self* from Carl F. Keppler, who used it to refer to the "double" or *Doppelgänger*. In Sufi terminology, this "second self" would be the essence, the inner self, or soul, who is afraid of being ridiculed, and who feels like a misfit, while the first self is the personality or the mask one can safely present to the world. Of course Sufism, then, aims to fuse the doubles, by giving greater and greater voice to the second self, or the soul, as is the case in *The Golden Notebook* in which Saul writes the opening lines, "The two women were alone in the London flat" (639).

20. Morgan finds that *The Golden Notebook* suffers from its author's alienation from the authentic female perspective" (480). She argues, "nowhere in their culture . . . do they see such perceptions corroborated" (472). Therefore Morgan likens Ella/Anna's emptiness, her inability to be herself and to acknowledge her feelings, to Lessing's "failure to come to terms with female authenticity" (472).

21. Sukenick argues that Lessing challenges the clique of woman writers who write about feeling, while men write about reason. Instead, Lessing offers "rational" and "tough" fiction about aspects of women that include *more* than "feminine" concerns: "Her fiction is tough, clumsy, rational, concerned with social roles, collective action and conscience, and unconcerned with niceties of style and subtlety of feeling for its own sake" (516). The reason for this, Sukenick argues, "is based upon [Lessing's] commitment to large issues and to the political" (519). As a result of this attitude, "Martha's intellect [often] mocks her feelings" (521). Sukenick celebrates Lessing's opposition to the irrational and upholds Lessing as a trustworthy guide who can see her contemporaries through hard

times. While this is true, Lessing also favors intuitive beings as the more intelligent ones and reveres them as the new saviors of humankind as, for example, in the ending of *The Four-Gated City*.

22. See also Fahim 113.

23. In "Woman of Many Summers" Tiger observes a similar stripping away of personality and getting to the core of essence in the character of Kate Brown in *The Summer before the Dark*. Having lived as Mrs. Michael Brown for forty-five years, Kate breaks down one summer, only to emerge as a more authentic human being who has the strength to say "*no*: no, no, no, NO" (270). In place of compliance and acquiescence, Kate discovers rage and freedom—freedom to let her greying hair show.

24. Hinz and Teunissen argue that "Saul Green is a projection and not a 'real' character" (458); therefore, like in Michelangelo's *Pietà*, Anna is the powerful creator, she is the "Great Mother" (460). This traps her, of course, in an archetypal relationship out of which she cannot break free. As Hinz and Teunissen further argue, The *Pietà* "best embodies the most basic archetypes of the Western mentality" (470). But at the same time, the "Great Mother" is not only a positive icon, but also carries with it the darker sides of maternal love (470). Hinz and Teunissen explain, this is why Anna and Saul are struck with horror when Anna holds him in a motherly embrace. When Sufism permeated Lessing's works beyond *The Golden Notebook* it became possible also to detect, in retrospect, the earlier signs of mystical inclinations even in *The Golden Notebook*. The idea that "projection," for instance, is a deadly trap is one of the teachings of Sufis, that one does not relate to real persons and events but to one's projections onto those around one. Hence, the horror in some embraces, such as that between Anna and Saul.

25. Rubenstein also views evolution in Lessing's fiction as cumulative: "the Martha Quest who emerges 'after' *The Golden Notebook* carries with her not only the seeds of Thomas

Stern's inner division but echoes of Anna Wulf's" (*Novelistic* 129). This is rightly so, considering Lessing's deepened and enhanced perception of the human psyche since her introduction to Sufi thought.

26. Fahim points out, "According to the Sufis, the colour black denotes wisdom and leadership" (119-20).

27. Malcolm Cowley both acknowledges that *The Memoirs* is about "a catastrophic breakdown of the affluent society" (23) and expresses his frustration with Lessing's vagueness and abstractness. He is uncomfortable with the visionary and prophetic Lessing, who will not offer a neat conclusion to the catastrophy she foresees: "But what shall we say about the end of the fable? . . . To this stubborn rationalist, [implying "to himself,"] it isn't an ending, really, but a cop-out" (24). Indeed, Lessing's solution can be seen as a cop-out if the Sufi context remains in the shadows. Among others disappointed by this sudden transformation is DuPlessis, who describes the conclusion of *The Memoirs* as having been "dealt . . . on a very flat cord" ("Feminist" 5). See also Fahim 119–35 on the ending of *The Memoirs*: "the ending is not 'a cop-out'" (122).

28. Of course Suvin is in turn indebted to the Russian formalists and to Bertolt Brecht. Fishburn uses this definition of science fiction as her point of departure in looking at Lessing's *Briefing*, *The Memoirs*, and the *Canopus* series. She argues for Lessing's technique of "recognition" and "re-cognition," which enables Lessing, and in turn her readers, to "modify reality" (11). For a discussion of "defamiliarization" Fishburn suggests "Art as Technique" by Victor Shklovsky 3–24. On Brecht's "estrangement effect," see *One-Dimensional Man* by Marcuse 66–70.

29. Sullivan draws a parallel between *The Golden Notebook* and the *Canopus* series, in that both are experiments with forms. Whereas the former negotiated between illusion/madness and reality/sanity, *Canopus* resorts to "the viewpoints of gods, devils, and whatever else may perch on a new

great chain of being" (77). Ahearn reminds readers that the inventiveness of space fiction allows Lessing to "use literature both to delight and to instruct. The form allows Lessing to pursue galactic voyages and inner journeys into the mind to provide insight into the human past, present, and possible future" (qtd. in Marchino 3). Knapp also approves of Lessing's turn to space fiction and observes how it enables her to elude compartmentalization and to avoid "the conventional demarcation lines between literary genres, between truth and fiction, the sane and the mad, the objective and the subjective" (131). Rowe best expresses critics' initial discomfort in her 1982 essay: "I remained bemused by the cold modernity, the metallic ring of the description itself. Science fiction—almost a contradiction in terms—as if there could be some alchemical metamorphosis which would produce a story out of the spanner, the laser, the atom" (191). Pickering's review of *Shikasta* and *The Marriages* echoes similar displeasure: "I am puzzled and disturbed by [Lessing's] two latest novels . . . as Virginia Tiger pointed out in her review of Lessing's stories, 'I'm surprised we didn't notice the cranky religious vision [Lessing] was developing'" (7). Bazin offers a sympathetic reading of *Shikasta*, arguing that in this novel "the quest for wholeness becomes that of the species rather than the individual" ("Evolution" 161). She looks back to Lessing's earlier novels for clues and suggests that the roots of the quest in *Shikasta* can be found particularly in *The Golden Notebook*. While the celebrated science-fiction author Ursula LeGuin is not completely happy with *Shikasta*, she praises its daring subject matter (Review 32). She warns us in her review of *Shikasta* that Lessing is neither a "realist" nor a "fantasist," and that the "old distinctions are useless and must be discarded" (32). Draine describes the *Canopus* series as "a work at odds with itself philosophically, stylistically, generically" (*Substance* 143). Oumhani explains, "*Canopus in Argos* is a science-fiction series but also a vision of the world" (93, my translation). And Stitzel adds, "Lessing uses . . . seven science-fiction novels to change our perception of reality by describing worlds that are simultaneously similar to and different from our own" ("Reading" 504).

30. Fishburn acknowledges this debt to Sufism in her discussion of *The Representative* when she credits particle physics and Eastern mysticism for the "defamiliarize[d] . . . fabric of reality" (122) in Lessing's space fiction. She discusses the role of particle physics in shaping Lessing's imagination, while I argue that within the context of Sufi mysticism, Lessing found new pathways she had not explored before and the possibility of a more profound and comprehensive study of the human race.

31. For a discussion of the title, *Canopus in Argos*, see Fahim 147.

32. See Fahim 217, on recreation, regeneration: "Nature as a constant flux of creativity."

33. Initial reviewers of *The Representative* pronounced it difficult to decipher. In his 1982 review when *The Representative* first came out Turner wrote, "Philosophically, it's a puzzler . . . Even though I know . . . [that Lessing] appears to believe in an afterlife, a sort of reincarnation and a journey toward salvation, I find [her] ending hard to figure out . . . Despite recent appearances, Doris Lessing really is a major author . . . and perhaps we should indulge her whim. But next time I hope she writes about Shammat. Pirates are a lot more fun than people freezing to death" (278). For other critics, acknowledging the Sufi context without understanding it has been equally futile: Linda Taylor writes in the *Times Literary Supplement*, "This Sufist regeneration is comforting and believable as far as Planet 8 and Canopus go. But this is where the 'space perspective' is found wanting . . . It's difficult for the reader . . . to identify with this mystical collectivism" (370).

34. Initial reviewers of *Shikasta* were frustrated and dissatisfied with what it had to offer. When it first came out DeView described it as "a jagged, fragmented narrative which

requires studious reading and rarely allows for any real feeling about the characters" (B3). This is true enough; but those fragments do amount to a whole picture, given the right viewing glasses. DeMott rejected *Shikasta*'s "tone of high prophetic solemnity." He wrote, "[I'm afraid] that many novel-readers won't find *Shikasta* to their taste" (53). Gray rejected the cosmic order and laws that, as Lessing implies, govern human life: "There is something unsatisfying about a vision of history that suggests humans could not, after all, help making the messes they have, that their blunders were all ordained by a small tic in the cosmos" (101). See also Fahim 153–234. Fahim studies the structure and narrative technique of *Shikasta* by looking at two Sufi concepts, the "Reflective Mirror" and the "Philosopher's Stone" (158), the former being the thing to which a Sufi aspires, and the latter being the means of achieving it (160). She identifies Johor's role as that of the Philosopher's Stone.

35. See also Oumhani; and Fahim 181–84.

36. On the other hand, arguing that Lessing's space fiction, like all her other fiction, is autobiographical, Carey Kaplan looks to "Britain's Imperialist Past" in order to understand "Lessing's Futuristic Fiction" (149) and sees Canopus as "a benevolent version of the British imperialism that formed Lessing's early consciousness and perceptions of the world" (150). According to Kaplan, Canopus is the imperialist power, while its surrounding planets and stars are the colonies that are inhabited by "imperfect, uncivilized, less than fully human natives, profoundly in need of the technology and wisdom of the master race" (150). Kaplan suggests, naturally, that nothing positive can (or does) come out of the dynamics of such power relations.

37. On the Sufi guide, see also Fahim 216.

38. This allegory will be discussed in chapter 3 in more detail.

39. Richey discusses an instance of this "sleep" state in *Briefing* in which Professor Watkins suffers from deep sleep.

Richey grounds his analysis in the teachings of Gurdjieff and Ouspensky, in which the state of being "asleep" is likened to being in prison. In fact, Professor Watkins refers frequently to "getting out of the trap, getting out of prison, escaping" (*Briefing* 241). Gurdjieff and the Sufis refer to such liberation from sleep when they speak of self-development and human evolution (Richey 11).

40. See also Fahim 181.

41. Mosier discusses similar experiences and awakening of a disciple in *The Sirian Experiments*.

42. As discussed in chapter 1, Sufis have been named after their professions, as well: *saqatî* (huckster), *hallâj* (cotton carder), *nassâj* (weaver), *warrâq* (bookseller or copyist), *qawârîrî* (glassmaker), *haddâd* (blacksmith), and *bannâ'* (mason) (Schimmel 84). Notice also some of the names of Sufis in appendix A.

Chapter 3

1. Greene discusses Sufi teaching stories in *Landlocked*: when Thomas is in the wilderness, his breakdown is accompanied by Sufi-like tales which he sends out of the wilderness. For instance, Greene argues that the tale about the man who escapes his enemy and then kills himself is an instance of Sufi-like break in logic. Sufism discourages habitual and predictable thoughts and behaviors, for its ultimate aim is to awaken (*Poetics* 60). See also Hardin's "Sufi Teaching Story and Doris Lessing."

2. On multiple levels in the teaching story, see also Fahim 133–34.

3. See Fishburn's *Unexpected* on the idea of Lessing's interest in changing our thought patterns. See also Draine's *Substance* 141 and "Changing Frames" 52–53, 61.

4. Capra observes the following in Zen Buddhist tales: "the joke . . . is meant to produce . . . [a] liberating laughter . . .

with a sudden intuitive insight . . . In the split-second [in which one understands] a joke, [one experiences] a moment of enlightenment. [And] it is well known that this moment must come spontaneously, that it cannot be achieved by explaining the joke" and by intellectual analysis (24).

5. Cf. D.T. Suzuki's *Zen and Japanese Culture.*

6. For discussions of quotations of Sufi teachings in *Landlocked,* see Rubenstein, *The Novelistic Vision of Doris Lessing* 121ff.

7. As Phelan elaborates, the mimetic, synthetic, and thematic dimensions are in turn sometimes converted into three distinctive functions that characters may perform to varying degrees in the narrative. Phelan's definition of "character" helps make the case for acknowledging the "mimetic dimension" and the "mimetic function" in Lessing's characters. Lessing criticism, by admitting this mimetic dimension, can move from dismissing Lessing's characters as mere rhetorical devices to considering them as plausible persons, as well.

8. For more on what Phelan means by progression, see *Reading People, Reading Plots.* Here I am primarily interested in characters.

9. In contrast, Fishburn treats them as constructs that represent an idea or that convey a message. She refers to them as "guide-leaders" who "translate" the alien world for us. Through them, "Lessing establishes the psychological framework by which she convinces us not of the existence of another world but, more central to her purpose, of the validity of her *ideas*" (*Unexpected* 13).

10. See also DuPlessis's "Feminist Apologues" (2) on flat characters that form clusters.

11. Shah points out in *The Sufis* that it *cannot* be coincidental that the Masons of the middle ages, members of a fraternal order involved in the development of human consciousness, were almost certainly intermingled with "Sufi Builders" (215).

12. Fishburn also states that in the space fiction series Lessing's message becomes more important than anything

else and her characters take second place to the narrator(s) (*Unexpected* 3).

13. The same is true in *Landlocked*, the first novel Lessing published following her introduction to Sufi thought. For a discussion of quotations from Sufi teachings in *Landlocked*, see Rubenstein, *Novelistic* 121 and Greene, *Poetics* 60; for a study of Sufism in *The Four-Gated City* and *Landlocked*, see Seligman's "The Sufi Quest." Seligman writes, "Sufism permeates these works because the Sufis share Lessing's own preoccupations" (193). See also M. Susan Lewis on Sufi concepts in *The Four-Gated City*.

14. In *The Tree outside the Window* Rose analyzes *The Four-Gated City* and the earlier *Children of Violence* novels as bildungsromans of Martha's life. The Sufi context would enhance Rose's reading of *The Four-Gated City* as a bildungsroman. Gamallo also places Lessing in the tradition of the feminine bildungsroman, seeing her as a practical example of the form. Knapp singles out *The Four-Gated City* as a work that straddles Lessing's oeuvre between South Africa and outer space, and between bildungsroman and space fiction. For instance, the central image of the tree in *The Four-Gated City* reappears in *Shikasta*, as the image of the utopian city also repeats itself in *Canopus in Argos*: "Somewhere in our minds there is an idea of a city. A City, rather!" (*Four-Gated* 302). Knapp asserts that *The Four-Gated City* serves as a bridge between the "old" and the "new" Lessing: "Lessing's later space fiction is visible already here, in the holistic concept of a thoroughly structured universe in which human beings need only recognize their rightful place" (102). This book follows Knapp's line of reasoning, among others, in that it casts Sufism as an influence that has been gaining momentum in Lessing's novels since the mid-1960s. Scott observes that *The Four-Gated City* uses Sufism only "on the 'edges' of the novel— in the dedication, and then in the transition between parts three and four of the book" (170). This initially marginal influence of Sufism later becomes much more central in Lessing's

space fiction. Scott discerns tensions in *The Four-Gated City* between Sufi and Christian imagery. One of these is "the Christian model of a voyage," that is, "the Stations of the Cross," and the Sufi Path of transformation. Scott sees such tensions also in *The Memoirs*, in which Sufi images tend to overpower Christian ones (176). For parallels to biblical stories about Jesus, Mary, and Martha, see Scott's "Sufism, Mysticism and Politics" 180ff. Jouve finds *The Children of Violence* series, which is concluded by *The Four-Gated City*, to be "strongly autobiographical" ("Of Mud" 77), but she is at the same time disturbed by "documentary 'truths'" (78) that do not add up. For Jouve, such is the case of Martha's wisdom at the end of *The Four-Gated City*. Considering Martha's earlier naiveté in Africa at the beginning of the series, Jouve sees no resemblance between the two Marthas. Fishburn recognizes a change in Lessing, starting with *The Four-Gated City*, which anticipates the space-fiction series in its apocalyptic vision. Fishburn also notes that the narrative style changes as well: "Most of the novel consists of narrative summary where we are told what happened and what to think about it. It is almost as though a new urgency possessed Lessing at the time of writing, convincing her that she no longer had the leisure to show how but must tell what" (*Unexpected* 17). On the other hand, Jouve is disturbed that "[a] change occurs, not a growth" (87)— a change "from rootedness, to the void" (88)—or, as the title of her article also suggests, a change "from 'mud' to the 'void'" (89). Greene sees a parallel between *The Four-Gated City* and *Jane Eyre*. Like Jane, Martha moves into the household where the mad wife lives in the house and where Martha becomes a governess, secretary, and later, lover, of the man of the house (*Poetics* 76).

15. On the fool, see also Scott's "Sufism, Mysticism and Politics" 170ff.

16. For a further discussion of "wholeness" in *The Four-Gated City* see Hardin's "Doris Lessing and The Sufi Way" 573.

17. Knapp introduces another angle to "madness" when she writes that although Lynda wants to get well, "she equates sanity with the enfeebling and abhorrent rituals of a proper marriage, and chooses to remain mad rather than resume this role" (97). In other words, Lynda is sane enough to know she is mad, and to choose madness over conformity. Pickering refers to Gilbert and Gubar's *The Madwoman in the Attic*, in which they describe works of female novelists in terms of a quest for the self. Pickering argues that Lessing "in her entire body of work has written and continues to write the story of her struggle to identify herself as a woman and as an author" (95). In other words, like Martha Quest, Lessing is on a "quest for her own story" (95). Like Jane Eyre's mad double Bertha Mason, Lynda Coldridge expresses Martha Quest's frustrations with the social and literary constraints placed upon her. Pickering points out a major difference between Lessing's doubles and Brontë's Jane Eyre/Bertha Mason or Woolf's Septimus Warren Smith/Clarissa Dalloway: Bertha has to die in order for Jane to marry Rochester, and Septimus dies in order for Mrs. Dalloway to appreciate life—whereas in the case of Lynda/Martha, it is not Lynda-the-mad-one who dies. On the contrary, she is thriving at the end of *The Four-Gated City*, "her visionary powers more fully developed than ever before" (97). Pickering does not attribute Lessing's upholding madness over sanity to Sufi influences, but she recognizes the uniqueness of Lynda's kind of madness. In fact she surmises that it could be Lynda who kept the memoirs in *The Memoirs of a Survivor*, since Lynda always used to test the walls for weakness in her basement apartment in *The Four-Gated City*. If so, then a decade later, she has broken through. Thus, unlike Brontë or Woolf, Lessing shows us the values of madness as an alternative to patriarchy. Furthermore, in the Sufi context, madness, with its attending insights, is regarded as a reasonable alternative to ordinary life on earth.

18. On new organs of perception, see also Fahim 207–8; and Seligman, "The Sufi Quest" 192–93.

19. Barnouw draws a parallel between Lessing and Robert Musil, from whose book *Man without Qualities* Lessing quotes in part 2 of *The Four-Gated City*. Barnouw recognizes Lessing's departure further into inner space, and she explains, "as [Lessing's] fear is more urgent, more immediate than Musil's was, her means to document it have to be more drastic, and her prescriptions for hope both more striking and more vulnerable" (514). Barnouw notes, in fact, how Lessing almost overdoes Martha's description of "the new children" (*Four-Gated* 608) in her letter to Francis. Nonetheless, she celebrates Lessing's inner-space travels in *The Four-Gated City*, referring to them as "the indispensable basis for [Lessing's] precise observation of things as they are" (514).

20. In "Doris Lessing's 'Città Felice'" Rose studies architectural metaphors in *The Four-Gated City* and looks at buildings as a running motif (369). She reminds Lessing readers of Lessing's profound interest in Jungianism as well as Sufism, both of which provide ample interpretations of the mythical city that represents psychic wholeness. Rose makes useful comparisons to the ideal city of the Italian Renaissance or the *Città Felice*, and in passing considers Singleton's evaluation of *The Four-Gated City* as a Sufi metaphor for hidden knowledge in a secret garden—a view that this book takes up with regard to Lessing's Sufism as her secret source of power. According to the philosopher-architects of the Renaissance, a perfect city had to be harmonious both with the human body and with the heavens. Rose uses examples of ideal architecture from Alberti, Campanella, and Filarete to understand Lessing's mythical city. She suggests that *The Four-Gated City* foreshadows Lessing's later heliocentric cosmology as well as recalling her earlier Martha Quest novels—a view upon which I expand by pointing to Sufism as the common denominator. With her ability to unite both Africa and Argos, Rose concludes that Mircea Eliade's term "zone of the sacred" (qtd. in Rose 383) can be useful in understanding Lessing's uses of inner and outer space. See Eliade's chapter, "The World, the City,

the House" in *Occultism, Witchcraft, and Cultural Fashions* for a discussion of sacred and profane space. See also Levin, "A Fourfold Vision," which argues that Lessing's *The Four-Gated City* is patterned after William Blake's *Jerusalem*: "[b]oth works are divided into four parts" (212) and both are concerned with "the Four-Gated City of Imagination" (213).

21. O'Rourke pays attention to Martha's status as exile and argues that "exile is central to Lessing's writing" (206). She refers to Eagleton's *Exiles and Émigrés* to point out that Lessing and Sylvia Plath are the only two women whom Britain "acknowledges as artists of classic stature—producers of Literature, capital L" (220) and that both are women in exile from home—Rhodesia, and the United States, respectively.

22. See Lessing's 1969 interview with Haas, in which she discusses her views on madness and ESP, as well as other subjects. Lessing also spoke openly about ESP in her interview with Bannon in 1969. Similarly, Rubenstein studies the madness of Charles Watkins in Lessing's *Briefing* as an inner space voyage in which Watkins "is periodically interrupted by the medical staff's observations on their patient's mental condition, and their disagreements about appropriate treatment" (*Novelistic Vision* 184). Rubenstein also quotes Lessing at length on the subject of ESP (184).

23. Rubenstein observes a connection in *Landlocked* between Thomas Sterne's madness and his potential for "a higher synthesis of being" (*Novelistic Vision* 121) as taught in Sufism. Spacks compares Lessing to Lillian Hellman, Anaïs Nin, and Colètte in her use of madness or introversion as a way out. Seligman captures the role of madness in Lessing: "In order to understand Lessing's sense of madness, her belief in the creative potential of all men, and her feelings about the application of this potential in the twentieth-century context, it is necessary first to understand the significance of Sufism for Lessing. It serves as an organized system which identifies and emphasizes certain otherwise ineffable capacities of twentieth-century man"

237

(204). Vlastos does a Laingian reading of *The Golden Notebook*, *The Four-Gated City*, and *Briefing*, in which she defines "madness as revelation and cure" (246). She recognizes Lessing's focus on the spiritual realm without belittling or compromising her preferences. She sees the collapse of political solutions to human misery making way for individual creativity and morality. Like Laing, Lessing believes "not in hearts but in psyches; not in Christian ethics but in the rhythms of nature and the order of the universe" (246). Vlastos adds that the only hope that Lessing has is, like Laing's, in an inner journey involving the loss of the ego (257). Fahim recognizes what she calls "the motif of descent" in many of Lessing's novels and looks at the recurrent theme of mental breakdown as the negative aspect of that motif, while an "existential rebirth" constitutes its positive aspect (8). Characters like Anna emerge from such a positive descent being able to face responsibility rather than withdrawing from it (9). Sufism offers Lessing what Fahim refers to as "the motif of ascent" (10). "Whereas [the motif of descent] is considered the end of the psychological journey, it is considered by Sufism an initial step towards attaining mystical heights of ascent" (Fahim 16).

24. Sukenick explains, it is "the mad who are sane" (530). She views Lessing's interest in madness as a way of Lessing's keeping up with the times. Sukenick writes, "Essentially a realist, [Lessing] travels parallel to the culture and keeps her eye on its movements . . . She wants . . . an abolition of the traditional hierarchy of the sane and insane, a recognition of the revolutionary nature of madness" (531).

25. Incidentally, Lessing's mother was named Emily Maud.

26. In the passages quoted from Lessing, of course, I left the wording as is; but I took liberties with paragraph indentations and sometimes by the addition of quotation marks in order to allow the Sufi teaching story in them to emerge.

27. For a more detailed discussion of the narrators in *The Representative* see Fishburn's chapter 6 in *The Unexpected*.

28. In *Substance* Draine argues the same point about *Briefing*, which is "a kind of mystical teaching-story" (92). She argues that Lessing is therefore a Sufi teacher who "prod[s] her students into a state of alertness and receptivity to that truth" (94). In *Briefing* Draine sees Charles Watkins as a seeker as well as a teacher: he is a man who "has lost sight of his place in this essential harmony" (94), and he is also a man "charged with the role of teaching this lesson to humanity" (94). See also Hardin's "The Sufi Teaching Story and Doris Lessing." In "Truth and Art in Women's Worlds," Khanna focuses on the role of art and music in *The Marriages*. She calls *The Marriages* "a delightful feminist utopia" (124) where "'song' or art . . . [is] the major concern" (125). She reads the novel as a merging of the teller and the tale (131) and asserts that "[i]n Lessing's dynamic utopian vision, it is art that facilitates and gives meaning to change" (133). In "Canopus in the Classroom" Khanna observes that "[m]ore than thirty utopian novels by women have been published in the last fifteen years" that have presented female visions of the "good society" (9). These visions differ greatly from men's utopias. They are not "static systems strictly ruled by law" (9) but dynamic systems that lead to growth and transformation. This is definitely the case in *The Marriages* in which there are no external laws except an inner drive toward enlightened states of being.

29. Perrakis gives distinct labels to these Zones from the Sufi perspective: "Zone Five suggests the animal spirit—the body without awareness or consciousness. Ben Ata awakens Zone Five to the human spirit, the condition of Zone Four . . . Zone Three suggests the greater consciousness of a more fully realized human spirit, while Zone Two hints at the angelic spirit . . . Zone One is mentioned only once . . . Presumably it represents a still higher spiritual state" ("Sufism" 116). Draine applies logic to these Zones, which is difficult, as illustrated by her analysis (*Substance* 156ff.). If, on the other hand, one reads the *Canopus* series with more abandon of one's habitual and rational thought patterns, the novels may offer a pleasant

surprise or two. See Knapp's chart of the Zones in *Doris Lessing* (156). Rowe sees symbols of the yin/yang, anima/animus, and matriarchy/patriarchy in *The Marriages* (202). She observes various archetypes and some stereotypes in the novel, which qualify it as both mythic (i.e., timeless) and naturalistic (i.e., grounded in time) (195). See also Fahim 161, 166ff., on her discussion of Zones in *Shikasta* and 137, 258 n. 5, on Zones as metaphors of states of consciousness.

30. In order to understand how Lessing uses the synthetic dimension of characters, it will be instructive to turn to Phelan's study of characters once again. In part 2 of *Reading People, Reading Plots*, Phelan studies "the effects created when the mimetic illusion is broken and the authorial audience's usually covert awareness that character is an artificial construct becomes overt" (133) in works ranging from John Fowles's *The French Lieutenant's Woman* and Charles Dickens's *Great Expectations* to an extreme case such as Italo Calvino's *If on a Winter's Night a Traveler*. Phelan observes that in *The French Lieutenant's Woman* the narrator is firmly rooted in the twentieth century while he appears to write a Victorian novel. This dual perspective allows Fowles to move between the modern view of the novel as fiction and characters as constructs, and the Victorian view of the story as real and characters as mimetic. The fact that the narrator distinctly places himself in 1967 and looks back at the nineteenth century aligns us with the narrator and encourages our engagement with the thematic aspects of the characters, that is, conflicts of the Victorian age. In chapters 13 and 55 the modern perspective and, with it, the synthetic component of characters, are foregrounded. This introduces a tension between the narrator and the authorial audience, and, along with the treatment of Sarah, sets up the narrative for the two endings. The authorial audience's attention on the thematic is strengthened by the occasional foregrounding of the synthetic component of characters, even while the narrator promises and attempts to reveal the inner world of, for instance, the mimetic Sarah, and insists

on engaging the authorial audience on the mimetic level. Yet Sarah Woodruff never fully functions mimetically. In fact the first mention of her refers to her as "it," a figure in the distance, and later, as "Tragedy." We never get an inside view of her, which makes the two endings possible. The character of Sarah functions both mimetically and thematically as a complicator of the instabilities in Charles's life established in chapters 2–12: Charles is engaged to Ernestina, a Victorian woman, while he remains uncertain about embracing Victorian values. Meeting Sarah offers him an alternative: loving the mimetic Sarah, an independent woman of the lower class, would also mean choosing the thematic Sarah, or the modern age, the anti-Victorian lover, and freedom. This choice is rewarded by the first ending that resolves the major instability in Charles's life, while the second ending in which Sarah rejects Charles hints at Charles's further growth into the free "modern man." The way in which John Fowles foregrounds the synthetic aspect of Sarah's character to draw attention to the theme of the Victorian conflict is similar to Lessing's treatment of Al·Ith in *The Marriages* and of Doeg in *The Representative*.

31. Without the benefit of an allegorical reading, Robert Towers wrote, "Apart from her visionary side, Doris Lessing's preoccupations are still so much those of her own time . . . that they remain like an unassimilated lump within a narrative mode deriving from a very different epoch . . . Finally, the fable itself is simply not enthralling or compelling enough on its own terms to carry the weight of significance that Mrs. Lessing has assigned to it" (1).

32. Rowe explains, "Through their appearance we see the habits of their respective zones. Al·Ith has light and grace, and eats fruits and nuts. Ben Ata is more gross, relies on animal protein" (199). Adjectives Rowe associates with the former are "gentle," "sexual," and "delicate," and with the latter, "macho" and "rough" (199).

33. Perrakis likens the Zones to the nine concentric spheres in Islamic cosmology between the realm of the Divine and the

realm of our physical existence ("Sufism" 104). Draine writes, "When, in *The Marriages*, the six ascending orders of being are developed in the context of a fabulous fantasy, the allegory (elaborated much more fully than in *Shikasta*) succeeds brilliantly" (*Substance* 157). On the concept of evolution in Lessing, see also Auberlen. Sizemore touches on the idea of a multilayered text in her discussion of the city as "palimpsest." She identifies Lessing as a novelist who can "decipher and portray the multiplicity of layers" in her own life as well as in a city. This is symbolized in *The Four-Gated City* by the "fragment of thirteen layers of wallpaper . . . that Martha scrapes off the wall of a bombed house" (177). Sizemore defines this as a miniature palimpsest. She then reads this and other palimpsests as an archeologist or a geologist would the earth. As the city grows, so build its layers. Sizemore's subsequent discussion of "invisible boundar[ies]" (185) between various districts anticipates the Zones in *The Marriages*. Not only is the text multilayered in *The Marriages*, so is space and so are the characters who occupy its various layers. Rubenstein argues along similar lines that Lessing moved from realistic space to symbolic, metaphysical, allegorical space "with its own invented territories" ("Alchemical" 201). She describes the hierarchy of Zones as levels of enlightenment that require "work," and discusses the alchemy involved in the marriages in terms of spiritual growth (215).

34. Fahim analyzes *Shikasta* by comparing the tale-within-tale technique of Oriental literature to Lessing's narrative technique. She analyzes the theme of Sufi equilibrium in terms of the space-fiction genre (156).

35. See also Hardin's "The Sufi Teaching Story and Doris Lessing."

36. Perhaps for this reason Peel describes *The Marriages* as a "fable of communication" ("Communicating" 11).

37. For more on Muslim names in the *Canopus* series, see Caracciolo's "What's in a Canopean Name?" Jouve considers the possibility that Al·Ith in *The Marriages* is Alice in Wonderland "with a lilt, and a childish lisp" going into Zone

Two through the looking glass ("Female Voice" 131). She also touches on the Arabic- and Hindu-sounding names and parts of names such as *Al* or *Ben*. Although she does not give definitions for these words, Jouve does acknowledge their "multifarious, across-the-borders glitter" (131). "But," she writes, "the glitter stops at the names" (131). In "What's in a Name?" Cleary discusses names in *The Marriages* as Greek and Middle English names, when transposed. She also argues that "[i]deas are central to Lessing's art" (8). Therefore it is necessary to pay attention to the names of Lessing's characters, since their names will signal their significance and the theme for which they stand. Cleary associates Lessing's characters' names with their thematic components: "By the names Lessing chooses for these protagonists, she encourages her readers to imagine a new pattern, not only for individuals, but for society" (8–9).

38. Greene also sees this connection: "[Ben Ata and Vahshi's] marriage represents another clash of cultures that produces another painful lurch forward—and so the process of change ripples from one character to the next and from one Zone to the next" (*Poetics* 183).

39. For a discussion of Doeg acting as Lessing's spokesman see also chapter 6 of Fishburn's *The Unexpected Universe*.

40. Their mimetic qualities, nonetheless, must also be taken seriously.

41. This is a central theme in Sufism and in many of Lessing's novels. See also *Substance under Pressure* 102 for Draine's discussion of the Sufi theme of "remembering" in *Briefing for a Descent into Hell*. Fahim recognizes the Sufi stress on remembering as an essential element in *The Memoirs* (98).

Chapter 4

1. These names are listed in the order that they come up in this chapter, not chronologically.

2. Lessing said in an interview with Josephine Hendin, "I used to go particularly to novels to find out how I ought to live my life. But to my loss, I see now I didn't find out" (47).

3. Among them were Bacon, Pope, Hobbes, Butler, Cowley, Dryden, Locke, Sprat, Rochester, Defoe, Mandeville, Swift, Shaftesbury, Addison, Steele, and Hume.

4. This is a saying of the prophet Muhammad heard frequently in Muslim countries.

5. Science fiction is diverse enough to include both works that represent science and technology as "the God" and works that represent things that are fantastic in the allegorical sense and that do some kind of spiritual teaching. The latter, however, usually do *not* expect the audience to act on their teachings. Lessing's emphasis is much less on the scientific and much more on the spiritual, which she asks her readers to take seriously.

6. Suvin builds here on the concept of "estrangement" from the Russian formalists. See also Fahim. She is interested in the ways that Lessing's fictive technique incorporates Sufi methods of writing so that not only is the *content* of Lessing's novels important, but what the novel does to the reader—the *estrangement* and *cognition*—becomes important (142).

7. On science and religion, see also Fahim 204–8, 247: "Religion, which is considered one of the oldest 'certainties,' is also challenged" in *Shikasta*.

8. Draine reasons, "If the six Zones were to be viewed as wholly immaterial and yet somehow existent, a science fiction writer would feel obligated to suggest a scientific or pseudo-scientific theory under which such an anomalous state could obtain . . . [yet] in her trips into Zone Six, Lessing seems to feel no such obligation." Therefore, Draine argues, Lessing must be defining science fiction more broadly to include sacred literature, because both are involved in "future-projection," one social and scientific, the other spiritual. She adds, "[m]ost writers on science fiction vigorously oppose this view and exclude from the canons of science fiction those works which

give prominent place to mystical or spiritual concerns." She explains that "[f]or all those critics who have attempted to set limits between science fiction and surrounding genres, a fundamental distinction is that science fiction, as its name implies, grounds itself in *science*" (*Substance* 146).

9. Traditionally, Zoroaster is believed to have lived in Iran during the sixth-century B.C.E. A new theory, however, places him in 1200–1100 B.C.E.

10. Similarly, for instance, Tolkien emulates and makes allusions to the Arthurian legend.

11. I realize that Obiwan Kanobi, an evolved soul in *Star Wars*, contradicts my argument. However, while Lessing's evolved soul, Al·Ith, is the protagonist around whom the story is woven, the focus of *Star Wars* is not on Obiwan Kanobi but on Luke.

Appendix A

1. As discussed in the opening chapter to this book, the term *Sufism* is problematic. Sufis in Islam do not use the term to refer to their Way; it is a West-based term that was devised for outsiders' use.

2. From the lectures of Marilyn Waldman, in her history of Islam class at The Ohio State University, 1987.

Bibliography

Abel, Elizabeth. "*The Golden Notebook*: 'Female Writing' and 'The Great Tradition.'" Sprague and Tiger 101–7.

Ahearn, Marie L. "Why Doris Lessing's Move into Science Fiction?" in MLA panel as cited by Louis Marchino, "Lessing and Science Fiction." *Doris Lessing Newsletter* 5.1 (Summer 1981): 3–4.

Aldiss, Brian. "Living in Catastrophe." Ingersoll, *Doris Lessing* 169–72.

Amis, Kingsley. *New Maps of Hell: A Survey of Science Fiction*. NewYork: Harcourt, 1960.

Araz, Nezihe. *Aşk Peygamberi Mevlâna*. N.p., Turkey: Kervan, n.d.

Arberry, A. J. *Aspects of Islamic Civilization*. Ann Arbor: U of Michigan P, 1983.

———. *Mystical Poems of Rûmî*. Boulder: Westview, 1979.

———. *Sufism: An Account of the Mystics of Islam*. New York: Macmillan, 1950.

'Attâr, Farîduddîn. *The Conference of the Birds*. 1177. Trans. Dick Davis and Afkham Darbandi. New York: Penguin, 1984.

Atwood, Margaret. *Surfacing*. New York: Popular Library, 1976.

Auberlen, Eckhard. "Great Creating Nature and the Human Experiment in *The Golden Notebook* and *Canopus in Argos*." *Doris Lessing Newsletter* 13.1 (Summer 1989): 12–15.

BIBLIOGRAPHY

Austen, Jane. *Pride and Prejudice*. Ed. Donald J. Gray. New York: Norton, 1966.

Bacon, Francis. *Advancement of Learning*. Great Books of the Western World. Vol. 30. Ed. Robert Maynard Hutchins. Chicago: Benton, Encyclopedia Britannica, 1952.

Bakhtin, M. M. *The Dialogic Imagination*. Ed. Michael Holquist. Trans. Caryl Emerson and Michael Holquist. Austin: U of Texas P, 1981.

Bannon, Barbara A. "Authors and Editors." *Publishers Weekly* 2 June 1969: 51–54.

Baranczak, Stanislaw. *Breathing under Water and Other East European Essays*. Cambridge: Harvard UP, 1990.

Barnouw, Dagmar. "'Disorderly Company': From *The Golden Notebook* to *The Four-Gated City*." *Contemporary Literature* 14 (Autumn 1973): 491–514.

Barr, Marleen, and Nicholas D. Smith, eds. *Women and Utopia: Critical Interpretations*. Lanham: UP of America, 1983.

Bazin, Nancy Topping. "The Evolution of Doris Lessing's Art from a Mystical Moment to Space Fiction." Reilly 157–67.

——— . "Madness, Mysticism, and Fantasy: Shifting Perspectives in the Novels of Doris Lessing, Bessie Head, and Nadine Gordimer." *Extrapolation: A Journal of Science Fiction and Fantasy* 33 (Spring 1992): 1, 73–87.

——— . "The Moment of Revelation in *Martha Quest* and Comparable Moments by Two Modernists." *Modern Fiction Studies Special Issue: Doris Lessing* 26.1 (Spring 1980): 87–98.

Bennett, John G., ed. *Gurdjieff: Making a New World*. London: Harper, 1973.

——— . The Sermon on the Mount: Future Communities One. 1001. Sherborne House Talk Tapes.

——— . Sherborne House Talk Tapes. Audiocassettes. Charles Town: Claymont Communications, 1976. 1001–54.

——— . *Witness: The Autobiography of John G. Bennett*. Charles Town: Claymont Communications, 1983.

Bergonzi, Bernard and Margaret Drabble. *Contemporary Novelists*. Ed. James Vinson. New York: St. Martin's, 1976. 373–74.

Bertelsen, Eve. "Acknowledging a New Frontier." Ingersoll, *Doris Lessing* 120–45.

———. "The Persistent Personal Voice: Lessing on Rhodesia and Marxism." *Doris Lessing Newsletter* 9.2 (1985): 8–10.

Bigsby, Christopher. "The Need to Tell Stories." Ingersoll, *Doris Lessing* 70–85.

Bikman, Minda. "Creating Your Own Demand." Ingersoll, *Doris Lessing* 57–63.

Bishop, Nick. *Remaking Poetry: Ted Hughes and a New Critical Psychology*. New York: St. Martin's, 1991.

Blake, William. "Auguries of Innocence." *Eighteenth-Century English Literature*. Ed. Geoffrey Tillotson, Paul Fussell, and Marshall Waingrow. New York: Harcourt, 1969. 1506.

———. "There is No Natural Religion." *Eighteenth-Century English Literature*. Ed. Geoffrey Tillotson, Paul Fussell, and Marshall Waingrow. New York: Harcourt, 1969. 1493.

Blish, James [as William Atheling]. "Cathedrals in Space." *The Issue at Hand*. Chicago: Advent, 1973.

Bloom, Harold, ed. *Modern Critical Views: Doris Lessing*. New York: Chelsea, 1986.

Bly, Robert, ed. *News of the Universe: Poems of Twofold Consciousness*. Chosen and introduced by Robert Bly. San Francisco: Sierra Club, 1980.

Booth, Wayne. *The Company We Keep: An Ethics of Fiction*. Berkeley: U of California P, 1988.

Brewster, Dorothy. *Doris Lessing*. New York: Twayne, 1965.

Britannica Book of the Year. 1995.

Brontë, Charlotte. *Jane Eyre*. Ed. Margaret Smith. Oxford: Oxford UP, 1975.

Brooks, Ellen W. "The Image of Women in Lessing's *Golden Notebook*." *Critique: Studies in Modern Fiction* 15.1 (1973): 101–9.

BIBLIOGRAPHY

Buckler, Ernest. "Against the Terror, the Spirit of Sisyphus." Rev. of *The Golden Notebook*, by Doris Lessing. *New York Times Book Review* 1 July 1962: 4, 18–19.

Bunyan, John. *The Pilgrim's Progress*. New York: Penguin, 1968.

Burgess, Anthony. *The Novel Now: A Guide to Contemporary Fiction*. New York: Norton, 1967.

Camus, Albert. *The Myth of Sisyphus, and Other Essays*. New York: Alfred Knopf, 1964.

———. *The Stranger*. New York: Vintage, 1946.

Capra, Fritjof. *The Tao of Physics*. Toronto: Bantam, 1984.

Caracciolo, Peter. "What's in a Canopean Name?" *Doris Lessing Newsletter* 8.1 (Spring 1984): 15.

Carey, John. "Art and Reality in *The Golden Notebook*." *Contemporary Literature* 14 (Autumn 1973): 437–56.

Carroll, Lewis. *Alice's Adventures in Wonderland and Through the Looking-Glass*. New York: Grosset, 1925.

Charnas, Suzy McKee. *Motherliness*. New York: Berkeley, 1978.

Cherry-Garrard, Apsley. *The Worst Journey in the World, Antarctic 1910–1913*. London: Chatto, 1937.

Clarke, Arthur Charles. *Childhood's End*. New York: Harcourt, 1953.

Cleary, Rochelle. "What's in a Name? Lessing's Message in *The Marriages between Zones Three, Four, and Five*." *Doris Lessing Newsletter* 6.2 (Winter 1982): 8–10.

Courtland, Lewis. "A Visit to Idries Shah." Lewin 82–100.

Cowley, Malcolm. "Future Notebook." Rev. of *The Memoirs of a Survivor*, by Doris Lessing. *Saturday Review* 28 June 1975: 23–24.

Daly, Mary. *Beyond God the Father: Towards a Philosophy of Women's Liberation*. Boston: Beacon, 1973.

Davis, Lennard J. *Resisting Novels: Ideology and Fiction*. New York: Methuen, 1987.

Dean, Michael. "Writing as Time Runs Out." Ingersoll, *Doris Lessing* 86–93.

de Montremy, Jean-Maurice. "A Writer Is Not a Professor." Ingersoll, *Doris Lessing* 193–99.

DeMott, Benjamin. "Tales of Two Writers." Rev. of *Shikasta*, by Doris Lessing. *Saturday Review* 24 Dec. 1979: 6, 54–55.

DeView, Lucille. "The World According to Lessing: Paradise Lost." Rev. of *Shikasta*, by Doris Lessing. *Christian Science Monitor* 14 Nov. 1979: B3.

Drabble, Margaret. "Doris Lessing: Cassandra in a World Under Siege." *Ramparts* Feb. 1972: 50–54.

Draine, Betsy. "Changing Frames: Doris Lessing's *Memoirs of a Survivor*." *Studies in the Novel* 11.1 (Spring 1979): 51–62.

———. *Substance under Pressure*. Madison: U of Wisconsin P, 1983.

Driver, C. J. "Profile 8: Doris Lessing." *New Review* Nov. 1974: 17–23.

DuPlessis, Rachel Blau. "The Feminist Apologues of Lessing, Piercy, and Russ." *Frontiers* 4.1 (1979): 1–8.

———. *Writing beyond the Ending: Narrative Strategies of Twentieth-Century Women Writers*. Bloomington: Indiana UP, 1985.

Eagleton, Terry. *Exiles and Émigrés*. London: Chatto, 1974.

———. *Literary Theory: An Introduction*. Minneapolis: U of Minnesota P, 1983.

Ean, Tan Gim, et al. "The Older I Get, the Less I Believe." Ingersoll, *Doris Lessing* 200–203.

Ebert, Robert. "Doris Lessing: An Idol on a Mercurial Pedestal." *Louisville Courier-Journal and Times* 22 June 1969: G4.

Eliade, Mircea. "The World, the City, the House." *Occultism, Witchcraft, and Cultural Fashions: Essays in Comparative Religions*. Chicago: U of Chicago P, 1976. 18–31.

Eliot, T. S. *The Waste Land*. Ellman and O'Clair 457–71.

Ellmann, Richard, and R. O'Clair, eds. *The Norton Anthology of Modern Poetry*. New York: Norton, 1973.

Elwell-Sutton, L. P. Letter to the Editor. "The Mysterious East." *New York Review of Books* 22 Oct. 1970: 51–52.

———. "Mystic Making." *New York Review of Books* 2 July 1970: 35–37.

———. "Sufism & Pseudo-Sufism." *Encounter* 44.5 (May 1975): 9–17.

———. "Sufism & Pseudo-Sufism." *Islam in the Modern World.* Ed. Denis MacEoin and Ahmed Al-Shahi. New York: St. Martin's, 1983. 49–56.

The Empire Strikes Back. Prod. Gary Kurtz. Dir. Irvin Kershner. 128 min. Lucas Film Ltd., 1980.

Ewing, Katherine Pratt. *Arguing Sainthood: Modernity, Psychoanalysis, and Islam.* Durham, NC: Duke UP, 1997.

Fahim, Shadia S. *Doris Lessing and Sufi Equilibrium: The Evolving Form of the Novel.* New York: St. Martin's, 1994.

Faulkner, William. *The Sound and The Fury.* Ed. David Minter. New York: Norton, 1987.

Fishburn, Katherine. *Doris Lessing: Life, Work, and Criticism.* Fredericton, NB: York, 1987.

———. *The Unexpected Universe of Doris Lessing.* Westport: Greenwood, 1985.

Forster, E. M. *A Passage to India.* San Diego: Harcourt, 1924.

Ford, Boris, ed. *The New Pelican Guide to English Literature: The Present.* Harmondsworth: Penguin, 1983.

Forde, Nigel. "Reporting from the Terrain of the Mind." Ingersoll, *Doris Lessing* 214–18.

Foster, William. "Sufi Studies Today." Lewin 123–37.

Foucault, Michel. *Madness and Civilization: A History of Insanity in the Age of Reason.* New York: Pantheon, 1965.

Frick, Thomas. "Caged by the Experts." Ingersoll, *Doris Lessing* 155–68.

Friedlander, Ira Shems. *The Whirling Dervishes.* New York: Macmillan, 1975.

Galin, Müge, ed. *Turkish Sampler: Writings for all Readers.* Indiana University Turkish Studies. 7. Bloomington: Indiana University, 1989.

Gamallo, Isabel Anievas. "The Feminine English Novel of Initiation: Doris Lessing in the Tradition of Bildungsroman." Diss. Universidad de Leon, Spain, 1994.

Gearhart, Sally Miller. *The Wanderground: Stories of the Hill Women*. Watertown: Persephone, 1979.

Ghazzâlî, Muhammad al. *Ihyâ 'Ulûm al-Dîn* [The revival of religious sciences]. Bayrut: Dar al-Nafais, 1982.

Gilbert, Sandra, and Susan Gubar. *The Madwoman in the Attic: The Woman Writer and the Nineteenth-Century Literary Imagination*. New Haven: Yale UP, 1979.

Gindin, James. *Postwar British Fiction: New Accents and Attitudes*. Berkeley: U of California P, 1962.

Graves, Robert. Introduction. *The Sufis*. By Idries Shah. New York: Doubleday, 1964. vii–xxii.

Gray, Paul. "Visit to a Small Planet." Rev. of *Shikasta*, by Doris Lessing. *Time* 22 Oct. 1979: 101–2.

Gray, Stephen. "Breaking Down These Forms." Ingersoll, *Doris Lessing* 109–19.

Green, Martin. "The Doom of Empire: *Memoirs of a Survivor*." *Doris Lessing Newsletter* 6 (Winter 1982): 6–7, 10.

Greene, Gayle. *Changing the Story: Feminist Fiction and the Tradition*. Bloomington: Indiana UP, 1991.

——— . *Doris Lessing: The Poetics of Change*. Ann Arbor: U of Michigan P, 1995.

Gunn, Giles. *The Interpretation of Otherness: Literature, Religion, and the American Imagination*. New York: Oxford UP, 1979.

Gurdjieff, George Ivanovich. *All and Everything: Beelzebub's Tales to His Grandson*. 3 vols. New York: Dutton, 1973.

——— . *Views From the Real World*. New York: Dutton, 1975.

Haas, Joseph. "Doris Lessing: Chronicler of the Cataclysm." *Panorama* [Chicago] 14 June 1969: 4–5.

Halliday, Patricia Young. *The Pursuit of Wholeness in the Work of Doris Lessing: Dualities, Multiplicities, and the Resolution of Patterns in Illumination*. Diss. U of Minnesota, 1973. Ann Arbor: UMI, 1973.

Hardin, Nancy Shields. "Doris Lessing and the Sufi Way." *Contemporary Literature* 14.4 (Autumn 1973): 565–81.

——— . "The Sufi Teaching Story and Doris Lessing." *Twentieth-Century Literature* 23.3 (Oct. 1977): 314–26.

BIBLIOGRAPHY

Hazleton, Lesley. "Doris Lessing on Feminism, Communism, and 'Space Fiction.'" *New York Times Magazine* 25 July 1982: 21–29.

Hendin, Josephine. "The Capacity to Look at a Situation Coolly." Ingersoll, *Doris Lessing* 41–56.

Hinz, Evelyn J., and John Teunissen. "The Pietà as Icon in *The Golden Notebook.*" *Contemporary Literature* 14 (Autumn 1973): 457–70.

Hodgson, Marshall G. S. *The Venture of Islam: The Classical Age of Islam.* 3 vols. Chicago: U of Chicago P, 1974.

Holloway, John. "The Literary Scene." Ford 417–49.

Howe, Florence. "A Conversation with Doris Lessing." *Contemporary Literature* 14 (Autumn 1973): 418–36.

Ingersoll, Earl. "Describing This Beautiful and Nasty Planet." Ingersoll, *Doris Lessing* 228–40.

———. *Doris Lessing: Conversations.* Princeton: Ontario Review, 1994.

Ishaq, Ibn. *The Life of Muhammad: A Translation of Ishaq's Sirat Rasûl Allah.* Ed. and trans. A. Guillaume. Oxford: Oxford UP, 1955.

James, William. *The Varieties of Religious Experience.* 1903. Ed. Frederick H. Burkhardt, Fredson Bowers, and Ignas K. Skrupskelis. Cambridge: Harvard UP, 1985.

Jouve, Nicole Ward. "Doris Lessing: A 'Female Voice'—Past, Present, or Future?" Kaplan and Rose 127–33.

———. "Of Mud and Other Matter—*The Children of Violence.*" Taylor, *Notebooks / Memoirs / Archives* 75–134.

Jung, Carl G. *Memories, Dreams, Reflections.* New York: Vintage, 1961.

———. *Inheritance of Dreams.* Prod. and dir. Stephen Segaller. Videocassette. 53 min. R. M. Arts Productions, 1989. Vol. 2 of *Wisdom of the Dream.* 3 vols. 1989.

———. *Matter of Heart.* Dir. Mark Whitney. Prod. Michael Whitney. Videocassette. 107 min. Kino Video, 1985. Vol. 1 of *Wisdom of the Dream.* 3 vols. 1989.

———. *A World of Dreams.* Prod. and dir. Stephen Segaller. Videocassette. 53 min. R. M. Arts Productions, 1989.

Vol. 3 of *Wisdom of the Dream*. 3 vols. 1989.

Kabîr. *The Kabîr Book: Forty-four of the Ecstatic Poems of Kabîr*. Trans. Robert Bly. Boston: Beacon, 1977.

Kaplan, Carey. "Britain's Imperialist Past in Doris Lessing's Futuristic Fiction." Kaplan and Rose 149–58.

Kaplan, Carey and Ellen Cronan Rose. *Doris Lessing: The Alchemy of Survival*. Athens: Ohio UP, 1988.

Kaplan, Sydney Janet. "The Limits of Consciousness in the Novels of Doris Lessing." *Contemporary Literature* 14 (Autumn 1973): 536–49.

Kelsey, Alice Geer. *Once the Hodja*. New York: Longmans, 1943.

Keppler, Carl F. *The Literature of the Second Self*. Tucson: U of Arizona P, 1972.

Ketterer, David. *New Worlds for Old: The Apocalyptic Imagination, Science Fiction, and American Literature*. Bloomington: Indiana UP, 1974.

Khanna, Lee Cullen. "*Canopus* in the Classroom." *Doris Lessing Newsletter* 7.1 (Summer 1983): 9–10.

———. "Truth and Art in Women's Worlds: Doris Lessing's *The Marriages between Zones Three, Four, and Five*." Barr and Smith 121–33.

Knapp, Mona. *Doris Lessing*. New York: Frederick Ungar, 1984.

Kumar, Sarla. "Sufism in Doris Lessing." *Paniah University Research Bulletin: Arts* 14.2 (Oct. 1983): 167–79.

Kurzweil, Edith. "Unexamined Mental Attitudes Left Behind by Communism." Ingersoll, *Doris Lessing* 204–13.

Langley, L. "Scenario for Salvation." *Guardian* 14 Apr. 1971: 8.

Leavis, F. R. *The Great Tradition*. New York: New York UP, 1964.

LeGuin, Ursula K. *The Left Hand of Darkness*. New York: Ace, 1976.

———. Rev. of *Re: Colonized Planet 5 Shikasta*, by Doris Lessing. *The New Republic* 13 Oct. 1979: 32–34.

Lem, Stanislav. *Die Astronauten [The Astronauts]*. 1951. Frankfurt am Main: Suhrkamp, 1978.

———. *Ozlowick z Marsa [The Man from Mars]*. Warszawa, Poland: Niczalezna Oficyna Wydawnicza, 1944.

―――― . *Solaris*. Warszawa: Wydawn, Ministerstwa Obrony Narodowej, 1961.

Leonard, John. "The Spacing Out of Doris Lessing." Rev. of *The Making of the Representative for Planet 8*, by Doris Lessing. *New York Times Book Review* 7 Feb. 1982: 1, 34–35.

Lessing, Doris. *African Laughter: Four Visits to Zimbabwe*. New York: Harper, 1992.

―――― . "An Ancient Way to New Freedom." Lewin 73–82.

―――― . *Briefing for a Descent into Hell*. New York: Vintage, 1971.

―――― . "Building a New Cultural Understanding with the People of the East." *Times* [London] 11 Oct. 1975: 8.

―――― . *The Diaries of Jane Somers*. New York: Alfred A. Knopf, 1983–84.

―――― . *The Diary of a Good Neighbour*. New York: Alfred A. Knopf, 1983.

―――― , ed. *The Doris Lessing Reader*. London: Cape, 1989.

―――― . "The East's New Dawn." *Books and Bookmen* 20 (June 1975): 26–27.

―――― . "An Elephant in the Dark." *Spectator* 213 (1964): 373.

―――― . *The Fifth Child*. New York: Knopf, 1988.

―――― . *The Four-Gated City*. New York: Knopf, 1969.

―――― . *The Golden Notebook*. 1962. New York: Bantam, 1979.

―――― . *The Good Terrorist*. New York: Knopf, 1985.

―――― . *The Grass is Singing*. New York: Popular Library, 1950.

―――― . "If You Knew Sufi . . ." *Guardian* 8 Jan. 1972: 12.

―――― . "In the World, Not of It." *Encounter* 39 (Aug. 1972): 61–64.

―――― . Introduction. *Learning How to Learn: Psychology and Spirituality in the Sufi Way* (French Edition). By Idries Shah. New York: Harper, 1981.

―――― . *Landlocked*. London: MacGibbon, 1965.

―――― . "Learning How to Learn." *Asia Magazine* July/ Aug. 1982: 12–15.

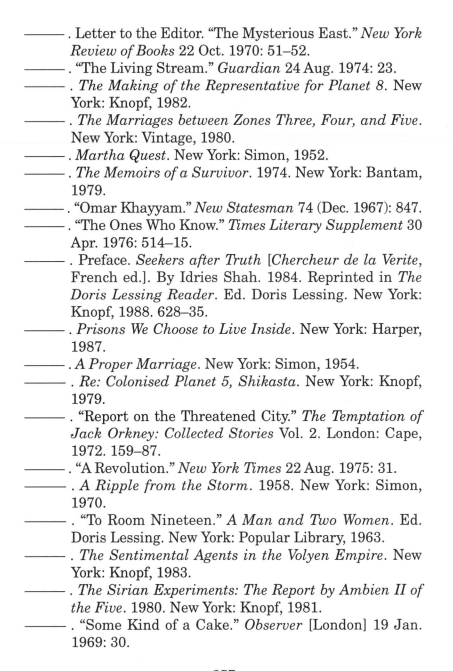

————. Letter to the Editor. "The Mysterious East." *New York Review of Books* 22 Oct. 1970: 51–52.

————. "The Living Stream." *Guardian* 24 Aug. 1974: 23.

————. *The Making of the Representative for Planet 8.* New York: Knopf, 1982.

————. *The Marriages between Zones Three, Four, and Five.* New York: Vintage, 1980.

————. *Martha Quest.* New York: Simon, 1952.

————. *The Memoirs of a Survivor.* 1974. New York: Bantam, 1979.

————. "Omar Khayyam." *New Statesman* 74 (Dec. 1967): 847.

————. "The Ones Who Know." *Times Literary Supplement* 30 Apr. 1976: 514–15.

————. Preface. *Seekers after Truth* [*Chercheur de la Verite*, French ed.]. By Idries Shah. 1984. Reprinted in *The Doris Lessing Reader.* Ed. Doris Lessing. New York: Knopf, 1988. 628–35.

————. *Prisons We Choose to Live Inside.* New York: Harper, 1987.

————. *A Proper Marriage.* New York: Simon, 1954.

————. *Re: Colonised Planet 5, Shikasta.* New York: Knopf, 1979.

————. "Report on the Threatened City." *The Temptation of Jack Orkney: Collected Stories* Vol. 2. London: Cape, 1972. 159–87.

————. "A Revolution." *New York Times* 22 Aug. 1975: 31.

————. *A Ripple from the Storm.* 1958. New York: Simon, 1970.

————. "To Room Nineteen." *A Man and Two Women.* Ed. Doris Lessing. New York: Popular Library, 1963.

————. *The Sentimental Agents in the Volyen Empire.* New York: Knopf, 1983.

————. *The Sirian Experiments: The Report by Ambien II of the Five.* 1980. New York: Knopf, 1981.

————. "Some Kind of a Cake." *Observer* [London] 19 Jan. 1969: 30.

———. "Sufic Samples." *Listener* 79 (June 1968): 744.

———. "Sufi Philosophy and Poetry." *Books and Bookmen* Oct. 1974: 38–39.

———. *The Summer before the Dark*. New York: Vintage, 1973.

———. "The Temptation of Jack Orkney." *The Temptation of Jack Orkney: Collected Stories*. Vol. 2. London: Cape, 1972. 213–72.

———. *Under My Skin*. New York: Harper, 1994.

———. "Unmasking Burton." *Guardian* 20 July 1974: 23.

———. "The Way of Mecca." *Books and Bookmen* Oct. 1974: 38–39.

———. "What Looks Like an Egg and Is an Egg?" *New York Times Book Review* 7 May 1972: 6, 41–43.

———. *The Wind Blows Away our Words*. New York: Vintage, 1987.

———. *Writer's Encounter with Sufism: Is There Something in it For Me?* Audiocassette. 23 mins. London: Norton Seminar Cassettes, 1973.

Levin, Susan. "A Fourfold Vision: William Blake and Doris Lessing." *William Blake and the Moderns*. Ed. Robert J. Bertholf and Annette S. Levitt. Albany: State U of New York P, 1982. 212–21.

Lewin, Leonard, ed. *An Elephant in the Dark*. New York: Dutton, 1976.

Lewis, C. S. *The Great Divorce*. New York: Macmillan, 1946.

———. *Perelandra*. New York: Macmillan, 1975.

Lewis, M. Susan. "Conscious Evolution in *The Four-Gated City*." *Anonymous: A Journal for the Woman Writer* 1 (Spring 1974): 56–71.

Lings, Martin. *The Secret of Shakespeare*. New York: Inner Traditions International, 1984.

Lott, Sandra. "The Evolving Consciousness of Feminine Identity in Doris Lessing's *The Memoirs of a Survivor* and Lewis Caroll's *Alice in Wonderland* and *Through the Looking Glass*." *Women Worldwalkers: New Dimensions of Science Fiction and Fantasy*. Ed. Jane B. Weedman. Lubbock: Texas Tech P, 1985. 165–79.

Maddocks, Melvin. "Ghosts and Portents." Rev. of *The Memoirs of a Survivor*, by Doris Lessing. *Time* 16 June 1975: 79.

Magie, Michael L. "Doris Lessing and Romanticism." *College English* Feb. 1977: 531–52.

Marchino, Louis. "Lessing and Science Fiction." *Doris Lessing Newsletter* 5.1 (Summer 1981): 3–4.

Marcuse, Herbert. *One-Dimensional Man: Studies in the Ideology of Advanced Industrial Society*. 1964. Boston: Beacon, 1966.

Markos, Alice Bradley. "The Pathology of Feminine Failure in the Fiction of Doris Lessing." *Critique: Studies in Modern Fiction* 16 Minneapolis: Bolingbroke Society, 1974.

McCrindle, Jean. "Reading *The Golden Notebook* in 1962." Taylor, *Notebooks/Memoirs/Archives* 43–56.

McDowell, P. W. Frederick. "The Fiction of Doris Lessing: An Interim View." *Arizona Quarterly* 21 (1965): 315–45.

The Meaning of the Glorious Koran. Ed. and trans. Mohammed Marmaduke Pickthall. New York: Mentor, 1953.

Middleton, Victoria. "Doris Lessing's 'Debt' to Olive Schreiner." Kaplan and Rose 135–47.

———. *Modern Fiction Studies Special Issue: Doris Lessing* 26.1 (Spring 1980).

Morgan, Ellen. "Alienation of the Woman Writer in *The Golden Notebook*." *Contemporary Literature* 14 (Autumn 1973): 471–80.

Mosier, M. Patricia. "A Sufi Model for the Teacher/Disciple Relationship in *The Sirian Experiments*." *Extrapolation: A Journal of Science Fiction and Fantasy* 32.3 (Fall 1991): 209–21.

Moskowitz, Sam. *Explorers of the Infinite: Shapers of Science Fiction*. Westport: Hyperion, 1974.

Musil, Robert. *The Man without Qualities*. New York: Coward, 1953.

"Mysticism." *Webster's Ninth New Collegiate Dictionary*. 1985.

Nasr, Seyyed Hossein. *Sufi Essays*. 1973. Albany: State U of New York P, 1991.

The New English Bible. London: Oxford UP, 1970.

Newquist, Roy. "Talking as a Person." Ingersoll, *Doris Lessing* 3–12.

Nicholson, Reynold A. *Studies in Islamic Mysticism*. Cambridge: Cambridge UP, 1980.

Nordell, Roderick. "Theme and Technique." Rev. of *The Golden Notebook*, by Doris Lessing. *Christian Science Monitor* 5 July 1962: 11.

Oates, Joyce Carol. "A Visit with Doris Lessing." *Southern Review* Oct. 1973: 873–82.

O'Connor, Flannery. *3 by Flannery O'Connor: Wise Blood, A Good Man is Hard to Find, The Violent Bear It Away*. New York: Signet, 1962.

Ornstein, Robert E. "Contemporary Sufism." Tart 355–88.

O'Rourke, Rebecca. "Doris Lessing: Exile and Exception." Taylor, *Notebooks / Memoirs / Archives* 206–26.

Oumhani, Cecile. "Doris Lessing et le Soufisme (*Shikasta* et *The Marriages between Zones Three, Four, and Five*)." *Revue de Litterature Compare* 225.1 (Jan.–Mar. 1983): 81–93.

Ouspensky, P. D. *In Search of the Miraculous*. New York: Harcourt, 1949.

———. *The Psychology of Man's Possible Evolution*. New York: Vintage, 1950.

Öztürk, Yaşar Nuri. *The Eye of the Heart*. Trans. Richard Blakney. İstanbul: Redhouse, 1988.

Peel, Ellen. "Communicating Differently: Lessing's *Marriages between Zones Three, Four, and Five*." *Doris Lessing Newsletter* 6 (Winter 1982): 11–13.

———. "The Self is Always an Other: Going the Long Way Home." *Twentieth-Century Literature* 35.1 (Spring 1989): 1–16.

Perrakis, Phyllis Sternberg. "The Marriage of Inner and Outer Space in Doris Lessing's *Shikasta*." *Science Fiction Studies* 17.2 (July 1990): 221–38.

———. "Sufism, Jung and the Myth of Kore: Revisionist Politics in Lessing's *Marriages*." *Mosaic: A Journal for the Interdisciplinary Study of Literature* 25.3 (Summer 1992): 99–120.

Phelan, James. *Reading People, Reading Plots: Character, Progression, and the Interpretation of Narrative.* Chicago: U of Chicago P, 1989.

Phelps, Gilbert. "The Post-War English Novel." Ford 65–125.

Pickering, Jean. "Martha Quest and 'The Anguish of Feminine Fragmentation.'" Sprague and Tiger 94–100.

———. *Understanding Doris Lessing.* Columbia: U of South Carolina P, 1990.

Piercy, Marge. *Woman on the Edge of Time.* New York: Fawcett, 1976.

Plato. *Symposium.* Cambridge: Cambridge UP, 1980.

Platzner, Robert L. "The Mystifiction of Outer Space: Pseudo-Mysticism and Science Fiction." *Studia Mystica* 1 (1978): 44–51.

Pratt, Annis, and L. S. Dembo, eds. *Doris Lessing: Critical Studies.* Madison: U of Wisconsin P, 1974.

Qur'ân. See *The Meaning of the Glorious Koran.*

Rapping, Elayne Antler. Review of *Cat's Eye* by Margaret Atwood. *Guardian* 12 Apr. 1989: 17.

Raskin, Jonah. "Doris Lessing at Stony Brook: An Interview by Jonah Raskin." Schlueter, *Small* 61–77.

Reilly, Robert, ed. *The Transcendent Adventure: Studies of Religion in Science Fiction/Fantasy.* Westport: Greenwood, 1985.

Rich, Adrienne. *Of Woman Born: Motherhood as Experience and Institution.* New York: Norton, 1976.

Richey, Clarence W. "Professor Watkins' 'Sleep of Necessity.'" *Notes on Contemporary Literature* Mar. 1972: 9–11.

Rigney, Barbara. *Margaret Atwood.* London: Macmillan, 1987.

Rose, Ellen Cronan. "Doris Lessing's 'Città Felice.'" *Massachusetts Review* 24.4 (Summer 1983): 369–86.

———. *The Tree outside the Window: Doris Lessing's Children of Violence.* Hanover: UP of New England, 1976.

Rousseau, Francois-Olivier. "The Habit of Observing." Ingersoll, *Doris Lessing* 146–54.

Rowe, Marsha. "If you Mate a Swan and a Gander, Who Will Ride?" Taylor, *Notebooks/Memoirs/Archives* 191–205.

Rubens, Robert. "Footnote to the *Golden Notebook*." *Queen* 21 Aug. 1962: 30–32.

Rubenstein, Roberta. *"The Marriages between Zones Three, Four, and Five.* Doris Lessing's Alchemical Allegory." *Extrapolation* 24.3 (Fall 1983): 201–15.

———. *The Novelistic Vision of Doris Lessing: Breaking the Forms of Consciousness.* Chicago: U of Illinois P, 1979.

———. "Outer Space, Inner Space: Doris Lessing's Metaphor of Science Fiction." *World Literature Written in English* Apr. 1975: 187–98.

———. Rev. of *Prisons We Choose to Live Inside*, by Doris Lessing. *Doris Lessing Newsletter* 12.1 (Spring 1988): 7.

Rûmî, Mawlânâ Jalâluddîn. *Divan-e Shams-e Tabrîzî.* Ed. Foruzanfar. Tehran: Amir Kabîr, 1984.

———. *Selected Poems from the Divan-e Shams-e Tabrîzî.* Trans. Reynold A. Nicholson. London: Cambridge UP, 1898.

———. *Jalâluddîn Rûmî, Mawlânâ. 1207–1273, Selections.* Trans. Robert Bly. Cambridge: Yellow Moon, 1983.

———. *The Mathnawî of Jalâluddîn Rûmî.* Trans. Reynold A. Nicholson. London: Luzac, 1940.

———. *Open Secret: Versions of Rûmî.* Trans. John Moyne and Coleman Barks. Putney: Threshold, 1984.

———. *This Longing: Poetry, Teaching Stories, and Letters of Rûmî.* Trans. Coleman Barks and John Moyne. Putney: Threshold, 1988.

———. *When Grapes Turn to Wine: Versions of Rûmî.* Trans. Robert Bly. Cambridge: Yellow Moon, 1983.

Rushdie, Salman. *The Satanic Verses.* New York: Viking, 1988.

Russ, Joanna. *The Female Man.* 1975. New York: Bantam, 1978.

Sage, Lorna. *Doris Lessing.* London: Methuen, 1983.

Said, Edward W. *Culture and Imperialism.* New York: Knopf, 1993.

———. *Orientalism.* New York: Vintage, 1979.

Sale, Roger. Rev. of *A Small Personal Voice*, by Doris Lessing. *New York Times Book Review* 22 Sept. 1974: 4.

Sardhana, Nawab. *Hu-Nama (Book of Hu)*. 1596. *Tales of the Dervishes*. Ed. and trans. Idries Shah. New York: Dutton, 1967. 35–38.

Saxton, Ruth. "The Female Body Veiled: From Crocus to Clitoris." Saxton and Tobin 95–122.

Saxton, Ruth, and Jean Tobin. *Woolf and Lessing: Breaking the Mold*. New York: St. Martin's, 1994.

Schimmel, Annemarie. *Mystical Dimensions of Islam*. Chapel Hill: U of North Carolina P, 1975.

Schlueter, Paul. *The Novels of Doris Lessing*. Carbondale: Southern Illinois UP, 1973.

——— . "A Sample Course on Lessing." *Doris Lessing Newsletter* 2 (Summer 1978): 3, 11.

——— . "Schlueter on Lessing Scholarship." *Doris Lessing Newsletter* 2 (Summer 1978): 6, 12.

——— , ed. *A Small Personal Voice*. New York: Knopf, 1974.

Schreiner, Olive. *The Story of an African Farm*. New York: Schocken, 1976.

Scott, Ann. "The More Recent Writings: Sufism, Mysticism, and Politics." Taylor, *Notebooks / Memoirs / Archives* 164–90.

Seaver, George. *Edward Wilson of the Antarctic: Naturalist and Friend*. New York: Dutton, 1937.

Seligman, Dee. "The Sufi Quest." *World Literature Written in English* Nov. 1973: 190–206.

Shabistarî, Sa'd ud Dîn Mahmûd. *The Secret Garden*. Trans. Johnson Pasha. London: Octagon, 1974.

Shah, Amina. *The Tale of the Four Dervishes and Other Sufi Tales*. San Francisco: Harper, 1975.

Shah, Idries. *The Exploits of the Incomparable Mulla Nasrudin*. New York: Dutton, 1972.

——— . *Learning How to Learn: Psychology and Spirituality in the Sufi Way*. New York: Harper, 1981.

——— . *A Perfumed Scorpion: The Way to the Way*. London: Octagon, 1978.

——— . *The Pleasantries of the Incredible Mulla Nasrudin*. New York: Dutton, 1973.

BIBLIOGRAPHY

———. *Seekers after Truth*. London: Octagon, 1982.

———. *The Subtleties of the Inimitable Mulla Nasrudin*. New York: Dutton, 1973.

———. *The Sufis*. New York: Doubleday, 1964.

———. *Tales of the Dervishes*. New York: Dutton, 1967.

———. *Thinkers of the East*. London: Cape, 1971.

———. *The Way of the Sufi*. 1968. New York: Dutton, 1970.

Shakespeare, William. *Hamlet*. Ed. Harold Bloom. New York: Chelsea, 1990.

Shklovsky, Victor. "Art as Technique." *Russian Formalist Criticism: Four Essays*. Ed. and trans. Lee T. Lemon and Marion J. Reis. Lincoln: U of Nebraska P, 1965. 3–24.

Showalter, Elaine. "Feminist Criticism in the Wilderness." *Critical Inquiry* 8.2 (1981): 179–205.

———. *A Literature of Their Own: British Women Novelists from Brontë to Lessing*. London: Virago, 1978.

Singer, Sandra. "Unleashing Human Potentialities: Doris Lessing's *The Memoirs of a Survivor* and Contemporary Cultural Theory." *Text and Context: A Journal of Interdisciplinary Studies* 1.1 (Autumn 1986): 79–95.

Singleton, Mary Ann. *The City and the Veld: The Fiction of Doris Lessing*. Lewisburg: Bucknell UP, 1977.

Sizemore, Christine W. "Reading the City as a Palimpest: The Experiential Perception of the City in Doris Lessing's *The Four-Gated City*." *Women Writers and the City: Essays in Feminist Literary Criticism*. Ed. Susan Merrill Squier. Knoxville: U of Tennessee P, 1984. 176–90.

Soos, Emese. "Revolution in the Historical Fiction of Jean-Paul Sartre and Doris Lessing." *Perspectives on Contemporary Literature* [Publication of the Conference on Twentieth-Century Literature] 2.1 (1976): 23–33.

Spacks, Patricia Meyer. "Free Women." *The Hudson Review* 24 (Winter 1971–72): 559–73.

Spencer, Edmund. *The Faerie Queene*. *The Norton Anthology of English Literature* Vol. 1. Ed. M. H. Abrams, et al. New York: Norton, 1979. 515–708.

Spiegel, Rotraut. *Doris Lessing: The Problem of Alienation and the Form of the Novel*. Frankfurt: Lang, 1980.

Spilka, Mark. "Lessing and Lawrence: The Battle of the Sexes." *Contemporary Literature* 16 (1975): 218–40.

Sprague, Claire. "Doubles Talk in *The Golden Notebook*." *Papers on Language and Literature* 17 (Spring 1982): 181–97.

——— . "Naming in *Marriages*: Another View." *Doris Lessing Newsletter* 7.1 (Summer 1983): 13.

——— . *Rereading Doris Lessing: Narrative Patterns of Doubling and Repetition*. Chapel Hill: U of North Carolina P, 1987.

Sprague, Claire, and Virginia Tiger, eds. *Critical Essays on Doris Lessing*. Boston: Hall, 1986.

Stamberg, Susan. "An Interview with Doris Lessing." Reprinted in *Doris Lessing Newsletter* 8.2 (Fall 1984): 3–4, 15.

Stapledon, Olaf. *Last and First Men*. London: Penguin, 1937.

——— . *Last and First Men and Star Maker*. New York: Dover, 1968.

Star Wars. Prod. and dir. George Lucas. 124 min. 20th-century Fox Film Corp., 1977.

Steinbeck, John. *The Grapes of Wrath*. Harmondsworth: Penguin, 1951.

Stimpson, Catharine R. "Doris Lessing and the Parables of Growth." *The Voyage In: Fictions of Female Development*. Ed. Elizabeth Abel, Marianne Hirsch, and Elizabeth Langland. Hanover: UP of New England, 1983. 186–205.

Stitzel, Judith. "Humor and Survival in the Works of Doris Lessing." *Regionalism and the Female Imagination* 4 (Fall 1978): 61–68.

——— . "Reading Doris Lessing." *College English* Jan. 1979: 498–505.

Stone, Laurie. "Narratives: The Doris Lessing Standard." *Ms* July–Aug. 1987: 29.

Sukenick, Lynn. "Feeling and Reason in Doris Lessing's Fiction." *Contemporary Literature* 14 (Autumn 1973): 515–35.

BIBLIOGRAPHY

Sullivan, Alvin. "Ideology and Form: Decentrism in *The Golden Notebook, Memoirs of a Survivor*, and *Shikasta*." Kaplan and Rose 71–79.

Summer, Bob. "Clear Some Shelf Space for Sufism." *Publishers Weekly* 9 Jan. 1995: 33–35.

Suvin, Darko. *Metamorphoses of Science Fiction: On the Poetics and History of a Literary Genre*. New Haven: Yale UP, 1979.

Suzuki, Daisetz T. *Zen and Japanese Culture*. New York: Pantheon, 1959.

Sviri, Sara. "Hakim Tirmidhi and the Malamati Movement in Early Sufism." *Classical Persian Sufism from its Origins to Rûmî*. Ed. Leonard Lewisohn. London and New York: Khaniqahi Nimatullahi, 1994. 583–613.

Tart, Charles T., ed. *Transpersonal Psychologies*. New York: Harper and Row, 1975.

Taylor, Jenny. "Memoirs was Made of This." Taylor, *Notebooks/Memoirs/Archives* 227–40.

——— . *Notebooks/Memoirs/Archives: Reading and Rereading Doris Lessing*. Boston: Routledge, 1982.

Taylor, Linda. "Through the Icy Wastes." Rev. of *The Making of the Representative for Planet 8*, by Doris Lessing. *Times Literary Supplement* 2 April 1982: 370.

Terkel, Studs. "Learning to Put the Questions Differently." Ingersoll, *Doris Lessing* 19–32.

Thomas, Disch. "Science Fiction as a Church." *Foundation* 25 (June 1982): 53–58.

Thomas, D. M. *The White Hotel*. New York: Pocket, 1981.

Thompson, Sedge. "Drawn to a Type of Landscape." Ingersoll, *Doris Lessing* 178–92.

Thorpe, Michael. *Doris Lessing*. London: Mildner, 1973.

——— . "Running through Stories in my Mind." Ingersoll, *Doris Lessing* 94–101.

Tiger, Virginia. "Candid Shot: Lessing in New York City, April 1 and 2, 1984." *Doris Lessing Newsletter* 8 (Fall 1984): 5–6.

————. "'Woman of Many Summers': *The Summer before the Dark*." Sprague and Tiger 86–94.

Tomalin, Claire. "Watching the Angry and Destructive Hordes Go By." Ingersoll, *Doris Lessing* 173–77.

Torrents, Nissa. "Testimony to Mysticism." Ingersoll, *Doris Lessing* 64–69.

Towers, Robert. "A Visionary Romance." Rev. of *The Marriages between Zones Three, Four, and Five*, by Doris Lessing. *The New York Times Book Review* 30 March 1980: 1, 23–24.

Trimmingham, Spencer. *The Sufi Orders in Islam*. Oxford: Clarendon, 1971.

Turner, Alice K. "Doris in Orbit." Rev. of *The Making of the Representative for Planet 8*, by Doris Lessing. *The Nation* 6 March 1982: 234, 278–80.

Tweedie, Irina. *The Chasm of Fire: A Woman's Experience of Liberation through the Teaching of a Sufi Master*. Longmead, Great Britain: Element, 1979.

————. *The Daughter of Fire: A Diary of a Spiritual Training with a Sufi Master*. Longmead, Gt. Brit.: Element, 1979.

Underhill, Evelyn. *Mysticism*. New York: Dutton, 1941.

Upchurch, Michael. "Voice of England, Voice of Africa." Ingersoll, *Doris Lessing* 219–27.

Vaughan-Lee, Llewellyn. *The Lover and the Serpent: Dreamwork within a Sufi Tradition*. Longmead, Gt. Brit.: Element, 1990.

————. *Sufism: The Transformation of the Heart*. Inverness: Golden Sufi Center, 1995.

————. *The Paradoxes of Love*. Inverness: Golden Sufi Center, 1996.

Von Schwarzkopf, Margarete. "Placing Their Fingers on the Wounds of Our Times." Ingersoll, *Doris Lessing* 102–8.

Vlastos, Marion. "Doris Lessing and R. D. Laing: Psychopolitics and Prophecy." *PMLA* 91 (March 1976): 245–58.

BIBLIOGRAPHY

Vonnegut, Kurt. *Slaughterhouse Five; or, The Children's Crusade: A Duty Dance with Death.* New York: Dell, 1968.

Waldman, Marilyn Robinson. "The Meandering Mainstream: Reimagining World History." Inaugural Address, The Ohio State University. March 2, 1988. Unpublished.

———, ed. *Muslims and Christians, Muslims and Jews: A Common Past, A Hopeful Future.* Columbus: Islamic Foundation of Central Ohio, The Catholic Diocese of Columbus, and Congregation Tifereth Israel, 1992.

———. *Toward a Theory of Historical Narrative: A Case Study in Perso-Islamicate Historiography.* Columbus: Ohio State UP, 1980.

Waldman, Marilyn Robinson, Artemis Leontis, and Müge Galin, eds. *Understanding Women: The Challenge of Cross-Cultural Perspectives.* Papers in Comparative Studies. 7. Columbus: The Ohio State University, Division of Comparative Studies in the Humanities, 1993.

Waldman, Marilyn Robinson, and Hao Chang, eds. *Religion in the Modern World.* Papers in Comparative Studies. 3. Columbus: The Ohio State University, Division of Comparative Studies in the Humanities, 1984.

Waldman, Marilyn Robinson, and William H. McNeill, eds. *The Islamic World.* Chicago: U of Chicago P, 1973.

Walker, Jeanne Murray. "Memory and Culture within the Individual: The Breakdown of Social Exchange in *Memoirs of a Survivor.*" Kaplan and Rose 93–114.

Willey, Basil. *The Seventeenth-Century Background.* London: Chatto, 1934.

Wilson, Elizabeth. "Yesterday's Heroines on Rereading Lessing and de Beauvoir." Taylor, *Notebooks / Memoirs / Archives* 57–74.

Wiseman, Thomas. "Mrs. Lessing's Kind of Life." *Time and Tide* 12 Apr. 1962: 26.

"The Witness as Prophet." *Time* 25 July 1969: 75–76.

Wollheim, Donald A. *The Universe Makers: Science Fiction Today.* New York: Harper, 1971.

Wood, Ramsay, ed. *Kalila and Dimna, Tales for Kings and Commoners*. Rochester: Inner Traditions, 1980.

Woolf, Virginia. *Mrs. Dalloway*. New York: Harcourt, 1981.

——— . *The Waves*. New York: Harcourt, 1931.

Yeats, William Butler. "The Second Coming." Ellman and O'Clair 131.

Index

271

INDEX

INDEX

Index

'*ishq. See* love
islam (surrender), 133, 142, 148, 155, 168, 184, 190, 192, 193, 197
Islam: awareness of, 217 n. 32, 218 n. 33; history of, 189–205; Nation of, 218 n. 33; scholars of, xviii, 14, 189; traditions of, 35, 170–71. *See also* Orientalists
Islamicate, xxii, 35, 211 n. 5
isnâd (chain of transmitters of *hadîth*), 192

J

Jalaliyyah, 17–18
Jamâ'î-Sunnî (majority), 191
James, William, 218 n. 1
Janna (Somers), 22, 33, 121–28, 149, 150
Javadi, Hasan, 47
Jesus, 54, 158–59
Joha. *See* Nasrudin
Johor, 23, 28, 33, 82–97; character of, 146–50; as a master, 108, 176; Sufi, 164
Jouve, Nicole Ward, 220 n. 15, 234 n. 14, 242–43 n. 37
Junayd, Abû'l Qasim al-, 195, 199
Jung, Carl, 30, 76, 160–62; God, 162, 171, 174, 179–80, 209
Jungianism, 12, 20, 82, 221 n. 5, 236 n. 20

K

kalâm (theological discourse), 192–93, 197
Kaplan, Carey, 20, 24, 28, 154, 223 n. 9, 230 n. 36
Karacaoğlan, 142–43
Kelsey, Alice Geer, 102

Keppler, Carl F., 225 n. 19
khalîfah (caliph), 191, 195
Khanna, Lee Cullen, 239 n. 28
Khayyam, Omar, 69, 117
Khidr, 200–201
Kinney, Jay, 9–10
Knapp, Mona, 24, 64, 111, 138, 145, 228, 233 n. 14, 235 n. 17, 240 n. 29
knowledge, self, 71, 73, 120
Koan, Zen, 105
Kumar, Sarla, 208

L

Laing, 25, 30, 120
Laingianism, 12, 20, 238 n. 23
Landlocked, 22, 51, 52, 78, 119
Lawrence, D. H., 24, 215 n. 23
Learning How to Learn (Shah), 100
LeGuin, Ursula, 178, 181, 228; *The Left Hand of Darkness*, 176
Lem, Stanislav, 178, 181
Leon, Moses de, 10
Leonard, John, 24
Levin, Susan, 237 n. 20
Lewis, C. S., 156, 177; *The Great Divorce*, 135
Lewis, M. Susan, 207, 233 n. 13
literature, Sufi, xvii, 8, 40, 46, 134, 175, 185. *See also* 'Attâr; Khayyam; Nasrudin; Rûmî; teaching stories
Lott, Sandra, 69, 224 n. 16
love (Sufi), 14, 39, 42–43; ecstatic, 194, 197; Path of, 46. *See also* Beloved, God the

M

Maddocks, Melvin, 223 n. 11
madhhab, 192

275

INDEX

madness, 71, 113, 117–20, 235 n.
17, 237 n. 23, 238 nn. 23–24
*Making of the Representative for
Planet 8, The.* See
Representative, The
Malâmatiyyah, 195
maqâm. See being, levels of
*Marriages between Zones Three,
Four, and Five, The,* xxii, 44,
87; Sufi, 176; teaching story,
128–46. *See also* Al·Ith
Martha (Quest), 22, 26, 51, 78,
95, 111, 113, 149, 157, 225 n.
20, 226 n. 25; awakening,
117–20; new organs, 116,
184; as a Sufi, 107
Marwanids, 191
Marx, 30, 167
Marxism, 12, 65, 68, 82, 160,
164–65
Masons, 94, 199, 232 n. 11
master/disciple (Sufi), 13, 42–44,
50, 105, 116, 131, 137, 138,
148, 194–205
Maudie, 33, 120–28, 164. See
also *Diary of a Good
Neighbour, The*
Mawlânâ (Our Master). *See*
Rûmî
Mawlawiyyah, 37, 199. *See also*
Whirling Dervishes, The
McCrindle, Jean, 215 n. 23
Memoirs of a Survivor, The,
xxii, 21, 22, 26, 32, 52–53,
62–83; carpet, 66, 222 n. 7;
madness, 120; teaching story,
100, 103, 107; wall, 67, 70,
75–81, 139, 223 n. 15; "work,"
70, 82. *See also* Emily;
Unreal City
Merrill, James, 175
Morgan, Ellen, 225 n. 20

Mosier, M. Patricia, 209, 231 n.
41
Moyne, John, 47
Mu'tazilites, 193
Muhammad, the prophet, 171,
244 n. 4; ascension to heaven,
12, 136–38; the first Sufi, 12,
197, 198; mosque, 39; revelation to, 190, 201; saint, 202
Mulla. *See* Nasrudin
Muslim. *See* Islam
Muslim: diaspora, xviii; Sufis, 7,
17, 38, 194; names, 242 n. 37

N

Naqshbandiyyah, 6, 199, 214 n.
22
Nasr, Seyyed Hossein, 9–10, 16,
73, 189, 213 n. 8
Nasreddin Hodja. *See* Nasrudin
Nasrudin, Mulla, x–xi, 4, 43, 45,
99, 102, 104–106, 157, 189,
212 n. 2; in *Diary of a Good
Neighbor, The,* 120–22,
125–28, 149; in *Four-Gated
City, The,* 110, 118; *imam*
(prayer leader), 104; in
Landlocked, 119; *medrese*
(theological school), 104; in
Representative, The, 130
nass (authority), 191
Nawab (of Sardhana): *Hu-
Nama,* 135
Nirvana, 49, 183
Nordell, Roderick, 222

O

O'Connor, Flannery. See *Wise
Blood*
O'Rourke, Rebecca, 237 n. 21
observation, self, 71
order. See *tarîqah*

INDEX

INDEX

Towers, Robert, 241 n. 31
transcendence, 129
transformation, 80, 123–24, 146–49
Trimmingham, 197, 198, 203, 204
Turner, Alice K., 229 n. 33
Tweedie, Irina, 214 n. 22

U

'ulamâ' (religious scholars), 192, 197, 203
'Umar (caliph), 191
'Uthmân (caliph), 191
Umayyads, 191
Ummah (Muslim community), 13, 19, 45, 118, 191
Under My Skin, 69
Underhill, Evelyn, 218 n. 1
Unreal City, 49–57; London, 50, 53; Planet 8, 50; Zone Four, 50
Upchurch, Michael, 23

V

Vaughan-Lee, Llewellyn, 214
Victorians, 159
Vlastos, Marion, 120, 237 n. 23
Vonnegut, Kurt, 178

W

Waldman, Marilyn Robinson, vii–xii, 190, 245 n. 2

Walker, Jeanne Murray, 67, 68, 223 n. 10, 12, &13
Wanderground, The (Gearhart), 56
Wasteland, The (Eliot), 51
Waves, The (Woolf), 166
Way. *See* Sufi, Way. *See also* Drunken Way; Sober Way
Whirling Dervishes, The, 14, 17–19, 37, 163–64
White Hotel, The (Thomas), 166
Wilson, Edward, 32, 33, 84, 85–86, 88
Wilson, Elizabeth, 25
Wise Blood, 167, 168
Wizard of Oz, The, 51
Wood, Ramsay: *Kalila and Dimna*, 100
Woolf, Virginia, 216 n. 25, 235 n. 17. See also *Waves, The*
"work," xix, 26, 31, 32, 33, 36, 41, 68, 70, 71, 90, 139; self-work, 74, 78, 81–82, 95–96, 128, 133, 242 n. 33

Y

Yarshater, Ehsan, 47
Yunus (Emre), 29

Z

Zoroaster, 245 n. 9
Zoroastrianism, 179, 180, 201
zuhd (rejection of the world), 193